Kings of the Chessboard

Paul van der Sterren

All sales or enquiries should be directed to Thinkers Publishing, 9850 Landegem, Belgium.

Email: info@thinkerspublishing.com
Website: www.thinkerspublishing.com

Managing Editor: Daniël Vanheirzeele

Assistant Editor: Dimitri ten Have

Software: Hub van de Laar

Photos: Frans Peeters, Cathy Rogers, Jos Sutmuller

Cover Design: Mieke Mertens

Graphic Artist: Philippe Tonnard

Production: BESTinGraphics

ISBN: 9789492510532

D/2019/3730/6

Kings of the Chessboard

Paul van der Sterren

Thinkers Publishing 2019

Contents

Introduction

People who are really, really good at something – unbelievably good, incomprehen-sibly good, have always held a strong fascination for those fellow humans who are less extraordinarily gifted. In this respect chess does not differ from other areas of human endeavour. To many chess lovers watching the great champions do battle with each other is even more thrilling than actually playing the game themselves. This book is about the greatest chess players who ever lived, who dominated their era and were looked upon as World Champions even at a time when this term, this very concept, did not yet exist. On the basis of a short biography, a selection of their most famous games and a brief characteristic of their playing style I will attempt to illuminate what made these great players great and what their significance is for the chess world. This will also give an overview of how chess itself has developed over the past two and a half centuries: how it has essentially remained the same, yet changed almost beyond recognition.

Chess is an inexhaustable game. When, around 2005, it became clear that even the world's very best players could no longer keep pace with chess engines, improving at a tremendous rate, it looked as if the game might be losing its charm, at least to humans. Yet the opposite of this gloomy scenario has happened! Computer tech-nology, with its superhuman calculating power, has added a new dimension to chess, which has given it a whole new worldwide appeal. In the past spectators at a chess tournament (a couple of hundred at best) could do little but watch and be silent. Nowadays an unlimited number of chess enthusiasts can follow tournaments from all over the world online, listen to live commentary by (human) experts and engines alike, and chat with other fans, simultaneously. It also has transformed 'vis-ibility' of the thinking process of the top players beyond recognition. Even a World Champion can now no longer hide behind the self-evident authority of his title ("I played this move, *therefore* it must have been best.") – and is constantly being cor-rected by those all-seeing, superior computer engines.

The same engines have also helped to considerably raise the levels of their owners, for when one is in constant dialogue with a superior 'mind' one's understanding of the game will improve automatically, whether intended or not. World class and or-dinary club players alike have learned a lot from computers. Diligent students are able to make much faster progress than before.

In a nutshell, chess has absorbed the latest technological revolution as easily as it has absorbed other fundamental changes in the past, such as the evolution of professionalism and the introduction of the chess clock. From the time of its origin – which is undocumented but likely goes back a couple of millennia to India – chess has adapted to changing cultures and different societies. It has survived devastating wars, religious persecution and gloomy episodes when it was thought that its possibilities had been exhausted. It has been a game for royalty as well as for the coffee houses, for the patient as well as for the impatient and – in a modern context – in the living room as well as on the internet.

This book does not give a complete overview of the history of chess. It is not until the 19th century that the chess world becomes more or less recognisable to the player of today so this is where we make our starting point. However, first we must look at someone from the 18th century, someone who was way ahead of his time and who must be viewed as the founder of chess as we know it today, not just because of his astounding success as a player, but also because he put down in writing his understanding of the game. He came, saw, conquered *and* analysed in detail why it was that he conquered. What more can a man do?

François-André Danican Philidor

François-André Danican Philidor (1726-1795) was born into a family of prominent musicians in France. Following in the footsteps of his father, grandfather and many other family members he too became a musician and it soon transpired that he was extremely talented. He became one of the leading composers of the day, specialising in the then highly popular genre of the *opéra comique*. From a very young age he also developed a passion – and perhaps an even greater talent – for the game of chess.

In those days chess was mainly being played in coffee houses in a few countries in Europe and nothing even faintly resembling a supraregional organisation existed. The concept of a World Championship was unknown and there was virtually no international contact. Yet the path to the top for a young, ambitious and talented chess player was basically the same as it is today, namely to go out into the world and beat the best players you meet, preferably in a match over many games in order to leave as little doubt as possible about your moral right to call yourself the strongest.

Yet at the end of this trajectory, having beaten everyone who stood in your way, there would be no official title for you, though *unofficial* recognition would be just the same as it is now.

A vital precondition for following such a career was of course the possibility to travel, which to the ordinary man was far from self-evident in the eighteenth century. However Philidor was able to do this thanks to his 'other' life as a famous musician. Having earned his first chess laurels in the famous Café de la Régence in Paris, his musical career brought him first to the Dutch Republic and then to England, where in 1747 he convincingly won a match against the Syrian-born Philippe Stamma, who until then held the reputation of being the best player in the world. He also demolished the best English player of the day, Abraham Janssen and when on his return to Paris Philidor formally defeated his former teacher François Antoine Kermur de Legal in a match as well he was widely acclaimed as the best player in the world.

Philidor's bust on the Opéra Garnier in Paris (photo Paul van der Sterren)

Yet Philidor's real claim to fame was still to come, because what really set him apart from anyone else in the history of chess was his incredible *longevity* as a champion. He would remain unbeaten in matches until his death in 1795, a period of half a century! Not even the generation of his grandchildren was able to overthrow him.

Wherever he went, Philidor would lecture, both on music and chess, and astonish large audiences with his demonstrations of blindfold chess. He was the first to play two or three games simultaneously without seeing the board (his opponents played without this handicap), which caused an absolute sensation at the time. He also wrote a manual of chess that would remain *the* standard text book for almost a century: *L'Analyze des Échecs*. In this book he gives a complete and systematic overview of all phases of the game and how they should be played and understood.

He was the first to point out that it is always the placement of the pawns that characterises any given position and that maintaining a healthy and flexible pawn structure should be a major strategic aim.
His axiom "the pawn is the soul of chess" has become a famous and popular saying. Based on these views, after the opening moves 1.e4 e5 2.♘f3 he advocated 2...d6 rather than the more popular 2...♘c6 which blocks the c-pawn. This opening was later named after him.

Since writing down your moves when playing a game of chess was still a practically unknown phenomenon in the eighteenth century, we unfortunately can't really appreciate how his many successes as a player came about. It is true that some fragments of his games have made it into today's databases, but their authenticity is doubtful and it is likely that these are mostly fictitious games invented by him for the purpose of teaching or demonstrating a particular point he wanted to make. A much better way for us to honour him is to look at one of the instructional positions from *L'Analyze des Échecs* that has stood the test of time magnificently. This is a position, or rather a defensive *method*, which was, is and always will be of fundamental importance to the theory – and practice! – of rook endings, and has gone down in history as 'Philidor's position':

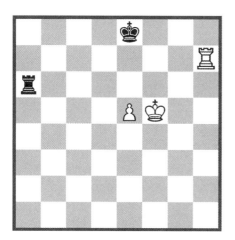

Rook endings occur remarkably often in practical play. Although they will usually start with many pawns on each side they very often result in one of a limited number of standard positions with just one or two pawns left.
This is one of those positions. White has succeeded in cutting off the black king on the back rank and advancing his king and pawn to the fifth rank.

Yet although the black king's movement is limited it does stop the white pawn from promoting on e8. The question is: can White make any progress from here?

What Philidor demonstrated is that black can hold this position fairly

easily if his rook keeps guarding the sixth rank until White pushes his pawn to e6. If it is White to move his only reasonable try is to play **1.e6**. This creates the threat of 2.♔f6, when Black either gets mated (for example 1.e6 ♖b6 2.♔f6 ♖b1 3.♖h8 mate) or has to give up the blockade of the pawn (for example 1.e6 ♖b6 2.♔f6 ♔d8 3.♖h8+ ♔c7 4.♔f7 and the pawn advance e6-e7-e8♕ becomes unstoppable).

Yet if Black is alert to this threat he can ward off the danger once and for all by playing **1...♖a1!** with the intention of meeting **2.♔f6** with **2...♖f1+**. White's king doesn't have a good hiding place: if **3.♔e5** Black will keep checking from behind (**3...♖e1+ 4.♔d6 ♖d1+**) until the white king moves away from his

pawn far enough for the danger to pass. If in the diagrammed position it is Black to move, he should do something which keeps this defensive mechanism intact, for instance **1...♖b6**. What he should most certainly *not* do is play the impatient 1...♖a1? for this allows White to play 2.♔f6! when it is too late to go back (2...♖a6+ 2.e6!), but also too early to start checking from behind: with his pawn still on e5 White now has the safe square e6 for his king (2...♖f1+ 3.♔e6!). Suddenly Black is in big trouble. It is true that he can still draw this position (only just) when he moves his king to the right side (2...♖f1+ 3.♔e6 ♔f8! 4.♖h8+ ♔g7) *and* finds one or two only moves in the ensuing position, but that particular defensive mechanism is much more difficult.

Philidor's position offers Black an *easy* draw if he is patient enough to wait for white's pawn to move to e6 and only then starts checking from behind. Anyone who has understood this principle well enough to use it in a practical game has laid a strong and necessary foundation for the study of more complex rook endings.

The match La Bourdonnais – McDonnell, 1834

Even before Philidor's death in 1795 chess life (and life in general) had come to an almost complete stop due to the revolution, civil war and terror that France had poured upon itself, then over the rest of Europe. It wasn't until the defeat of Napoleon at Waterloo in 1815 that peace finally settled over the ravaged continent, leaving millions of people dead and most of the countries involved devastated. Perhaps chess was still popular during these terrible years, but it could of course only be played on a small scale. There were no major events and consequently no famous names emerged.

The first player to make a name for himself after the Napoleonic Wars was a veteran of the French Army, Alexandre Deschapelles (1780-1847). He was the archetypal *player*, a man who never read a chess book, wouldn't have dreamed of writing one himself and excelled not just at chess, but also at whist, backgammon and billiards.
However it wasn't until around 1820 when a brilliant pupil of his, Louis-Charles Mahé de La Bourdonnais (1797?-1840), arrived on the scene, and sporadic encounters between English and French players were resumed, that chess really started to come to life again. La Bourdonnais soon overtook his teacher as France's leading player. He followed in the footsteps of Philidor by writing a textbook (*Nouveau Traité du Jeu des échecs*) and co-founded the first ever chess journal (*Le Palamède*).

Having crushed all opposition in France, La Bourdonnais left for England to seek new challenges and there he was to become legendary for winning the first truly epoch-making *and* well-publicised match in the history of chess. His opponent in this historic encounter, which took place in 1834, was Alexander McDonnell (1798-1835), an Irishman who lived in London and was considered the best of the 'British' players. (At that time Ireland was still part of the United Kingdom.) Their marathon match was in reality six consecutive matches, probably because the loser of each match would insist upon an immediate rematch, and it was only in hindsight that this came to be regarded as one long epic battle. La Bourdonnais won four of the first five matches and lost one. The final match of the series was abandoned for reasons which have never been clear, with the score slightly in McDonnell's favour. Another mystery that surrounds the match is the total num-ber of games played. One source quotes a number of 85, another says 88, a third and a fourth say 91 and 92, while La Bourdonnais himself in *Le Palamède* makes it a round 100. One thing is clear though: La Bourdonnais scored an over-whelming victory. Based on the most of-ten quoted number of 85, the overall score was 45-27 in his favour with just 13 draws.

La Bourdonnais

Interest in the match was huge. For the first time all moves were recorded, pub-lished and annotated. The moves were not recorded by the players themselves – that would not become standard until several decades later – but by a secretary. One of the consequences was that chess players from all over the world started to model their own opening repertoire on that of the top players. Those openings were thoroughly investigated and criticised, making opening theory a more public affair than it had ever been.

The players themselves also made a significant impression on the audience, main-ly because of their very different characters. La Bourdonnais played fast, was ex-troverted and let his emotions run wild as the course of the battle gave him rea-son to do so. He was a *bon vivant*, conversed loudly with people in the audience, and if a game was finished he would immediately start playing for money against all comers, often until late into the night. McDonnell on the other hand, played extremely slowly (there were no limitations at all on how long a player was allowed to think), went home exhausted after every game and always kept a stiff upper lip, no matter what happened. They must have nettled each other tremendously.

A match over so many games is of course a treasure trove of memorable moments, yet one position in particular has become so famous that it can be seen as emblematic of the whole match. Say "La Bourdonnais-McDonnell" and you say this:

♙ McDonnell, Alexander
♟ La Bourdonnais, Louis Charles Mahé de
🌐 London 1834

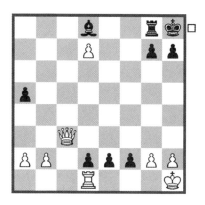

This is the final position of game 62, or more accurately game 16 of the fourth match. Black's last move was

37... e2

White, McDonnell, resigned. He is a queen up, but against the tidal wave of black pawns he is as powerless as a sandcastle against incoming water. If people ask me what is so beautiful about chess I like to show them this position.

La Bourdonnais has been called the first chess professional, because for at least the last ten years of his life he had no income other than his chess earnings. He died in poverty in London at the age of (probably) 43 yet by then McDonnell had been dead for six years. He died less then a year after the match, possibly of physical and mental exhaustion. Even in those days chess was not taken lightly by those who truly loved it.

The First Tournament: London 1851

When La Bourdonnais died in 1840 the chess world was left with a power vacuum. Neither his home country France, which had dominated chess for well over a century, nor the United Kingdom, where the most recent challengers had come from, could provide a player of La Bourdonnais' stature. However, before the chess world would finally spread its wings, representatives of these two countries were to battle it out for the highest honour one last time. The Frenchman Pierre de Saint-Amant (1800-1872) and the Englishman Howard Staunton (1810-1874) met in Paris in 1843 to decide who would have the moral right to call himself La Bourdonnais' successor. Staunton won with a score of 13-8 (11 victories, six losses and four draws). He impressed with the quality of his opening preparation, an aspect of the game that had only just begun to come under serious scrutiny now that people were beginning to write down their moves and

Howard Staunton

chess literature was taking shape. Staunton introduced the opening move 1.c4, which was named the English Opening after him. He was also the first to bring along helpers, who were called seconds, after the assistants in a duel.

Yet even before Staunton's match was over chess players from several countries were calling out for a more modern way to decide who was best. In common with the world in general, the chess world was changing, becoming more lively, more international and perhaps even more democratic. The concept of a tournament (instead of a match) was introduced and the term 'World Champion' could be heard. (The honour of being the first to be thus called – albeit incidentally – goes to Staunton.) And so the first modern chess tournament was held in London in 1851. All the best players of the day were invited to take part, so the unmistakable (yet not official) intention was to determine the best player in the world. But the tournament was still widely seen as an experiment only, so the winner (about whom we will have a little more to say below) didn't quite come to have the general acclaim he perhaps deserved.

However new the formula, in many respects this first tournament was still firmly rooted in tradition, consisting of matches in what we would today call a knock-out format. In round one sixteen participants played eight matches, the eight winners going through to the next round and so on until the two strongest players faced each other in the final. In this way sixteen players rather than just two, were given the chance to prove themselves. This principle, to involve many more than two players in the struggle for world supremacy, would not be widely accepted until after the Second World War, so in this respect "London 1851" was far ahead of its time. Purely as a way to organise a chess event, the tournament formula was an immediate success. Within decades tournaments became the backbone not only of international chess, but of chess on all levels. It turned out to be simply more fun to have a group of opponents competing against each other instead of just two: a tournament provided more tension, more drama and many more beautiful games. However, matches, being head-to-head fights, did not disappear. They remained what they had always been: the purest of all formats, ideal for establishing which of just two players was the strongest: ideal for a World Championship.

Adolf Anderssen (1818-1879) from Germany was the winner of the London 1851 tournament. He won all his matches with a clear margin, defeating pre-tournament favourite Staunton in the semi-finals. His victory meant that the chess world finally transcended the long rivalry between England and France and became more truly international. Anderssen was to remain one of the world's best players until his death in 1879 and many of his major rivals (and successors if we call him the world's best) originated, like him, from Central Europe.

Adolf Anderssen

For Staunton, London 1851 signalled the end of his active career. From a chess player he turned into a chess writer. Until his death in 1874 he devoted himself not only to his professional career as a Shakespeare expert, but also to his work for the first English chess magazine *Chess Player's Chronicle*, (founded by him), his chess column in the *London Illustrated News* and to the writing of books.

He wrote the first-ever tournament book (about London 1851) and a number of very well-received chess manuals, of which *The Chess-Player's Handbook* has become the most famous – still in print, some 170 years after first publication! Staunton's name is also inextricably bound up with the first chess set to be used as an international standard and in this way made an important contribution to the unification of the chess world. The Staunton design set is still the preferred set for almost every major tournament today.

If Staunton was what we might call a veritable chess *scholar*, his 'successor' Adolf Anderssen was a *player* above all. In matches he would be defeated by Paul Morphy in 1858 and by Wilhelm Steinitz in 1866 – see the next two chapters – but as a tournament player he was astoundingly successful. After his victory in London 1851 he also won the first ever round-robin tournament in 1862, again in London, with the fantastic score of 12 points from 13 games. In fact after 1866, at a time when tournament life all over Europe virtually exploded, he won almost everywhere he played. Yet Anderssen's most enduring claim to fame lies in his extremely imaginative playing style. Always on the lookout for attacking chances and gifted with unique combinative vision he destroyed many of his opponents in brilliant style. His two most famous games have even been given nicknames, a rarity in chess

Jean Dufresne

literature: one is called the Immortal Game, the other the Evergreen Game. Here is the finish of the Evergreen Game:

♙ Anderssen, Adolf
♟ Dufresne, Jean
🌐 Berlin 1852

Position after: 18... ♖g8

White is a piece down, but that doesn't trouble him, because Black's knight on e7 is pinned and can't be saved. A more serious problem is that Black is threatening to capture another piece (19...♕xf3), when White's king would be in grave danger. Anderssen's solution is as simple as it is far-sighted.

19. ♖ad1!

At first glance this move seems to betray an almost astonishing degree of naivety. Not only does White not take immediate action, he doesn't even parry the big threat. What the move does do however is involve the second rook in the attack and that outweighs all the negatives.

In a position where all eyes are on e7 Anderssen has seen that it is not this square but d7 which is the real weak link in Black's defence. It is a superb demonstration of cool-headedness and combinative power at the very highest level. Rather more mundanely you might also call it setting a trap, into which Dufresne falls.

19... ♕xf3?

The position is enormously complex. Later analysis has shown that Black has a whole series of better moves, including   19...♖g4,   19...♖xg2+, 19...♗d4 and 19...♕h3. But what concerns us here is what follows now:

20. ♖xe7+! ♘xe7?

Dufresne obviously doesn't see what is coming. He could still have put up a fierce resistance with 20... ♔d8! 21. ♖xd7+! ♔c8!.

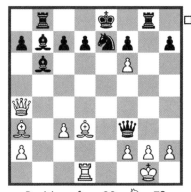

Position after: 20... ♘xe7?

21. ♕xd7+!

Having already sacrificed a rook and a knight and under severe threat of mate himself White sacrifices his queen as well – and forces mate.

21... ♔xd7 22. ♗f5+

Double check! Both the rook on d1 and the bishop on f5 are unprotected, but neither can be taken.

22... ♔e8

22... ♔c6 23. ♗d7 is mate in one.

23. ♗d7+ ♔f8 24. ♗xe7 Mate.

Anderssen must have had a nose for combinations like this. It is not just a matter of being able to calculate the variations to perfection (though that is most certainly a requirement!), but of somehow 'knowing' they are there.

Perhaps even more spectacular is the finale of the Immortal Game:

Image from the tournament where the 'Immortal Game' was played.

♙ Anderssen, Adolf
♟ Kieseritzky, Lionel
⊕ London 1851

Position after: 18... ♗xg1

White has already sacrificed a rook and a bishop and there is another rook *en prise* on a1 with check. Yet a player like Anderssen is unconcerned by material considerations like this, spotting underneath something of a higher order: a mating net, and with his next move he closes it.

19. e5!

Cutting off Black's queen from the defence of his king. The threat is mate in two: 20.♘xg7+ ♔d8 21.♗c7+. Black has no way of protecting g7, so his only hope is covering the c7-square. First he captures the rook.

19... ♕xa1+ 20. ♔e2

The white king is in no danger here. Now Black has to make the defensive move

20... ♘a6

but it is just not good enough.

21. ♘xg7+ ♔d8

Position after: 21... ♔d8

22. ♕f6+! ♘xf6 23. ♗e7

Mate. Three minor pieces defeating an almost entirely intact army. The possibility of such a concept is one of the factors that makes chess such a beautiful game.

Paul Morphy

And then suddenly there was ... Paul Morphy. How can one describe such a unique phenomenon in the history of chess? Out of the blue Morphy appeared on the scene, shook the chess world to its foundations and then, as suddenly as he had come, he was gone again, leaving behind an utterly confused legion of admirers. Had this been an earthquake, a dream?

Well, it wasn't a dream, but a coherent explanation – or even a thorough description – of Morphy's comet-like appearance and disappearance has rarely been offered. Perhaps it is impossible to do so without digging far deeper than is normal for a chess biography.

With Paul Morhpy (1837-1884) America makes its grand entrance into the expanding chess world. Born in New Orleans, Louisiana, he grew up in a wealthy and distinguished family. Morphy supposedly learned chess at the age of three, just by watching his father and uncle play, a story which *could* be true, though it sounds incredible. (Half a century later the same would be said about Capablanca.) Little Paul was certainly an unusually gifted child. His parents stimulated him, he was 'allowed' to play against ever stronger opponents and by the time he was twelve years old he was by far the best player in New Orleans.

Whether because of a lack of new challenges or because he simply did as he was told by his parents, Morphy then devoted himself completely to his studies (wherein he again excelled) for the next seven years. However when in 1857 Morphy had completed his education and could finally call himself a free man, he immediately resumed his chess career. Morphy travelled to New York to play in *the First American Chess Congress* with overwhelming success. He easily overcame the strongest American players of the time *and* Louis Paulsen (1833-1891), a

German then living in America, who was already considered one of the world's best players and would remain so for several more decades. After his defeat of Paulsen in the final – the format of the tournament was a knock-out as in London 1851 – Morphy was instantly (and explicitly) recognised as the new American Champion. This was the start of a career that was in essence a triumphal procession, yet one which was to last for only two years, an incredibly short period. Travelling to Europe in the summer of 1858, Morphy sought out the strongest possible opponents there, demolishing every one who was willing to play him, including Anderssen. Having completed his mission, Morphy returned to America the next year. Although his countrymen showered him with honours, he then publicly declared his retirement from chess, a 'promise' Morphy went on to keep – with a few unimportant exceptions – for the rest of his life. He had shown himself to be the best and that was enough for him.

Paul Morphy

There are many good reasons to take a closer look at Morphy's life and his personality: his having lived through the American Civil War (1861-1865), his increasing isolation after he quit chess, his early death and the likelihood that he suffered from some undiagnosed mental disease. However such an examination would be beyond the scope of this book. What made Morphy stand out in chess is a question that many experts have tried to answer. Some have pointed out his decisiveness in attack, others his indomitability in defence, his accuracy in technical positions and many other attributes. Yet is it not self-evident from his results that his technical skills were of the very highest quality? What seems to me much more relevant is a remark on Morphy's psyche, made by Adolf Anderssen in 1859: "Morphy approaches chess with the earnestness and solemnity of an artist. To us, chess is merely a pleasant way of passing time. To him it is a sacred duty, never trivial, always deserving of his full attention. Chess is a vocation to him, a life fulfilment".

Paul Morphy (left) against Hungarian master Johann Löwenthal

Chess as a matter of sacred earnestness. There are other famous chess players of whom this can be said, but Morphy is perhaps the ultimate example of an attitude of this kind. If chess were a religion, Paul Morphy would be our prophet.

It is typical of the many legends that surround him that Morphy's most famous game was not a proper game at all – at least not in the sense of being a serious game against a worthy opponent. The game was played *during* an opera performance in Paris, in the private box of Charles II, Duke of Brunswick, who had invited Morphy to join him in his box, but was apparently more interested in chess than in opera. Morphy was forced to play a game against the Duke in consultation with another of his guests, a Count Isoard, with his back to the stage. It must have given him great satisfaction that the game turned out to be one of the most devastating victories of his career.

♙ Morphy
♟ Brunswick/Isoard
🌐 Paris 1858

---

1. e4 e5 2. ♘f3 d6 3. d4 ♗g4 4. dxe5

Morphy's play is simple yet forcing. If Black wants to restore the material balance he has to exchange on f3 when White's lead in development becomes a telling factor.

4... ♗xf3 5. ♕xf3 dxe5 6. ♗c4

Threatening mate in one.

6... ♘f6

This prevents the mate but it overlooks a second, more subtle threat. 6...♕d7 or 6...♕f6 were better moves, keeping everything under control.

Position after: 6... ♘f6

7. ♕b3!

Again attacking f7, but now b7 is also under threat. Since Black cannot cover both squares he is already in serious trouble.

7... ♕e7

A clever defence. Black not only protects f7 but also makes sure that 8.♕xb7 can now be countered with 8...♕b4+, when Black remains a pawn down but at least he has taken the sting out of White's initiative.

8. ♘c3

Apart from 8. ♕xb7 Morphy must also have considered 8. ♗xf7+ when 8... ♕xf7 9. ♕xb7 now causes more damage than just a pawn. But the problem is that after 9... ♗c5 10. ♕xa8 0-0, although Black is an exchange and a pawn behind, he takes over the initiative, with moves like ♘f6xe4 and ♘f6-g4 casting a shadow over White's kingside.

Morphy does not want to lose the initiative. He much prefers to increase the pressure by bringing another piece into the battle, thus forcing Black's queen to remain on her uncomfortable position on e7, bottling up the bishop on f8.

8... c6 9. ♗g5 b5?

Position after: 9... b5?

Although this move gives White a forced win and therefore fully deserves its question mark, it is also quite understandable. Driving away the aggressively placed bishop from c4 *seems* like a good idea. The only problem is that the bishop does not *have* to retreat.

10. ♘xb5! cxb5 11. ♗xb5+ ♘bd7 12. 0-0-0

Just two moves and the game has transformed beyond recognition. Black is completely tied up and there is no way to free himself.

12... ♖d8

This still looks like a decent defence, but Morphy has no trouble at all smashing it to pieces.

13. ♖xd7! ♖xd7 14. ♖d1

Making good use of *all* his pieces. Now d7 can no longer be protected.

14... ♕e6

White could simply play 15.♗xf6 now, since 15...♕xb3 16.♗xd7 is mate and 15...gxf6 16.♗xd7+ loses the queen. Morphy plays it a little differently and ... more cruelly.

15. ♗xd7+ ♘xd7

The natural move, yet it loses instantly. Only by giving up his queen with 15...♕xd7 would Black have been able to prolong the game. Needless to say his huge material deficit would have made further resistance quite useless.

Position after: 15... ♘xd7

16. ♕b8+! ♘xb8 17. ♖d8

Mate.

Wilhelm Steinitz

Most if not all modern-day sources list Wilhelm Steinitz (1836-1900) as the first official World Champion of chess. Yet the transition between the age of what we now call the 'unofficial' and the official World Champions is surprisingly vague, to say the least.

To begin with, Steinitz's predecessor Paul Morphy was already often called a World Champion. The term, which probably dates from the beginning of the 19th century, was well established in Morphy's day and the chess world saw no reason not to adopt it for its great new champion. But it was still very much an honorary title, not a formal one, and when Morphy retired from chess he took this honorary title with him. No other player dared call himself World Champion while Morphy was alive.

Besides, even in Steinitz's time nothing really changed. There was still no governing body of the chess world, so it was still left to the top players themselves to challenge each other to a match to decide who was the best. In fact this situation would essentially remain unchanged until 1946, with the title of World Champion being to all intents and purposes the private property of the reigning Champion. It was for him to decide whether or not he wished to risk losing his title, though it must be admitted that the chess world always kept a critical eye on the Champion's decisions.

So regarding Steinitz as the first World Champion is, to a certain extent at least, an arbitrary choice. It is true that the contract for the 1886 match between Steinitz and Zukertort (1842-1888) was the first to state explicitly that "the title of World Champion" would be awarded to the winner, so if we *have* to put a starting point somewhere 1886 is not a bad choice. But it remains a choice. Steinitz himself later backdated the beginning of his reign to 1866, the year when he beat Anderssen in a match.

Wilhelm Steinitz was born in Prague in 1836, then lived in Vienna and London before he settled in America in 1883. He had the bulk of his chess career already behind him when he beat Zukertort in 1886 and claimed the World Championship title. While still a student (and a journalist) in Vienna, capital of the Austro-Hungarian Empire, Steinitz discovered that he could make good money with chess and he became a professional player. His nickname, the *Austrian Morphy*, suggests that he was hugely successful, but he was too late to measure his strength against the real Morphy who, although a year younger, had already retired by the time Steinitz made his way to the top.

Wilhelm Steinitz

In 1862 Steinitz moved to London, where he developed his strength and his reputation further in matches against the best British players.

In 1866 he was deemed strong enough to take on Anderssen who, after Morphy's retirement, was again regarded as the best *active* player in the world. Steinitz won that match, so his claim of many years later that he had been World Champion since 1866 is not completely unfounded.

However by now the chess world was becoming too big for a single player to dominate. Tournaments were being held all over Europe and America and no one was able to take part in, let alone win, all these events. The list of winners of major tournaments between 1870 and 1890 includes, apart from Steinitz and the aforementioned Anderssen, Zukertort and Paulsen, people such as Szymon Winawer (1838-1919), Isidor Gunsberg (1854-1930), Joseph Blackburne (1841-1924), Mikhail Chigorin (1850-1908) and Siegbert Tarrasch (1862-1934).

Of these, Chigorin and Tarrasch in particular do not appear to have considered themselves in any way inferior to Steinitz.

However in match play Steinitz turned out to be virtually unbeatable. He destroyed Blackburne 7-0 in 1876 and in the 1886 "Match for the World Championship" against Zukertort he turned a 1-4 deficit into a 10-5 victory. (The winner of the match was the first to score ten wins and five games were drawn.)

It wasn't until 1894, when he was already 58 years of age, that Steinitz was finally dethroned.

Emanuel Lasker, 32 (!) years his junior, beat Steinitz 10-4 (with five draws) in a match that was held in New York, Philadelphia and Montreal.

By then, after twenty years in England, Steinitz had settled in New York. Steinitz became an American citizen, though he would continue to travel back and forth between America and Europe to play tournaments until his death; international chess had become a truly transatlantic affair.

Regardless of how vague the term 'World Champion' was in Steinitz's time, chess was clearly moving towards a more serious, professional and 'modern' image, recognisable to a player of today. The chess clock was introduced, more and more newspapers and magazines were running a chess column – often at a very high level – and chess was clearly moving away from the old coffeehouses into the modern tournament halls. Money was also finding its way into the chess world, making it easier for players who had no other income to make a living from chess. The money involved was not just prize money for tournaments. Top players could also demand good, sometimes huge fees for simultaneous exhibitions and the like. In World Championship matches, money was even becoming a crucial factor. It became

customary to play for huge stakes, making it necessary for challengers to find finan-
cial backing from investors (or gamblers) who would then get a share of the win-
nings if their player won. Not every prospective challenger was able to raise enough
money, whereupon there would simply be no match, a situation about which Steinitz was aware and with which he was unhappy. Steinitz was the first to try to turn
the World Championship into a fair and well-organised competition. However, although he met with a lot of support for this idea, especially in America, a breakthrough was never realised and when Lasker took the title from him in 1894 the
plan disappeared altogether.

Like Philidor before him, Steinitz's fame is not only based on his excellent results in
practical play but also on his writings which could, with only the slightest of exag-
gerations even be called scientific work, for Steinitz was one of the greatest re-
searchers and theorists in chess history. He analysed the game in great depth, rein-
vented everything that was already known and formulated a new theory of chess,
based on a positional understanding of the game. Again, like Philidor, he underlined
the importance of strategical thinking. According to him, combinations, or tactical
solutions, could only work if they had a solid base in strategy or if the opponent had
made a clear mistake which demanded punishment. Steinitz's theoretical work
earned him many an honorary nickname such as "the Michelangelo of chess", but
he shared the fate of many other great reformers who where ahead of their time:
recognition came only after he was dead. Among his contemporaries there was little understanding for his 'bizarre' emphasis on strategy and many even felt re-
pulsed by his uncompromising and aggressively polemic style (one of his many
broadsides was aptly titled "Ink War"). However Steinitz's successors, most notably
Lasker and Tarrasch, had great admiration for his theoretical writings. Steinitz published his ideas in many magazines, mainly in England and America, in his own *International Chess Magazine*, and in a book, *The Modern Chess Instructor*, which is
still in print today.

Although his writings strongly emphasised (and advocated) positional chess, it
would be a grave misunderstanding to think that Steinitz was a onesided, possibly
even 'dull' *player*. His view of the interconnectedness of strategy and tactics is wonderfully illustrated by one of his most famous games, that also gives us a chance to
eliminate some of the most persistent misunderstandings about what 'positional
play' really is.

♙ Steinitz, William
♟ Von Bardeleben, Curt
🕐 Hastings 1895

"Hastings 1895" is generally regarded as a highlight in the history of chess. Every great player of the time took part, making a total of no less than 22 participants. These 22 played each other once – the round-robin format had by now become the norm – so the tournament consisted of 21 rounds; the strain and the effort involved must have been tremendous for all players. Surprise winner of the event was the young American Harry Nelson Pillsbury (1872-1906), who scored 16½ points from 21 games, finishing ahead of Chigorin (16 points), World Champion Lasker (15½), Tarrasch (14) and Steinitz (13). Steinitz, by now sixty years old, is unlikely to have been happy with his fifth place, but in all fairness one can only be impressed by the way he held his own in this exhausting tournament amongst a pack of hungry young wolves. Von Bardeleben finished seventh with 11½ points, still an excellent performance. This game was played in round ten. At that point Von Bardeleben was the only player not yet to have lost a game.

1. e4 e5 2. ♘f3 ♘c6 3. ♗c4 ♗c5 4. c3 ♘f6 5. d4

This was the main line of this opening, called the Italian Game, for many decades. Nowadays a more prudent set-up based on d2-d3 is almost universally preferred.

5... exd4 6. cxd4

If White were able to consolidate his 'ideal' pawn centre (pawns on e4 and d4) his opening strategy would be a great success. The problem is that Black is able to strike back just in time.

6... ♗b4+ 7. ♘c3

A pawn sacrifice, designed to keep the initiative. 7. ♗d2 ♗xd2+ 8. ♘bxd2 is a more careful approach, to which 8... d5 is the intended reply. Steinitz however, is not interested in taking care.

⚠ *MISUNDERSTANDING*
Number 1:

Positional play is not the same as a careful approach!

7... d5

Black avoids the critical move 7...♘xe4, accepting the sacrifice. White would then sacrifice another pawn by playing 8.0-0, based on the assumption that his lead in development outweighs the material deficit. This variation has been known since the 17th century and is still played today.

8. exd5 ♘xd5 9. 0-0

White's opening strategy is based on a rapid development of all his pieces. The 'sacrifice' he makes in order to achieve this is of a *positional* nature: his d-pawn has become isolated. As a consequence not only will the pawn itself be a liability from now on (for it can't be defended by other pawns), but also the so-called blockading square in front of it (d5) becomes an ideal square for Black to place his pieces since they can never be attacked by pawns.

Ironically, it was Steinitz himself who formulated this principle as a basic rule of positional chess. However, being the great strategist he was, Steinitz also knew the *advantages* of having an isolated pawn: White has more space and this tends to give him the initiative. What Steinitz understood better than most is that White really has to *do* something with his initiative, for if he doesn't it will gradually pass to Black. This game is a prime example.

⚠ *MISUNDERSTANDING*

Number 2:

The 'laws' of positional chess are never dogma

9... ♗e6 10. ♗g5 ♗e7 11. ♗xd5 ♗xd5 12. ♘xd5 ♕xd5 13. ♗xe7 ♘xe7 14. ♖e1

Position after: 14. ♖e1

The point of the previous exchanges: Black is unable to castle so he somehow has to wriggle his king into safety. Still, in a strategic sense White is walking a tightrope. *If* Black manages to get his rooks into play the large-scale piece exchanges will start working to *his* advantage.

14... f6 15. ♕e2 ♕d7 16. ♖ac1 c6?

In the end it is Black who is overcareful! Contemporary commentators suggested that Von Bardeleben probably decided against the more natural 16...♔f7! because of the exchange sacrifice 17.♕xe7+ ♕xe7 18.♖xe7+ ♔xe7 19.♖xc7+ followed by either 20.♖xb7 or 20.♖xg7. Yet this endgame would have been infinitely preferable to the text move.

(see diagram next page)

17. d5!

A powerful pawn sacrifice, which turns

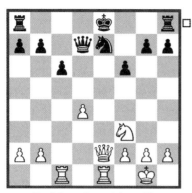

Position after: 16... c6?

the tables. Black cannot capture the pawn with either queen or knight, so after

17... cxd5 18. ♘d4

it is now White who enjoys all the advantages of an ideal blockading square. The immediate threat is 19.♘f5.

⚠ *MISUNDERSTANDING*

Number 3:

Strategy and tactics go together well!

18... ♔f7 19. ♘e6

Threatening 20.♖c7.

19... ♖hc8

At first glance it may look as if this move solves Black's problems but in reality

White's attack now begins in earnest.

20. ♕g4!

This of course threatens 21.♕xg7+, but it also exposes a crucial flaw in Black's defences: his unprotected queen at d7.

20... g6 21. ♘g5+ ♔e8

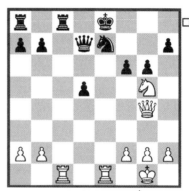

Position after: 21... ♔e8

22. ♖xe7+!!

The brilliance of this move lies not so much in what happens if Black captures the rook, but in what happens if he does not take *and* in what White does *not* play here. He could have gone for 22.♘xh7! which leaves him a safe pawn up in the endgame after 22...♕xg4 23.♘xf6+ ♔f7 24.♘xg4. Steinitz's move brings far greater rewards in the end, but the depth and accuracy of the calculation required are huge. Many players would not have had the courage or the self-confidence to go for it, even if they had spotted 27.♖xe7+.

22... ♔f8!

It is easy to see that 22...♕xe7 23.♖xc8+ loses. Calculating the winning variations after 22...♔xe7 23.♖e1+ accurately (23...♔d6 24.♕b4+ ♔c7 25.♘e6+ ♔b8 26.♕f4+ and 23...♔d8 24.♘e6+ ♔d7 25.♘c5+) is a little more difficult, but nothing an experienced player couldn't manage. Yet to see that White has a win even after 22...♔f8!, with pieces hanging on e7, g4 and g5 *and* the threat of mate on c1 is brilliant and transforms what would otherwise be a good but unexceptional attacking game into a masterpiece.

23. ♖f7+

Alright, this move is perhaps not so difficult to spot (23...♕xf7 24.♖xc8+ is easy enough), but what does it achieve after Black's next move?

23... ♔g8

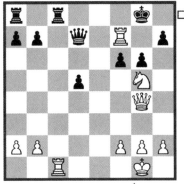

Position after: 23... ♔g8

24. ♖g7+!

Continuing to riff on the same theme. Black cannot take this rook with his king because White then captures the queen with check (24...♔xg7 25.♕xd7+) nor can he take with the queen (24...♕xg7) because of 25.♖xc8+. Since 24...♔f8 loses instantly to 25.♘xh7+ Black is left with only one move.

24... ♔h8 25. ♖xh7+!

And Black resigned, that is to say: he left the playing hall and didn't come back. Steinitz had to wait for his opponent's time to run out before the arbiters could declare him the winner. It was not exactly the behaviour of a gentleman, but it shows how much losing a game can mean to a real chess player. And Von Bardeleben's resignation at this point shows that he *was* a real chess player, for the final move of White's combination still lies no less than ten moves ahead and is not obvious. After the forced 25...♔g8 White again plays 26.♖g7+! when after 26...♔h8 the absence of Black's h-pawn makes itself felt, giving White a forced mate in nine moves: 27.♕h4+! ♔xg7 28.♕h7+ ♔f8 29.♕h8+ ♔e7 30. ♕g7+ ♔e8 31.♕g8+ ♔e7 32.♕f7+ ♔d8 33.♕f8+ ♕e8 34.♘f7+ ♔d7 35.♕d6 mate.

The top five placegetters from this legendary event were then invited to another tournament a few months later in Saint Petersburg 1895/96. Tarrasch declined, but the other four, Lasker, Steinitz, Chigorin and Pillsbury, battled it out in 18 extremely tough rounds, each player meeting every other six times.

Again Steinitz did surprisingly well, scoring 9½/18 and finishing second behind Lasker. However in a return match for the World Championship, a year later in Moscow, Steinitz didn't have a chance and Lasker won with 10 wins, 2 losses and 5 draws. After this match Steinitz's health began to fail, both physically and mentally. He kept playing tournaments and still managed some good results, although not for long as he died in 1900 in a psychiatric hospital in New York.

Emanuel Lasker

World Champion from 1894 to 1921, the reign of Emanuel Lasker over the chess world was not only exceptionally long, but also coincided with one of the worst periods of international warfare and social upheaval in human history.

Born in the kingdom of Prussia in 1868, Lasker witnessed not just his own country but almost the whole of Europe being torn up and reconfigured several times and when he died in New York in 1941 stability and peace seemed further away than ever. Apart from all the horror and persecution Lasker also lived through a period of scientific invention and new technologies which completely changed day-to-day life: electricity, telephony, bicycles and cars, the spread of which contributed to making the world smaller and life more comfortable.

That Lasker managed to retain the title of World Champion for as long as he did in these tumultuous times is of course a tremendous feat. However Lasker was helped by the fact that, in contrast with the wider world, the *chess* world did not change so much, at least not as far as the World Championship was concerned. The reigning Champion still had to be challenged and beaten (and those were *two* great hurdles to overcome), otherwise nothing would change.

Lasker was acutely aware of the drawbacks of this situation and worked tirelessly to modernise and professionalise the chess world. He aimed for an increase in prize money in both tournaments and matches for the World Championship and in 1900 he even founded a (not very succesful) trade union for chess players. Towards the end of his reign Lasker suggested he might step down as World Champion and during the laborious negotiations that preceded his match against Capablanca in 1921 he actually *did* step down – but the unorganised chess world somehow refused to accept this, so the match still went down in history as between *World Champion* Lasker and *challenger* Capablanca, regardless of what the two combatants themselves had to say about it at the time.

Lasker's defeat of Steinitz in 1894 heralded the start of a long and brilliant career. Even for a World Champion Lasker was exceptionally successful, both in matches and tournaments and he has often been called 'the greatest chess player who ever lived'. It is not much of an exaggeration to say that he won wherever he went and it is certainly true that – unlike Morphy – he continued to do so almost until the end of his life. This is made even more impressive when you consider that Lasker – unlike Philidor – always had to compete against very strong rivals, players who would have made worthy World Champions themselves... if there had been no Las-

Emanuel Lasker

ker to stand in their way. Lasker's most narrow escape came in 1910 when, in a ten game contest against the Austrian Carl Schlechter (1874-1918) he had to win the last game in order to tie the match and did so after a tremendous fight. This was the only match for the World Championship (apart from the one against Capablanca) which Lasker did not win by a large margin.

Equally legendary was his victory in Saint Petersburg in 1914. Though the World Championship was not officially at stake here, a new 'proof of superiority' was urgently needed for Lasker after no less than four years of abstinence from any form of tournament activity.

Many people had been writing him off, not just because he was already 45 years of age, but also because two bright young stars, José Raúl Capablanca from Cuba and Akiba Rubinstein (1880-1961) from Poland, had been extremely successful during these four years. It was felt that each of them fully deserved a match against Lasker and would probably beat him.

Rubinstein had a disappointing tournament in Saint Petersburg, but Capablanca played phenomenally well. The Cuban seemed to be heading for a huge success until, in one of the most thrilling finales of any tournament in history, Lasker suc-

Two legends at the board: Capablanca and Lasker (right)

ceeded in catching up with his rival just before the end and overtaking him on the finish line. A few months later the First World War broke out, making a match between Lasker and Capablanca an impossibility.

Even when that match finally came in 1921 and Capablanca took the crown – Lasker abandoning the match after 14 games, having not won a single game while losing four – Lasker was by no means finished. In yet another legendary tournament, in 1924 in New York, Lasker celebrated one of the greatest triumphs of his career, winning first prize with 16 points from 20 extremely tough games, ahead of Capablanca and several other young stars, one of them the future World Champion Alexander Alekhine. A year later Lasker finished second in another very strong tournament in Moscow, behind Efim Bogoljubov (1889-1952) but again ahead of Capablanca. Lasker then ended his chess career, only to be forced to resume it nine years later when, like so many others, he had to flee his native Germany after Hitler came to power in 1933. Urgently needing money, Lasker played in several top tournaments between 1934 and 1936 and, although by now in his sixties, his results remained very impressive. In Moscow 1935, when 66, Lasker finished just half a point behind the winners, future World Champion Mikhail Botvinnik and Czech Salo Flohr, but (again) ahead of Capablanca plus all the best players the Soviet Union then had to offer. Lasker's score was 12½/19 without a single defeat.

This leads us to one of the most significant changes the chess world underwent during Lasker's lifetime and which could be described as 'the coming of age' of the draw. Until about 1900 draws were generally looked upon as wasted effort: necessary because there is an inherent drawing margin in chess – stalemate, repetition of moves, the impossibility of mate in certain endgames – but not as a desirable or even a useful result. In matches draws were usually not counted, while in tournaments drawn games were often replayed in order to get a 'proper' result. As a consequence draws were rare. The mindset of chess players in the 19th century was geared to winning or losing only, to take no prisoners.

This attitude to draws began to change when Steinitz (and science in general) taught the world to look at phenomena in a more scientific way. Steinitz analysed chess games assessing *positional* factors, not just tactical calculations. He showed that there is such a thing as 'positional equilibrium', which will only be disturbed if one of the players makes a mistake. When no mistakes are made a draw is the natural, logical and just outcome of a game.

The generation after Steinitz embraced this new and at the time revolutionary insight. Tarrasch for instance, who wrote about chess mostly in a didactic and sometimes pedantic manner and who had a tremendous influence on future generations, was a severe critic of everything which was not logical and correct. Tarrasch thoroughly disapproved of games which could not be explained in terms of logic, even when they contained a brilliant combination. Even the games of Lasker, then a young World Champion, did not escape his criticisms. From his writings one gains the impression that Tarrasch thought of himself as a much better player than Lasker until the latter beat him soundly (8-3 plus 5 draws) in a World Championship match in 1908.

Yet even Lasker, who is universally and justly considered one of the greatest fighters in the history of chess, understood and accepted the 'scientific' structure of chess, which Steinitz had brought to light. Lasker felt no shame if a game of his ended in a draw and indeed the abovementioned match Lasker-Schlechter saw eight out of ten games end in a draw. In a way players like Schlechter embodied a new approach to the game: winning is of course good, but a draw is not a bad result either. Schlechter was exceptionally tough to beat, even for Lasker, and that became his trademark. The draw had become socially acceptable.

During the Lasker era chess evolved into what we would now call a professional sport, with most of the top players earning their living from chess. Lasker was one

of these professionals, yet he also had an amazing number of other interests, talents and even professional activities, which sometimes kept him away from the
tournament arena for years and some of which he seems to have valued higher
than his achievements in chess.

The extent of Lasker's involvement with and interest in other games was unusually high. He was a very good bridge and Go player, published extensively on these
and other board and card games, and even invented a game of his own, based on
draughts, which he called Lasca.

In addition Lasker also studied mathematics and philosophy, obtaining a PhD in
the former in 1901 and publishing a number of books and articles in both areas.
At a time when so much fighting, murder and suffering was going on (the First
World War, the Russian Revolution and Civil War, Nazi Germany, Stalin) it is probably not a coincidence that the central theme of his thinking and writing is 'struggle': a theme that characterises him both as a human being and as a chess player.
Lasker was a fighter through and through. Although he wrote several influential
instructional manuals (*Lasker's Manual of Chess* and *Common Sense in Chess* being the most famous) it is often said of him that he "founded no school" in the
way several of his contemporaries did (Steinitz, Tarrasch, Euwe).

This misunderstanding of Lasker – for that is what it is – is something he has in
common with other truly independent thinkers. His attitude was not to encourage
a doctrinaire copying of examples or a following of 'methods', but to encourage
people to investigate and find out for themselves. A teacher like that does not
surround himself with pupils, but sends them out into the world to inspire others.

Lasker's games are completely modern in almost every way so they are as thrilling
and instructive today as they were to his contemporaries. This makes selecting his
best games rather difficult and very much a matter of taste, though there can be
little dispute that one of his greatest efforts was the abovementioned game
against Capablanca from Saint Petersburg 1914.

♙ Lasker, Emanuel
♟ Capablanca, José Raúl
🌐 Saint Petersburg 1914

1. e4 e5 2. ♘f3 ♘c6 3. ♗b5 a6 4. ♗xc6

The Exchange Variation has always been considered a sideline, an occasional choice for people wanting to get away from the main lines starting with 4.♗a4. But Lasker truly believed in 4.♗xc6 and regarded the general opinion that "4.♗a4 must be stronger" as prejudice. Even so to play this line in a game of such vital importance, *and* against an opponent who had a reputation for being unbeatable, must have felt like an act of provocation. Lasker is silently challenging his opponent to prove that the 'theoretical' evaluation of 4.♗xc6 as being impotent is correct. Indeed the Exchange Variation enjoyed a certain popularity during the Saint Petersburg tournament. Capablanca had tried it himself against Janowski and only one round earlier Lasker had had to face it on the black side, against Alekhine. So Lasker's choice of 4.♗xc6 also contained the element of being 'hot', which always has a slightly intimidating effect.

4... dxc6 5. d4 exd4 6. ♕xd4 ♕xd4 7. ♘xd4 ♗d6 8. ♘c3 ♘e7 9. 0-0 0-0 10. f4!

Position after: 10. f4!

A powerful move, the originality and depth of which can still be felt today. In the tournament book Tarrasch shows himself so impressed with it that he even casts doubt on the correctness of 3...a6. His comments, along with Capablanca's inability to come up with a convincing reply in the game, are clear proof of the depth and complexity of the problems posed by Lasker's opening play. The triumph of an independent mind!

10... ♖e8

A hesitant reply. Tarrasch remarks that if nothing else Black should at least have played 10... ♗c5 and only after 11.♗e3 should he have played 11...♖e8.

His view on the position is that Black should somehow attack White's central formation with ...f7-f5 in order to provoke e4-e5, which would turn e6 and d5 into beautiful squares for Black's pieces.

11. ♘b3! f6

Not an uncommon move in this type of position, yet this gets a '?' from Tarrasch. Black prevents e4-e5 and prepares possible development of his queen's bishop via e6 to f7. What *is* unusual is Lasker's next move, putting his finger with unerring accuracy on Black's key problem: his lack of space.

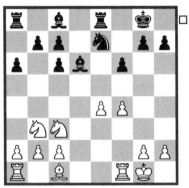

Position after: 11... f6

12. f5!

If 10.f4 was already a novel idea at the time, this move caused a sensation. White voluntarily yields control over the e5 square, which on the face of it now becomes an ideal outpost for Black's pieces. What is more, White voluntarily breaks up the flexibility of his pawn chain, making it more difficult to turn his majority on the kingside into a passed pawn.

However Lasker has looked more deeply into the position. He has seen that Black is unable to permanently occupy

e5 since on 12...♗e5 the reply 13.♗f4 prevents Black from consolidating his grip on e5 by playing ...b7-b6, ...c6-c5 followed by ♘e7-c6.

Moreover Black's queen's bishop is now stuck on c8, making it difficult for Black to develop and connect his rooks. Capablanca's next moves deal with these problems, but White keeps the initiative.

12... b6 13. ♗f4 ♗b7

A hard decision to make. It seems natural to allow White to 'repair' Black's pawn structure by exchanging bishops on d6, but the d6-pawn will be vulnerable and the 'repaired' pawn chain does not in itself provide Black with chances to regain the initiative. In all likelihood the alternative 13... ♗xf4 14. ♖xf4 c5 (to stop ♘b3-d4) would have been a better choice.

14. ♗xd6 cxd6 15. ♘d4 ♖ad8 16. ♘e6

A commanding position for the knight. Not only does it sit annoyingly close to Black's king, it also blocks off any pressure the black rooks might exert on the e-file. It is clear that Lasker has won the opening battle.

16... ♖d7 17. ♖ad1

Again Black faces a difficult choice. Should he try to free himself by playing 17...c5 or 17...d5 at the cost of weakening his position? Capablanca decides to keep his pawn structure intact and the position closed.

17... ♞c8 18. ♖f2 b5 19. ♖fd2

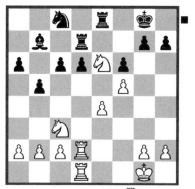

Position after: 19. ♖fd2

White has succeeded in locking his opponent up in a passive position, but what is the next step? Lasker's approach is highly instructive. Without any hurry he starts improving every single detail of his position that *can* be improved. His first priority is to discourage any possible attempt at a breakout. The d6-pawn is kept under pressure so that Black's knight on c8 cannot move which in turn makes it impossible for Black's bishop to attack the knight on e6 via c8. In the long term White is planning to open a file for his rooks.

19... ♖de7 20. b4

Preventing both ...b5-b4 and ...c6-c5, while fixing the pawn on b5 in order to

eventually open either the a- or the c-file with a2-a4 or c2-c4.

20... ♚f7 21. a3

No hurry.

21... ♝a8 22. ♚f2 ♖a7 23. g4

After thorough preparation White finally reveals his master plan: an attack on the kingside with g4-g5. Yet it soon becomes transparent that he is in no hurry to actually *execute* this plan. Keeping any possible counterplay in check remains firmly at the top of his agenda.

23... h6 24. ♖d3 a5

Is this a counterattack? As long as White has a knight on c3 there is no danger at all for White on the queenside and later this pawn push will turn against Black. Still, it is almost impossible for a defender to refrain from any form of counterplay whatsoever and whether this would have been a better strategy objectively is moot in any case.

25. h4 axb4 26. axb4 ♖ae7

This yielding of the open a-file to White could be taken as an admission that Black's attempt at counterplay has failed, but nothing is decided yet. Black is protecting every weak point in his position very well and keeps an eye out for counterattacks. One option for Black is to sacrifice an exchange on e6. Lasker does not prevent this, but takes great care not to make it more attractive than it currently is. For instance, he keeps his knight firmly on c3 in order not to weaken e4.

27. ♔f3 ♖g8 28. ♔f4

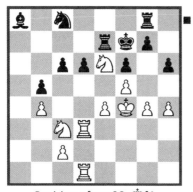

Position after: 28. ♔f4

One would expect White to use his rooks to prepare the g4-g5 advance, yet Lasker uses his king, to great effect. This is a prime example of the unconventional thinking which was characteristic of Lasker. The following moves suggest that Capablanca doesn't really know how to cope with this 'straightforward yet not straightforward' approach. Lasker often had such an effect on his opponents. His play and, according to eyewitnesses, his whole personality often exuded a feeling of superiority unsettling to even the strongest opponents.

28... g6 29. ♖g3 g5+

This move is severely criticised by Tarrasch, who recommends 29...gxf5. Is he right? There is a deep and clever idea behind this move, except that it does not work out the way Capablanca has envisaged.

30. ♔f3!

White won't open the h-file until his rooks are ready to take control of it. 30...gxh4 31.♖h3 is nothing to worry about.

30... ♘b6

All things considered, this is a truly fantastic defensive ploy. Black sacrifices his d- pawn in order to get a knight to ...e5 via ...c4. If this works (31.♖xd6? ♘c4) the game assumes a wholly different character and White will have to start all over again. However White's attack on the kingside is just in time, a strong indication that Lasker foresaw Capablanca's idea.

31. hxg5 hxg5 32. ♖h3!

If now 32...♘c4 the knight does indeed get to ...e5, but in the meantime White's rook invasion is decisive: 33.♖h7+ ♔e8 34.♘c7+ ♔d7 35. ♖xe7+ ♔xe7 36. ♖a1 ♗b7 37.♖a7.

32... ♖d7 33. ♔g3!

Again Lasker displays an impressive degree of self-control. As long as Black's knight remains on ...b6 (to cover d7) the exchange of rooks is not yet decisive. So he calmly steps away from a possible knight check on e5, making sure that the ...♘b6-c4-e5 manoeuvre will never gain Black a tempo. Now an invasion is threatened on both sides of the board.

33... ♔e8 34. ♖dh1 ♗b7

It seems Black has managed to cover all his weak spots; although a rook invasion via h7 or h8 remains unpleasant it doesn't seem lethal yet. So how does White proceed?

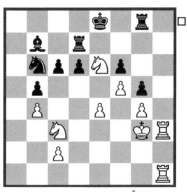

Position after: 34... ♗b7

35. e5!

A marvellous, purely positional pawn sacrifice. The white knight joins the battle via e4. All White's pieces are working together harmoniously in the final attack.

35... dxe5 36. ♘e4 ♘d5

This covers f6 at least, but there are now weaknesses everywhere.

37. ♘6c5

Winning the exchange without in any way diminishing the force of the attack.

37... ♗c8 38. ♘xd7 ♗xd7 39. ♖h7 ♖f8 40. ♖a1 ♔d8 41. ♖a8+ ♗c8 42. ♘c5

Black resigned. His once impregnable fortress is completely destroyed.

This game is an impressive demonstration of how Lasker fully concentrated his efforts in the middlegame and endgame while he kept the opening phase as short and simple as possible. To be successful with an attitude like this requires not just a deep understanding of chess in all its aspects, but a phenomenal tenacity in converting even the slightest of positional advantages. Lasker's will to win was one of his greatest assets.

Yet what set him apart from his contemporaries even more was his tenacity as a defender. Many strong players, even some of the great ones, are prepared to do their utmost to win an *advantageous* position, but lack the dogged perseverance needed to defend an *inferior* position.

A classic example from Lasker's day is Dawid Janowksi (1868-1917), originally from Poland, later a French citizen. So long as he held the initiative Janowski could beat anyone, but if a game took a turn for the worse he was inclined simply to lose interest. Endgames in particular were not to his liking. Such a player will either win brilliantly or lose horribly. Lasker, on the contrary, had all the patience for a protracted defence when needed. Under no circumstances would he ever lose his intensity, his motivation, his fighting spirit.

Here is one example of Lasker's defensive skills in the endgame, taken from the same tournament as the game above:

 Lasker, Emanuel
 Tarrasch, Siegbert
Saint Petersburg 1914

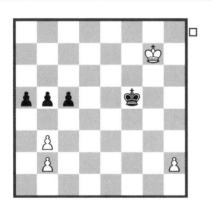

Tarrasch had gone straight for this pawn endgame, convinced that it was an easy win for him. And why shouldn't it be? Black's majority on the queenside is unstoppable while White's h-pawn is within reach of Black's king. But Lasker demonstrates that this is in fact an optical illusion. By looking at the position in a *concrete* way instead

of relying on general considerations, it is possible to find a *concrete* path to salvation for Black.

40. h4 ♚g4

Now what? After 41.♚f6 (to try to get back to the queenside) 41...c4 42.bxc4 bxc4 43.♚e5 c3! 44.bxc3 a4, White's king is too late to stop the a-pawn.

41. ♚g6!

On the one hand this move is obvious, for (unlike after 41.♚f6) White now threatens to play 42.h5. On the other hand it is counter-intuitive, for the route back to the queenside seems longer via g6. Yet that is precisely the sort of 'lazy' thinking that Lasker was impervious to.

41... ♚xh4 42. ♚f5

And all is clear: White is just in time. If 42...c4 43.bxc4 bxc4 44. ♚e4 c3

45.bxc3 a4 46.♔d3, Black's a-pawn is within reach of White's king. Suddenly it is Black who has to be careful.

42... ♔g3 **43.** ♔e4 ♔f2 **44.** ♔d5 ♔e3 **45.** ♔xc5 ♔d3 **46.** ♔xb5 ♔c2 **47.** ♔xa5 ♔xb3   **Draw**

The theme of this endgame, the successful combining of two totally different and seemingly impossible tasks, by a king far away from the scene of action, was probably the inspiration for what has perhaps become *the* most famous endgame study of all time.

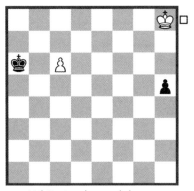

White to play and draw.

Ever since 1921, the year when this study by the Austro-Hungarian, later Czechoslovak player and composer Richard Réti (1889-1929) was published, students of the game have looked at this position in wonder and disbelief. How on earth can White's king get back in time? He needs two extra moves to catch Black's h-pawn *and* he needs two extra moves to support his own c-pawn.

Again, to put the problem like this is to fall prey to an optical illusion. Paradoxically, the solution is not at all difficult. White saves himself by playing the most obvious moves. Only the *strength* of these moves is not obvious. Even so,

imagine getting this position in a practical game. Who would not resign at this point in sheer desperation?

1. ♔g7! h4

1...♔b6 is met by the same reply.

2. ♔f6!

Now there is a first glimmer of hope, for if 2...h3 White's king can support his pawn by playing 3. ♔e6 (or 3.♔e7) when 3...h2 4.c7 ♔b7 5.♔d7 is indeed a draw.

2... ♔b6

But now what?

3. ♔e5!

The impossible has been achieved. If 4...♔xc6 White has 5.♔f4, neutralising Black's h-pawn, while if 4...h3 there is 5.♔d6 and White's c-pawn becomes unstoppable so that *both* pawns will queen, resulting in a drawn queen endgame: 5...h2 6.c7 ♔b7 7.♔d7.

It is a mathematical impossibility, but not in chess: by moving diagonally (h8-g7-f6-e5) instead of in a straight line (h8-h7-h6-h5 or h8-g8-f8-e8) White forces his opponent to make two king moves (♔a6-b6xc6) and thus gets back

exactly the two tempi that he seemed to be missing in the starting position. In honour of this truly brilliant endgame study, this motif has been called the Réti manoeuvre ever since.

A similarly famous endgame study was composed by Lasker himself. Here, too, the impossible becomes a reality. Yet in this case the key to the solution lies not so much in overcoming of a sense of disbelief as in the tenacity to keep on calculating a logical variation to its very end. Typical Lasker.

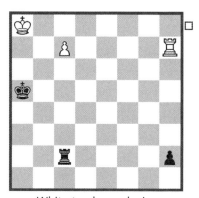

White to play and win.

Equal material, both sides have a pawn on the seventh rank. Why should White be better in the first place? Because his king supports his own pawn and the black king doesn't, although this in itself is not enough to win. Specific moves by White's king are crucial.

1. ♔b7

Simple enough. White now threatens to promote his pawn. There is only one defence.

1... ♖b2+

Now how can White make any progress? If his king walks back to 'silence' the Black rook, say 2.♔c6 ♖c2+ 3.♔d6 ♖d2+ 4.♔e5, Black will simply attack the c-pawn at a convenient moment (e.g. 4...♖c2), when the dual threats of 5...h1=♕ and 5...♖xc7 force White to protect his pawn again (5.♔d6) and Black starts checking all over again (5...♖d2+).

2. ♔a7!

At first glance this is not a better square for the king than any other, but after the forced reply

2... ♖c2

it turns out that there is one crucial difference...

3. ♖h5+!

A *zwischenzug* or rather a *zwischenschach*. Before White protects his pawn again he forces the Black king to a different square and it immediately becomes clear that there isn't a great choice: b6, which would be ideal, is obviously inaccessible and if 3...♔b4? White forces pawn promotion by going back to b7 (4.♔b7) when Black has no check along the b-file. So there is only one move.

3... ♔a4

Now 4.♔b7 ♖b2+ is the same as before, so what is the problem?

4. ♔b6!

Admittedly, this does not threaten 4.c8=♕ (as 4.♔b7 would have done), but what it does threaten is 4.♖xh2, resulting in a queen versus rook endgame which is theoretically winning. So a check on the b-file is still compulsory.

4... ♖b2+ 5. ♔a6! ♖c2 6. ♖h4+!

Repeating the procedure. Again White pushes the Black king backwards before he protects his pawn.

6... ♔a3 7. ♔b6!

And again 8.♖xh2 is threatened. Black has no choice: he has to keep alternately checking White's king and attacking the c-pawn.

7... ♖b2+ 8. ♔a5! ♖c2 9. ♖h3+! ♔a2

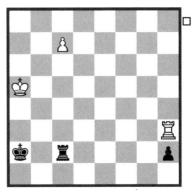

Position after: 9... ♔a2

White has managed to push the Black king all the way back to the second rank. This introduces a new motif...

10. ♖xh2!

Because Black's king is on a2 his rook is now pinned so he cannot take on c7. The queen versus rook endgame has become unavoidable. White wins.

This motif, like that of Réti, has been named after its inventor, becoming the Lasker manoeuvre.

Lasker didn't care much for 'artificial' endgame studies. But in the above – highly realistic – endgame he managed to combine the artistic element of the endgame study with the 'feel' of an ordinary practical game (it is not a coincidence that this motif has occurred quite a few times in practical games). *Common Sense in Chess*: Lasker's philosophy in a nutshell.

José Raúl Capablanca

José Raúl Capablanca (1888-1942) from Cuba, the man who succeeded Lasker to the chess throne in 1921, was in more ways than one the complete opposite of his predecessor. The start of his career reminds one very strongly of Paul Morphy. Both were child prodigies, left their native cities at an early age to go to New York, conquered the American chess world in a flash and then crossed the Atlantic to conquer Europe as well.

However that is where every similarity between the two ends. To begin with, Capablanca met *one* opponent who wouldn't budge (Lasker). More importantly in the long run, Capablanca did not retire from chess and in fact remained one of the best players in the world until his death.

Yet what separates Capablanca the most, not just from his immediate predecessor but from all other World Champions (except perhaps Morphy!), is the apparent ease with which he played. Capablanca's speed, and above that his elegance and simplicity, somehow made his games, seemingly of their own accord, go *his* way not his opponent's. Capablanca's play seemed effortless. He didn't spend much time studying the game and he seems to have been a stranger to self-criticism or introspection. Typically, he once commented on a game where the opening had not gone to his liking by writing "I don't know where I went wrong, for I have the fortunate habit to forget not just games by other players, but even my own games". He made laziness and nonchalance look like virtues, defeating earnestness and a capacity for hard work in others. In reality it was of course pure, dispassionate talent, only this talent manifested itself in a non-intellectual, handsome, charming, self-assured man of the world, rather than in someone like

Lasker, who was a scientist, a philosopher, a man of the mind. Nevertheless, the speed with which Capablanca grasped a position at the chessboard and the ease with which he played were held in high esteem by his contemporaries and have since become legendary.

Capablanca's results speak for themselves. The superiority with which he won his first match against an established world class player (8-1 with 14 draws against Frank Marshall in 1909 in New York), his glorious debut in Europe (winning the tournament of San Sebastian 1911, ahead of all the best players in the world except Lasker), his incredible results in huge and exhausting simultaneous exhibitions (the high point being his 102½ out of 103 in an exhibition in Cleveland in 1922), his near invincibility (between 1916 and 1924 he did not lose a single game) – all these are feats that can't be explained in words. Capablanca was a unique phenomenon in the world of chess and it is not surprising that there have always been more than a few admirers who regard *him* as 'the best player that ever lived'. In this light it is perhaps a little sur-

José Raúl Capablanca

prising that his reign as World Champion did not last very long. If, as we saw in the previous chapter, there is some room for discussion about when it began (though the year 1921, when Capablanca beat Lasker, is almost universally accepted, not 1920, when Lasker announced he had stepped down in favour of the Cuban), there can be no argument about when it ended. In 1927 Alekhine defeated Capablanca 6-3 with 25 draws and took over the world title.

It was a completely unexpected, sensational defeat. Perhaps Capablanca had become a little *too* assured of his own superiority, coming to the match psychologically unprepared for a tough battle against an evenly matched and fully determined opponent. Alekhine himself has said that Capablanca underestimated him but whatever the reason for his victory, Alekhine showed himself a worthy successor, who went on to rule over the chess world with an iron fist.

After the loss of his title Capablanca remained one of the best players in the world until his death in 1942. If the World Championship hadn't been 'enjoying' its final spell as a form of private property, Capablanca would almost certainly have received a chance for revenge, but under Alekhine's reign it was not to be. The extensive correspondence between Alekhine and Capablanca about a possible rematch contains many acrimonious and uncompromising passages, sadly inflaming their personal relationship.

With Capablanca chess became even further removed from the romantic nineteenth century path. Adolf Anderssen would not have recognised his beloved game in the ultra-efficient playing style of the legendary Cuban, who was a past master at creating and exploiting even the tiniest of positional advantages. This is not to say that Capablanca did not have an eye for the combinational side of chess. On the contrary, he was famous and much feared for his *petites combinaisons*: surprising, yet not overly complicated, combinations – but only if it was the shortest way to the desired result!

The games of Capablanca are living proof that strategy and tactics differ only in name. Both are dependent on a clear understanding of a position and the capacity to distinguish between what is essential and what is not. A famous example of this merging of strategy and tactics is the following game.

♙   Bernstein, Ossip
♟   Capablanca, José Raúl
🕐   Moscow 1914

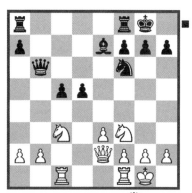

Position after: 15. ♕e2

A strategically tense position. Black's pawns on c5 and d5, a configuration called 'hanging pawns', could become weak *or* strong. Without hesitation Capablanca takes the initiative.

15... c4!

Black 'sacrifices' the d4-square in order to give scope to his bishop and to create a target on b2 before White gets the chance to consolidate his queenside with b2-b3. This is a courageous strategic decision from which many players would have shied away.

16. ♖fd1 ♖fd8 17. ♘d4 ♗b4!

Introducing the option to take on c3,

followed by ♘f6-e4 and possibly ♘e4-c5-d3. In response White decides to attack the pawn on c4, a logical yet risky decision because it is not yet clear whether this pawn is going to be strong or weak. As a result the character of the game immediately changes; a polite, philosophical conversation between two gentlemen turns into a street fight.

18. b3 ♖ac8 19. bxc4 dxc4 20. ♖c2 ♗xc3 21. ♖xc3 ♘d5!

Now 22.♖xc4 is forbidden because of 22...♘c3! when White has to give up rook for knight. Yet the question remains: is Black's c-pawn weak or strong?

**22. ♖c2 c3 23. ♖dc1 ♖c5 24. ♘b3
♖c6 25. ♘d4 ♖c7**

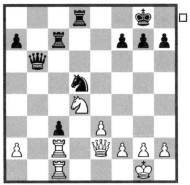

Position after: 25... ♖c7

Avoiding a draw by repetition, Black increases the pressure. Black has no direct threat, but with moves like ♖d8-c8 en ♘d5-b4 in the offing, it is understandable that Bernstein now succumbs to the temptation to eliminate the c-pawn once and for all and liquidate this tense middlegame into what looks like a tenable endgame. To continue to bear the tension even when the pressure seems unbearable is one of the greatest challenges for any defender.

26. ♘b5? ♖c5 27. ♘xc3?

Bernstein probably counted on

27...♘xc3 28.♖xc3 ♖xc3 29.♖xc3 ♕b1+ 30.♕f1 when 30...♖d1? fails to 31.♖c8+, while 30...♕xa2 offers Black no more than minimal winning chances. The next two moves seem to confirm this train of thought, until ...

27... ♘xc3 28. ♖xc3 ♖xc3 29. ♖xc3

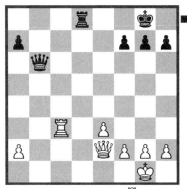

Position after: 29. ♖xc3

29... ♕b2!!

A simple move, yet with tremendous impact. The queen can't be taken because of the back rank mate on d1, so both White's queen and rook find themselves under attack. If 30.♕e1 Black repeats the same motif with 30...♕xc3!.

The game is over. Devastated, White resigned.

It is little wonder that Capablanca's purposeful and businesslike playing style also made him a formidable endgame virtuoso, yet even in this area he was never a dry and dull technician. Capablanca's knack of elegantly and harmoniously combining strategy and tactics resulted in some of the most beautiful and famous endgames ever played, for example...

♙ Capablanca, José Raúl
♟ Tartakower, Saviely
🌐 New York 1924

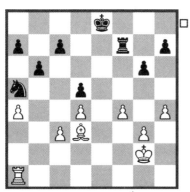

Position after: 26... ♚xe8

Material is equal and if Black's knight were on a slightly more central square, say d6 or f6, there would be no question of White having the better chances.

27. h5!

Capablanca seizes his chance without hesitation. If Black now plays 27...gxh5, the reply 28.♖h1 immediately wins back the pawn and a further pawn will be lost, on h7 or d5. So Black has no choice but to accept a weakness on g6.

27... ♖f6!

A powerful move, combining the defence of g6 with the possibility of a counterattack against c3 (♖f6-c6). Tartakower's idea seems to put White's

initiative in doubt, but Capablanca rises to the challenge magnificently.

28. hxg6 hxg6 29. ♖h1!

Fearless, purposeful, clinical. One can't help wondering if Capablanca had foreseen the full consequences of his plan or whether his hand was merely guided by that all too rare phenomenon, unerring intuition.

29... ♚f8

The immediate 29... ♖c6 would have been a blunder (30. ♗b5), but now ... ♖c6 is a serious threat. Many players would have started looking for an emergency exit at this point (e.g. 30.♗b5, provoking 30...c6), but not Capablanca.

30. ♖h7! ♖c6 31. g4!

It is now clear that White's plan is to surrender his c-pawn for Black's g-pawn and, anticipating this exchange, White starts moving his kingside pawns forward. Afraid that these pawns will steamroller him after 31...♖xc3 32.♗xg6, Black decides to bring his knight into play.

31... ♘c4 32. g5!

Introducing the threat 33.♖h6 ♚g7 34.f5.

32... ♘e3+ 33. ♚f3!

Much stronger than 33. ♔g3, when the aggressive 33... ♘d1! would have caused a lot of problems, due to the threat of 34...♖xc3 pinning and winning the bishop. The difference between the two king moves is that after the text 33...♘d1 can be met by 34.♖h6 ♖xc3 35.♔e2!, when g6 falls. Nor does 34...♔g7 (instead of 34...♖xc3) 35.f5! constitute an adequate defence. Therefore Black changes tack: he uses his knight to obstruct the diagonal of White's bishop.

33... ♘f5

And it is true: this move *does* seem to pose White some serious problems. The pawn on c3 is doomed and what has White achieved with his aggression on the kingside? Capablanca's solution is mind-bogglingly simple.

34. ♗xf5 gxf5

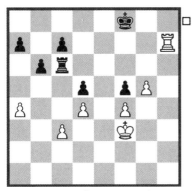

Position after: 34... gxf5

35. ♔g3!!

Not only does Capablanca sacrifice the c-pawn with check, he is prepared to do the same with his f-pawn as well. However it soon transpires that penetrating the enemy position with his king outweighs any material considerations. Now, is this strategy, tactics or just plain endgame virtuosity? It is all of that and more – typical Capablanca.

35... ♖xc3+ 36. ♔h4 ♖f3

Perhaps this succumbing to the temptation of winning a second pawn is Tartakower's only mistake in this endgame. The outcome would have remained in more doubt if he had immediately created a passed pawn with 36...c5!. It is true that even in this case White appears to be winning, but the variations are very tricky, for instance 37.dxc5 ♖xc5 38.g6 ♖c6 39.♔g5 ♖d6 40.♔xf5 (40.♖xa7 ♖d8! 41.♔h6 ♔g8 leads nowhere) 40...d4 41.♔g5 d3 42.f5 d2 43.f6 ♖d5+ 44.♔h4! (None of the alternatives, 44.♔h6 ♖h5+!, 44.♔f4 ♖d4+ 45.♔g3 ♖g4+!, or in the latter variation 45.♔e3 ♖d3+! 46.♔f2 ♖f3+! produce the desired result.) 44...♖d4+ 45.♔h3! ♖d3+ 46.♔g2 and White wins because after 46...♔e8 47.♖e7+ ♔d8 48.g7, mate has become unavoidable.

37. g6 ♖xf4+ 38. ♔g5

With his king now a powerful attacking unit, White's double pawn sacrifice turns out to be fully justified. Black must find a defence against the threat of 39.♔f6, so he can't afford to take another pawn (38...♖xd4), when 39.♔f6 would force him to play 39...♔e8 (If 39...♔g8 40.♖d7! and Black's king is trapped.) and then 40.g7 ♖g4 41.♖h8+ would be winning.

38... ♖e4 39. ♔f6

White's *material* disadvantage is a *positional* advantage here: without the f-pawn his king would be vulnerable to checks from behind.

39... ♔g8 40. ♖g7+ ♔h8 41. ♖xc7 ♖e8

By retreating his rook to the back rank Black has managed to avoid being mated *and* he has kept his king in front of the passed pawn on g6. If now 42. ♔f7

♖d8 43.g7+ ♔h7, Black hangs on by the skin of his teeth. However Black's position is so passive that White can safely switch to a much more simple plan, capturing as many Black pawns as possible and creating a second passed pawn. As a start Black's f-pawn can be eliminated.

42. ♔xf5 ♖e4 43. ♔f6 ♖f4+ 44. ♔e5 ♖g4 45. g7+!

The final blow. If 45...♖xg7 46.♖xg7 ♔xg7 47.♔xd5 the pawn ending is an easy win.

45... ♔g8 46. ♖xa7 ♖g1 47. ♔xd5

All is clear. Tartakower carried on for a few more moves, but resigned after **47... ♖c1 48. ♔d6 ♖c2 49. d5 ♖c1 50. ♖c7 ♖a1 51. ♔c6 ♖xa4 52. d6.**

Capablanca produced dozens of gems like this: no one was ever safe from his all-seeing eye.

♙   Van den Bosch, Johannes
♟   Capablanca, José Raúl
🌐   Budapest 1929

At first glance this position doesn't look very interesting. White's last move was 33.♔a3-b4, an attempt to free his position from the pressure exerted by Black's queen. It is a tremendous error

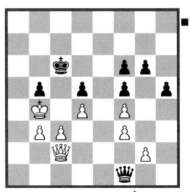

Position after: 33. ♔b4

of judgment, but this is made clear only by Capablanca's next move.

33... ♛e1!

Could a move be more simple yet more powerful simultaneously? All of a sudden there is the threat of 34...♛e7+ 35.♚a5 ♛a3 mate and, strange as it may seem, there is simply no defence against this. If 34. ♛b2 ♛e7+ 35.♚a5 ♛a7+ 36.♚b4 ♚b6 White is mated anyway, as is the case after 34.♚a3 ♛a1+ 35.♚b4 ♚b6. If in the latter variation White plays 35.♛a2 instead of 35. ♚b4, the pawn ending after 35...♛xa2+ 36.♚xa2 g5 is lost because the h-pawn is unstoppable.

Van den Bosch chose the only sensible option left and resigned.

Capablanca was the archetypal champion of the roaring twenties. He brought glamour to the chess world, attracting a larger audience for the game. In this respect his appearance in *Chess Fever*, a Russian movie shot during the famous tournament in Moscow in 1925, was exemplary. Here Capablanca manages, by simply being his charming self, to reconcile a young woman, driven to distraction by her 'chess fanatic' fiancé, not only with her fiancé but also with chess itself.

No doubt it was thanks to Capablanca that chess became very popular in Cuba and beyond. Cuba already had a chess history to be proud of, for it was here that Steinitz had played two matches for the World Championship against Chigorin in 1889 and 1892. However when in 1927 Argentina hosted the title match between Capablanca and Alekhine in Buenos Aires, this was a first for South America. Argentina was also where Capablanca played his last tournament, the Buenos Aires Olympiad in 1939. Though by now aged fifty, he won the individual gold medal for the best performance on board one.

Capablanca was also sometimes criticised, especially in his later years, for a playing style that was *too* businesslike, with not enough spirit of adventure. He took this to heart and in 1922 even went so far as to make a public statement that he "proposed to play with greater liberty from now on, regardless of the result". Like Lasker before him Capablanca expressed concern about chess becoming increasingly drawish, because the general level of play had become so high that it was getting more and more difficult to win a game. Both of them proposed several remedies. Lasker suggested that castling might be ruled out, making it more difficult for both kings to reach safety, thus stimulating an attacking spirit or that a stalemate might be counted not as a draw but as 0.7-0.3 or a similar score. Capablanca's idea was to enlarge the board and add an extra pair of pieces. None of these ideas met with great enthusiasm.

One might argue that criticisms of Capablanca's style were the unavoidable downside of the unparalleled ease with which he played. Capablanca often made it look as if he really had solved "the mystery of chess", thus robbing the game – at least in the eyes of some members of the public – of its romantic aura. His self-assured attitude ('I am invincible and I know it') probably added to the general public's somewhat exaggerated view of his chess skills.

Yet even a World Champion can only be one of a multitude of factors determining the course of chess history. Among Capablanca's contemporaries there were several

Alekhine against Capablanca

top players who pioneered new and sometimes revolutionary strategic concepts, such as Aron Nimzowitsch (1886-1935) from Latvia, and Richard Réti, mentioned previously. These two and others showed that there were still depths to be discovered in chess, invigorating the game with a new charm and a higher degree of complexity. When Capablanca's apparent invincibility finally came to an end, and the games of his successor Alekhine made it dazzlingly clear that even with a romantic style success at the very highest level was still possible, all fear that chess had been analysed to death subsided. Not until the computer era were these anxieties to return and even then (*now!*) they haven't been realised ... yet.

After Capablanca had taken the title from Lasker in 1921, in a match that lasted only fourteen games, he submitted to his fellow world class players a detailed plan (known as the *London Rules*, after the city where the plan was discussed and signed by many of those present), intended to put the World Championship on a firmer and more structured footing. Part of the proposal was that a match for the world title would always be played until one of the contestants had won six games, draws not counting, and with no limit to the total number of games. It also fixed the time limit at forty moves per two and a half hours and stipulated that "the Champion will not be compelled to defend his title for a purse below $10000."

Although the *London Rules* was considered an important document by many, it didn't have a huge impact. The continuing problem was that the World Champion needed to be challenged, forcing potential candidates to have or acquire money raising skills *and* the Champion also had the last say as to whether the challenge was acceptable or not, and the *London Rules* left this unaffected. In the end the only match ever played under the *London Rules* was Capablanca-Alekhine in 1927.

Even so, with or without these attempts, chess was inexorably moving forward to a more modern organisational structure. When in 1924 in Paris an 'Olympic' chess tournament was held as a side event to the Olympic Games, a small number (15) of representatives of national chess federations founded FIDE (Fédération Internationale des Échecs). It was a breakthrough, albeit a very modest one. Many countries didn't have a national federation yet, so these countries were called upon to create one and then apply for FIDE-membership. FIDE's first president was Alexander Rueb from the Netherlands. His main goal was to promote the game of chess on a global scale, with the first practical success the introduction of the Chess Olympiad, a chess equivalent of the 'real' Olympic Games. It wasn't until after World War II and the death of Alekhine that FIDE grew into a truly global organisation, taking over 'ownership' of the World Championship from the individual Champion.

Alexander Alekhine

Alexander Alekhine (1892-1946) was born in Moscow and grew up in a wealthy family environment in the final years of the Russian Empire. Though not a child prodigy he showed a remarkable talent for chess at an early age. Alekhine soon rose to the top of Russian chess which had been at a high level since the days of Mikhail Chigorin, the loser of two matches for the World Championship against Steinitz. When in the legendary tournament of Saint Petersburg 1914 Alekhine passed his first major test against the world's best with a brilliant third place behind Lasker and Capablanca, he seemed on the verge of an international breakthrough. However shortly afterwards World War I broke out and was followed in 1917 by the Russian Revolution and Civil War. Alekhine, like so many others, found himself destitute and caught in the middle of a country in great turmoil.

Alekhine was a fierce anti-Bolshevik, publicly criticising the Soviet regime in 1928, and in retaliation was declared an 'Enemy of the People'. Yet in spite of this, Alekhine is remembered in history as a Russian player. This is largely the effect of later Soviet propaganda, which 'rehabilitated' Alekhine and – retroactively – declared him to have been the great forerunner of the famed Soviet Chess School. There is certainly some truth in Alekhine being first and foremost a Russian, but this does not change the fact that he was a very vocal anti-Bolshevik. It may have been his hatred and fear of the Bolsheviks that determined his highly controversial public position during World War II. Having been anti-German and an outspoken French patriot during the early Hitler years, Alekhine started collaborating with the Nazis in 1941 when Hitler invaded the Soviet Union. This allowed him to continue to play chess, for only tournaments that were approved by the Nazis could be held in Nazi-occupied Europe.

Later in the war Alekhine sought a safe haven in Spain and later Portugal, presumably because he had lost faith in the possibility of a German victory and feared the advancing Soviet army and/or French reprisals against collaborators.

Whether Alekhine did find the safety he was looking for is moot. His death, in 1946 at the age of 53 in the Portugese coastal resort Estoril, is shrouded in mystery. This is mainly because Portugal was then a dictatorship, where by definition nothing could happen without the government either knowing about it, having a hand in it, or at the very least dictating the official version of what happened afterwards. The official version of Alekhine's

Alexander Alekhine

death was that he had choked on a piece of meat. At a time when almost everybody had other more pressing matters to worry about, this went unquestioned, but precisely *because* this was the official version by a dictatorship, rumours and speculative theories about what 'really' happened deserve consideration. In all probability the mystery will never be solved, but considering that the likelihood of a cruel dictatorial regime issuing a statement containing any degree of thruth (about any subject whatsoever) is exceedingly small, it seems to me that the case for Alekhine having been murdered by either the French or the Russian secret police is at least as strong as the official version of his death.

What is clear is that after the collapse of Nazi Germany Alekhine came under severe criticism for his collaboration, and in particular for a series of anti-semitic articles published under his name in 1941, offering 'scientific proof' of the inferiority of 'Jewish chess'. Alekhine denied responsiblity for these articles, but his attempts to clear his name were largely unsuccessful, although the matter was never fully resolved. By the time he died few still wanted Alekhine as World Champion. Judging from his final games, played against local champions in Spain and Portugal, Alekhine had by this time lost most of his once formidable playing strength and wouldn't have stood a chance against a young challenger such as Botvinnik.

Bogoljubov and Alekhine at the board

Just how formidable Alekhine was in his heyday becomes strikingly clear if we take a look at some of his tournament victories in the early 1930s. His 14 out of 15 in San Remo 1930, 3½ points ahead of runner-up Nimzowitsch, and his 20½ out of 26 in Bled 1931, 5½ points ahead of runner-up Bogoljubov, are legendary and betray the unsatiable ambition that must have burned inside him.

Alekhine's combinations were deep and brilliant, yet his style was universal, with a special talent for creating the complications he so loved in even the simplest of positions. A stranger to indolence, Alekhine worked very hard on his chess, often experimenting with openings that nobody else dared to play, such as 1...♘f6 against 1.e4, an opening that was soon named after him. He beat the unbeatable Capablanca in 1927 in a gruelling match lasting 34 games (6 wins, 3 losses and 25 draws), largely thanks to his excellent preparation, both chesswise and pychologically. Alekhine was the first World Champion to lose his title (against Max Euwe in 1935) and regain it (in 1937) and so far he is also the only Word Champion who died while still holding the title. In a word, Alekhine has a unique place in chess history and it is only natural that he, too, is often named as 'the best chess player in history'.

One should look at *all* of Alekhine's games for sheer enjoyment, but in this book we'll restrict ourselves to his two most famous combinations; the virtuosity that made him immortal.

♙ Réti, Richard
♟ Alekhine, Alexander
🌐 Baden-Baden 1925

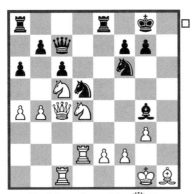

Position after: 24... ♕c7

25. b5

Things are looking good for White, but Alekhine is well prepared for this advance. His plan is to combine a minimum of defensive measures on the queenside with the creation of counterthreats on the kingside, his speciality. Alekhine is often called the greatest attacking player who ever lived; even in positions were he was on the defensive he was always looking for a chance to counterattack.

25... axb5 26. axb5 ♖e3!

So this is what someone like Alekhine calls defending the queenside! The rook cannot be taken (27.fxe3?? ♕xg3+ and White is mated) and 27... ♖xg3+ is a threat.

How does White solve this problem without giving up his offensive against the queenside? 27. ♔h2 is not good enough, because Black then reinforces his counterattack with moves like ♖a8-a3 and ♕c7-e5.

In his annotations to the game Alekhine offers the variations 27.♔h2? ♖aa3! 28.♘cb3 (If 28.fxe3 ♘xe3 there is the double threat of 29...♘xc4 and 29...♘f1+ followed by 30...♕xg3+.) 28...♕e5! 29.bxc6 bxc6 30.fxe3? ♕h5+ 31.♔g1 ♕h3 winning.

27. ♘f3?

A mistake, but this was incredibly hard to see over the board. Alekhine recommends 27. ♗f3! ♗xf3 28. exf3! while later analyses have brought 27. ♖d3 to light as a viable alternative. In both cases White's attack on the queenside has lost some of its force, exactly what Black was aiming for. The text move, however, swings the balance rather surprisingly in Black's favour.

27... cxb5 28. ♕xb5 ♘c3!

In complications like these Alekhine was in his element. It has taken him just three moves to completely disorganise White's attack.

29. ♕xb7

This amounts to a queen sacrifice, but White has little choice because after 29. ♕c4? b5! the damage to his position would be even worse.

29... ♕xb7!

Few could have resisted the temptation to win material with 29... ♘xe2+, when White's only chance is to try to build a fortress with 30. ♖xe2! ♕xb7 31. ♖xe3!.

Whether this fortress is strong enough to hold out against longterm assaults is difficult to say, but it would certainly give Black an advantage with no risk. Eagle-eyed as always, Alekhine has spotted a more promising alternative. This is not just a matter of being able to calculate exceptionally deeply, it also takes courage and self-confidence to *rely* on one's calculations.

30. ♘xb7 ♘xe2+ 31. ♔h2

With the queens off and little material left, there is no danger for White in the slight weakening of his pawn structure after 31...♘xc1 32.fxe3.

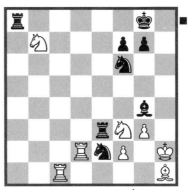

Position after: 31. ♔h2

31... ♘e4!

Alekhine's precision in calculating this move calls to mind that supercalculator of the 21st century: the computer.

32. ♖c4!

Réti replies in style. The obvious 32. fxe3 would have been met by 32... ♘xd2! costing White at least the exchange.

32... ♘xf2!

If 32... ♘xd2 White saves himself with 33. ♘xd2! ♖d3 34. ♘c5! ♖xd2 35.♗xa8, while 32...♗xf3 also only draws provided White finds 33.♖xe4! ♖xe4 34.♗xf3.

Alekhine's move wins a pawn, but with only two pawns against one left on the kingside this is hardly a decisive advantage. The real problem for White is that his pieces do not cooperate well. To begin with, there is the threat of 33...♘xh1.

33. ♗g2 ♗e6!

There were other moves (e.g. 33...
♘e4), but again Alekhine's is the
strongest. The precarious position of
White's king leads to further material
losses.

**34. ♖cc2 ♘g4+ 35. ♔h3 ♘e5+ 36.
♔h2 ♖xf3! 37. ♖xe2 ♘g4+ 38. ♔h3**

Again White is forced to expose his
king to a discovered check (38. ♔g1?
loses to 38...♖a1+). Now comes the final touch, which Alekhine must have
foreseen a very long time ago.

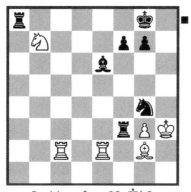

Position after: 38. ♔h3

**38... ♘e3+! 39. ♔h2 ♘xc2 40. ♗xf3
♘d4**

And White resigned as after 41. ♖f2
♘xf3+ 42. ♖xf3 ♗d5! he loses a full
piece.

♙ Bogoljubov, Efim
♟ Alekhine, Alexander
♞ Hastings 1922

Position after: 28. ♘d1

White's position looks battle-scarred.
He has lost a pawn, his kingside pawn
structure is weakened and his bishop
on h1 is badly out of play. But he is still
fighting. If, for example, 28...bxc4
29.♘xc4, his positon is not hopeless.
His knight will find an excellent square
on e5, thus more or less compensating
for Black's control over d5. The 'ideal'
move would be 28...♘d3, but this is
met by 29. ♖xa5. What should Black
play?

28... ♘d3!

There is nothing wrong with a good,
solid move like 28...c6, but Alekhine
never went for anything less than 'the
perfect solution'. Again this is based on
very deep calculation and a hidden tactical point.

29. ♖xa5

With hindsight, 29. cxb5 was the better choice, although Black then gets a strong position at no material cost after 29... ♗xb5 30. ♖xa5 ♘d5. Like Alekhine, Bogoljubov is trying to squeeze the utmost out of every move.

29... b4 30. ♖xa8

If 30. ♕a1 ♖xa5 31. ♕xa5 ♕a8 32. ♕xa8 ♖xa8 Black's control over the a-file, in combination with his passed b-pawn gives him a decisive advantage without any problems.

Position after: 30. ♖xa8

30... bxc3!

It isn't that this queen sacrifice is *better* than the simple 30... ♕xa8, (which gives Black a winning position as well, e.g. 31. ♕b3 [Or 31. ♕c2 ♘e1] 31... ♕a1 threatening 32...♗a4), but it is immeasurably more *beautiful*. Alekhine reminds us that chess should always

give us aesthetic pleasure; a true artist of the chessboard.

31. ♖xe8 c2!

Being already one rook down Black sacrifices another one, with check! Yet it is White's position which is imploding.

32. ♖xf8+ ♔h7

Promotion of Black's passed pawn on c2 is unavoidable so all White can do is make sure that he doesn't lose one of his knights as well.

33. ♘f2 c1=♕+ 34. ♘f1 ♘e1!

Threatening 35...♘f3 mate! There is only one defence.

35. ♖h2 ♕xc4

White has maintained the material balance but Black's pieces are hugely more active.
Black threatens 36...♗b5 with a mating attack and this can only be stopped by an exchange sacrifice.

36. ♖b8 ♗b5 37. ♖xb5 ♕xb5 38. g4

By advancing his g-pawn to g5 White tries to increase his chances of building a fortress. However again Alekhine cuts through with a sacrificial variation that required very accurate calculation.

38... ♘f3+ 39. ♗xf3 exf3 40. gxf5
♕e2!

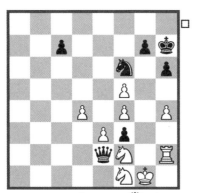

Position after: 40... ♕e2!

Now Alekhine introduces a new and
deadly weapon: *zugzwang*. There is no
threat, but White's only sensible
moves, 41. ♖h3 and 41. ♘h3 both lose
to 41...♘g4!, e.g. 41. ♘h3 ♘g4!
42. ♖xe2 fxe2 and the e-pawn promotes.

Bogoljubov could have resigned at this
point, but he carried on with **41. d5
♔g8 42. h5 ♔h7 43. e4 ♘xe4 44.
♘xe4 ♕xe4 45. d6 cxd6 46. f6 gxf6**

47. ♖d2 whereupon **47... ♕e2!** Black's
third queen sacrifice of the game(!)
gave Black an easily winning pawn ending. The game concluded **48. ♖xe2
fxe2 49. ♔f2 exf1=♕+ 50. ♔xf1 ♔g7
51. ♔f2 ♔f7 52. ♔e3 ♔e6 53. ♔e4
d5+** and White finally resigned.

Alekhine was particularly proud of these games. They are a lasting monument to
his wonderfully imaginative and highly powerful attacking play.

Apart from being a great player, Alekhine is also widely recognised as one of the
game's greatest analysts. He carefully annotated both his own games and those of
his rivals, authoring several tournament books, the volumes on New York 1924
and 1927 being the two most famous, and two volumes of his own games, *My
Best Games 1908-1923* and *1924-1937*. He introduced many new ideas in the
openings, most notably 1.e4 ♘f6, the opening which carries his name.

Alekhine was the first World Champion to turn opening preparation into a weapon, whereas his predecessors had usually been content to treat the opening

merely as a way of getting the game started. This gave him a clear edge over his contemporaries and inspired the generations after him to do the same. In this respect Alekhine really *was* a forerunner of what came to be known as the Soviet School of Chess, as the Soviets later claimed him to have been. In reality Alekhine's influence was far greater than that: he was the midwife at the birth of modern, professional opening preparation as it is still practised today.

The author at the grave of Alekhine in Paris.

Until Alekhine lost to Euwe in 1935 his world title was never in any serious danger. He would not grant Capablanca a revenge match, choosing instead Bogoljubov no less than twice (in 1929 and 1934) and winning both matches fairly easily.

In his second term as World Champion, after he had won the return match against Euwe in 1937, Alekhine's supremacy was less marked. He vehemently resisted all attempts by FIDE to take control of 'his' World Championship, but public demand for a match against a new challenger was very strong and couldn't be ignored. The outbreak of war in 1939 put an end to match negotations going on with young Soviet champion Mikhail Botvinnik (1911-1995) and with Paul Keres from Estonia (1916-1975), younger still. Alekhine was to take the world title with him to his grave. This of course gave FIDE a unique chance to finally seize control of the running of the World Championship. However, as we shall see later, in the end it was first and foremost Max Euwe, World Champion before *and* after Alekhine, who must be credited with bringing this great and fundamental change about.

Max Euwe

Dutchman Max Euwe (1901-1981) was a rare bird among the World Champions. He was an amateur, not a professional player except for a short period between 1946 and 1949, when he was in the service of the Dutch National Chess Federation. He led a perfectly 'normal' life, always had a fulltime job, married and had children. Euwe was never forced to move from one country to another by fate or war. Firmly rooted in Dutch culture and society he took on responsible positions in the chess world, firstly as a member of the board of the Dutch Chess Federation, later (from 1970 to 1978) as FIDE President. He actively campaigned for FIDE to become a truly global organisation after WW II and he was the first World Champion who didn't regard the title as his private property. After he had taken the world title from Alekhine in 1935 he immediately agreed to a revenge match, simply because in his view Alekhine deserved it. It was the fair thing to do, so he did it, generously and without hesitation. *Fair play*: it could have been the motto of Euwe's life.

However in one essential respect Euwe was *not* an exception. Although he held the title for only two years, he too left his mark on the chess world. His victory over Alekhine in 1935, though expected by no one, was fully deserved. He played with great vigour, showed himself to be at least as well-prepared theoretically as Alekhine (who was famous for his opening preparation) and, most importantly perhaps, he was totally fearless despite his formidable opponent. That must have been an unsettling experience for Alekhine who, like Capablanca before him, may have become a little too accustomed to his own superiority.

It is often suggested that Euwe's victory in 1935 was largely a matter of luck, and that Alekhine, having come to his senses, simply came back two years later to reestablish the natural world order, but this is definitely not true. In my view the brevity of Euwe's World Championship reign was entirely due to the fact that he really was an amateur through and through. It would have been completely out of character for him to sacrifice his family life, his social position and his many other interests in life for his chess career. Once or twice in his life, if he saw a very good reason for it, Euwe was willing to put everything aside *for a short period of time* in order to devote himself fully to chess. However once the goal was achieved he would resume his normal life immediately. The World Championship match in 1935 was the ultimate demonstration of Euwe's mentality.

Euwe's attitude is usually met with a lack of understanding, even downright hostility by those who *do* sacrifice everything on the altar of chess and this has led many a chess historian to underestimate Euwe. Yet his victory over Alekhine in 1935, which earned him a place in history, was by no means a one-off. He remained one of the best players in the world for many more years until his final appearance in a top class event at the Candidates Tournament in Zürich in 1953. After that he still occasionally participated in Olympiads and smaller events, but only if they did not take up too much of his time. When a much younger Hein Donner (1927-1988) finally dethroned him as the best player in the Netherlands – not before time! – Euwe was nearing sixty years of age and hardly devoting any time to chess.

When Max Euwe won his first Dutch Championship in 1921 he was already well estabished as a highly promising young player. However because he was a very 'normal' boy, attending school and playing football with his friends like everybody else, and because in those days the Dutch chess world was a very provincial one, totally unable to provide an extraordinary young talent with extraordinary chances, he had to grow up first before he could get his chess career properly started. He was also unlucky in that his adolescent years coincided with World War I which, although it left the Netherlands unscathed, made international contacts a virtual impossibility. However, this changed abruptly after 1918, when the Dutch chess scene was greatly enlivened by the arrival of many strong foreign players, attracted by the relative peace and prosperity the Netherlands then had to offer. Chess giants like Réti, Lasker and Géza Maroczy (1870-1951) all lived in the Netherlands for some time and Euwe must have benefited greatly from contact with them.

When Euwe finally embarked on an international career he quickly made a name for himself, but his refusal to devote himself completely to chess prevented him from realising his full potential. Euwe studied mathematics, married, started a family, completed his PhD and became a maths teacher in Amsterdam. He was ex-

Max Euwe (source: Max Euwe Centre Amsterdam)

tremely well-known and popular in the Netherlands and spent a lot of time pro-moting chess, involving himself in activities such as simultaneous exhibitions, small tournaments and journalism. Euwe became a prolific writer, turning out more newspaper articles and books then anyone else. Although this meant that he was 'working' on chess in one way or another almost continuously, it also hampered him in focussing entirely on reaching the top of the chess ladder.

In a strange twist Euwe didn't break through to the top of the game until he be-came World Champion! Ironically, it was Alekhine who invited Euwe to challenge him for the title. The two had first contested a training match in 1926/27. That match was won by Alekhine by the smallest of margins (5½-4½), though the de-feat was considered a great success for Euwe at the time. Now, eight years later, Alekhine wanted to play 'for real'. Euwe considered the proposal very carefully before accepting, for he was – as ever – very busy. Besides, did he honestly see himself as a realistic contender for the World Championship? Nonetheless, when Euwe *did* make up his mind he devoted himself totally to the task he had set him-self. Not only did he prepare for the match mentally and theoretically (i.e. he worked hard on his openings), he also worked on his *physique*, something Ale-khine had never done. To almost everyone's surprise, Euwe showed himself to be in no way inferior to his mighty opponent despite a hesitant start. The match, which was played in several different locations in the Netherlands, was extremely tense and hard-fought, the outcome unclear until the very last game. In the end, to the roaring applause of his countrymen, Euwe won 15½–14½. His energy, de-termination, level-headedness and perhaps most importantly his powers of recu-peration after even the toughest of setbacks carried the day over Alekhine's geni-us and experience. Euwe's powerful play in this match is perfectly illustrated by the 26th game, which has gone down in history as 'the Pearl of Zandvoort', Zand-voort being the city where the game was played.

 Euwe, Max
 Alekhine, Alexander
🌐 26th matchgame Zandvoort 1935

By game 26 the match had reached boiling point. In the previous game Eu-we had taken the lead for the first time, having trailed by three points earlier in the match. Since a maximum

of 30 games had been agreed for the match, Alekhine had five games left to catch or overtake his rival.

1. d4 e6 2. c4 f5

The Dutch Defence, a fighting opening *par excellence*.

3. g3 ♗b4+ 4. ♗d2 ♗e7

Alekhine had been the first to intro-
duce this subtle bishop manoeuvre,
which is based on the theory that
White's bishop might be slightly worse
placed on d2 than on c1.

**5. ♗g2 ♘f6 6. ♘c3 0-0 7. ♘f3 ♘e4 8.
0-0 b6**

In the 24th game Alekhine had played
8... ♗f6. Apparently unimpressed by
Alekhine's novelty, Euwe continues to
develop his pieces naturally.

9. ♕c2 ♗b7 10. ♘e5 ♘xc3

A typical Alekhine idea. White is invited
to play 11.♗xb7 which wins the exchange in return for two pawns after
11...♘xe2+ 12.♔h1 ♘xd4 13.♕d3
♘bc6 14.♗xa8 ♕xa8 after which the
position is murky, but probably good
for Black thanks to his strong knight on
d4. Euwe remains unruffled and continues to play logically and according to
plan.

11. ♗xc3 ♗xg2 12. ♔xg2 ♕c8 13. d5!

This consolidates White's space advantage and opens a beautiful diagonal
for the bishop so one can say that
White has won the opening battle.
Naturally, when playing against an opponent like Alekhine this is only the
first step, but it is a very important one
all the same. It should be kept in mind
that Alekhine was used to winning
opening battles, not losing them.

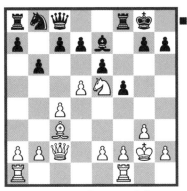

Position after: 13. d5!

13... d6 14. ♘d3 e5 15. ♔h1

The immediate 15. f4 would have been
more straightforward. Apparently Euwe doesn't want to commit himself
yet.

**15... c6 16. ♕b3 ♔h8 17. f4! e4 18.
♘b4**

The positional threat of 19.dxc6 ♘xc6
20.♘d5 now forces Black to close the
queenside. When he played 15...c6 Alekhine probably hoped to create counterplay along the c-file so this must
have been a slight disappointment.

18... c5 19. ♘c2 ♘d7 20. ♘e3

The knight is now ideally placed, both
for putting pressure on f5 and for supporting the strategically important advance of his g-pawn.

20... ♗f6?

It is understandable that Black wants to neutralise the pressure against g7. Should White now simply continue 21.♗xf6 ♘xf6 22.h3 (or 21.♖g1 ♗xc3 22.♕xc3 ♘f6) Black's play would have been justified and he would greatly have improved upon the immediate 20... ♘f6. However he is also taking a huge risk and Euwe pounces on it without hesitation.

Position after: 20... ♗f6?

21. ♘xf5! ♗xc3 22. ♘xd6 ♕b8 23. ♘xe4 ♗f6

White has given up his bishop for three pawns, so we can't really call 21. ♘xf5 a sacrifice. Yet to exchange an already promising risk-free position for this very complicated, potentially double-edged situation requires courage that few would have brought to such a crucial game, especially when being a point ahead. Euwe now wastes no time in getting his impressive central pawn phalanx moving.

24. ♘d2! g5!

Nor does Alekhine beat about the bush. Before the advance of White's e-pawn can smother him he starts counterplay on the kingside.

25. e4 gxf4 26. gxf4 ♗d4

What looked like a totally invulnerable pawn chain only a minute ago now suddenly contains a weak spot: the pawn on f4 requires protection. White is thus prevented from continuing with the 'ideal' move ♘d2-f3.

27. e5 ♕e8 28. e6

Now if 28...♘f6 White can finally play 29.♘f3 and eliminate Black's bishop, thus greatly reducing Black's counter-chances, e.g. 29...♘h5 30.♘xd4 cxd4 31.♕d3.

28... ♖g8!

Black makes optimal use of the open g-file. If 29.exd7? White even loses after 29...♕e2!.

29. ♘f3

At first glance this seems a perfectly straightforward, logical, even powerful move, yet in his annotations to this game Euwe points out that 29. ♕h3! would have been infinitely stronger. However although 29. ♘f3 may not be the best, it is undeniably a fearless move for it involves another – and this time very real – sacrifice.

29... ♕g6

Position after: 29... ♕g6

30. ♖g1!

The seemingly strong *and* safe 30. ♘g5? would have been met with the surprising 30... ♘e5! and White's attack comes to a halt. The force of the counterattack, which Alekhine has conjured up, seemingly out of nothing, is indeed astonishing, but again Euwe does not allow himself to be intimidated.

30... ♗xg1 31. ♖xg1 ♕f6

What could be more natural than covering the c3-h8 diagonal? Yet a ruthlessly accurate calculation of variations tells a different story. Black could have held the balance here with 31...♕f5! when 32.exd7 ♖xg1+ 33.♔xg1 ♕xd7 gives White two pawns for the exchange, but no advantage due to the exposed position of his king, while 32.♘g5 (as in the game) is now totally

harmless for Black after 32...h6 33.♘f7+ ♔h7.

32. ♘g5!

Now this is very strong. The threat is 33.♘f7+ while 32...h6 33.♘f7+ ♔h7 runs into 34.♕d3+, forcing Black into a deadly self-pin with 34...♖g6 after which Euwe gives the pretty variation 35.♘e5! ♘xe5 36.fxe5 ♕g7 37.d6 winning. Since giving back the exchange with 32...♖xg5 33.fxg5 looks fairly hopeless as well Alekhine finds the only way to keep fighting. He sacrifices a knight, making sure that at least one of White's dangerous passed pawns is eliminated.

32... ♖g7 33. exd7 ♖xd7 34. ♕e3 ♖e7

If 34... ♕xb2 35. ♕e6 is winning on the spot.

35. ♘e6

It goes without saying that this is an excellent square for the knight, but some very precise calculation was needed to make this move work, for if Black could now simply play 35...♕xb2 he would be out of trouble. Euwe must have seen that then 36.d6 is winning in all variations, e.g. 36...♖ee8 37.d7 ♖e7 38.d8♕! ♖xd8 39.♘xd8 ♖xe3 40.♘f7 ends in mate, while 36...♖d7 loses more prosaically to 37.♘c7 ♖f8

*Max Euwe together with his
wife in the 1970s
(Source: Max Euwe Centre Amsterdam)*

38. ♕e5+ ♕xe5 39.fxe5 and the passed pawns are too strong.

35... ♖f8

Alekhine continues to fight back, posing new problems almost every move. To keep on finding the right answers against such tenacious defence requires enormous perseverance.

36. ♕e5

The transition to a rook ending (again) had to be calculated accurately.

36... ♕xe5 37. fxe5

Position after: 37. fxe5

37... ♖f5

If 37... ♖xe6 38. dxe6 ♖e8 the rook ending after 39. ♔g2 ♖xe6 40. ♖e1 ♔g7 41. ♔f3 is hopeless for Black. White not only has a well-protected passed pawn, he also has much the more active pieces. However 38...♖f5! (instead of 38...♖e8), as suggested by Euwe, would have made White's task much more difficult. Although Black is then (temporarily at least) no less than two pawns down, his pieces are much more active than White's, a major factor in any kind of endgame. The text move is based on the same idea, but the execution is less accurate. (It is worth noting that both players were very short on time here.)

38. ♖e1

In his notes Euwe gives 38. ♖g5! as the strongest move, but this must have been almost impossible to calculate with any degree of accuracy in time trouble. For instance it would have been essential to foresee that after 38... ♖xg5 39. ♘xg5 ♔g7 [39... h6? 40. d6!] 40. d6 ♖xe5 41. d7 ♖e1+ 42. ♔g2 ♖d1, there is the pretty combination 43. d8=♕! *and* that 40...♖d7 (instead of 40...♖xe5) 41.♘e6+! ♔f7 42.♘f4 ♔e8 43.♔g2 allows White just enough time to centralise his king.

The text move gives Black a second chance to go for 38...♖xe6 39.dxe6 ♔g8, while 38...♔g8 would also have been a difficult move to meet, forcing White, after 39.♖g1+ ♔h8! (not 39...♔f7 40.♘d8+! and White's pawns get moving), to find the solution 40.♖g5! after all.

38... h6?

Perhaps the only moment in the entire game where Alekhine really slips up.

He overlooks a *petite combinaison*, which liberates White's passed pawns'.

39. ♘d8!

The final blow. The pawn on e5 is safe because of the knight fork on f7. The rest is (relatively) easy.

39... ♖f2 40. e6 ♖d2

The game was adjourned here. No deep analysis is needed. When the game was resumed Alekhine tried everything he could but after **41. ♘c6 ♖e8 42. e7 b5 43. ♘d8** (Euwe does not let himself be distracted.) **43... ♔g7** (The threat was 44.♘f7+ ♔g7 45.♘d6.) **44. ♘b7! ♔f6 45. ♖e6+ ♔g5 46. ♘d6 ♖xe7 47. ♘e4+** there was nothing left for Alekhine but to resign.

Alekhine won the next game but couldn't break Euwe's resistance in the remaining three, which meant he had lost the match. Not since Lasker-Schlechter in 1910 had a match for the World Championship been this exciting and this close.

Analysing one's adjourned position had long been considered bad form (and was often expressly forbidden by the tournament rules). Alekhine-Euwe 1935 was the first match where adjournment analysis was explicitly allowed as was the cooperation of seconds. Alekhine's second was the Dutchman(!) Salo Landau (1903-1944); Euwe's his old friend Géza Maróczy. Thus the match was an important step in the transition of chess from a purely individual sport towards being (partly) a team effort, signalling a new phase in the ongoing professionalisation of chess that was to be perfected in the Soviet Union in the years to come.

Two years later Euwe lost the revenge match and with it the world title. He remained one of the world's very best however, for over a decade. When in 1946 the Dutch city of Groningen organized the first elite post-war international tournament, including many of the Soviet stars that were to dominate the chess world for many years to come, Euwe, though by now 45 years of age, had one of his best results ever. Together with a much younger Botvinnik he dominated the field. They were neck and neck until the very last round when they both lost(!). Botvinnik thus won the tournament half a point ahead of Euwe.

The following endgame is almost a mirror image of the course of the tournament. It is also a highly instructive – and very famous – rook endgame.

 Botvinnik, Mikhail
 Euwe, Max
🌐 Groningen 1946

Position after: 39... h6

Material is equal, but Black's rook is *behind* his passed pawn whereas White's is in front of it and thus doomed to passivity, making the situation very dangerous for White. However, due to the simplified nature of the position Black does not have a great deal of choice. The only possible winning plan is to exchange the c-pawn for White's e-pawn in such a way that ensures Black's king will be the first to

reach (and eat) the kingside pawns. What can White do to defend himself?

40. g5!

If 40. ♔e3 ♔e5 of 40. h5 g5+ 41. ♔e3 ♔e5 Black is winning. The difference is not immediately obvious, but Botvinnik must have seen it.

40... h5 41. ♔e3 ♔e5

In this position the game was adjourned. At first glance the situation looks hopeless for White, yet "to the amazement of all participants" (Euwe) it turns out that Black cannot win.

42. ♖c2! c3 43. ♔d3 ♖d8+

As explained by Euwe in his annotations in the tournament book, the basic winning strategy would be to play for zugzwang: 43...♖c7, when 44.♔e3 ♖c4 is indeed winning for Black. The only problem is that it is not zugzwang! White plays 44.♖xc3! and is just in time to draw the pawn endgame after 44...♖xc3+ 45.♔xc3 ♔xe4 46.♔c4

♔f4 47.♔d4 ♔g4 48. ♔e5 ♔xh4 49.♔f6 when White is saved by his g-pawn. Every other pawn configuration on the kingside, which had to be determined by White's 40th move, would have been winning for Black.

Euwe decides to stay with the rook ending, but here too it turns out that White has just enough resources to save himself.

44. ♔e3! ♖d4 45. ♖xc3 ♖xe4+ 46. ♔f3 ♖xh4 47. ♖c6

Position after: 47. ♖c6

If now 47...♔f5 then 48.♖c5+ ♔e6 49.♖c6+ is an easy draw. Euwe's idea is more dangerous, yet it contains one little loophole.

47... ♖f4+ 48. ♔e3 ♖e4+ 49. ♔f3 ♔f5

Now 50.♖c5+ does not work because of 50...♖e5. Unfortunately the insecure position of Black's rook on e4 offers White a new escape route.

50. ♖f6+ ♔xg5 51. ♖xg6+!

And a draw was agreed. "You can't argue with that" was Euwe's matter of fact comment. I know quite a few players who would have run away from the board howling and wailing.

The 1948 tournament for the World Championship, held partly in The Hague, partly in Moscow and featured in the next chapter, was a fiasco for Euwe and perhaps the biggest disappointment in his career. His play was unrecognisable, he lacked self-confidence and he blundered in many of his games, throwing away points left, right and centre.

However Euwe's final appearance at world elite level was very impressive, although in the end physical and mental tiredness – in short old age – prevented him from finishing near the top. The event was the legendary Zürich 1953 Candidates Tournament, where fifteen grandmasters played a double round robin tournament to determine which of them was to be Botvinnik's next challenger. After 28 gruelling rounds Euwe, by far the oldest participant, finished on 11½ points in second last place.

Nonetheless, in the first half of the tournament he had been among the very best, winning several games in brilliant style. For example, the way he defended against a blistering kingside attack from Efim Geller (1925-1998) is unforgettable. (Geller was at the time one of the rising stars from the Soviet Union, by then in almost complete control of the chess world.)

♙ Geller, Efim
♟ Euwe, Max
♙ Zürich 1953

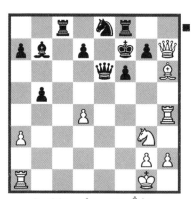

Position after: 22. ♗h6

White is threatening to strengthen his attack decisively by bringing his queen's rook into play with 23.♖f1. Black has no means of reinforcing his fragile defences so his only chance lies in a counterattack. What is White's weakest point? The g2 square – but

how to target this? The obvious move would be 22...♕d5, but this allows White to simply block the diagonal with 23.♗e4. Theoretically the only other move to target g2 is 22...♖c2, but this simply puts a rook *en prise*. Euwe finds another solution, as simple as it is stunning.

22... ♖h8!

One of the most famous *and* most effective suboptimal moves in all chess literature! Thorough analysis later revealed that 22... ♖c4!! was actually stronger, although Black would then have needed the nerve to endure onslaughts such as 23. ♖f1 ♕d5 24. ♖e4 ♖xd4 25. ♖xf6+ ♔xf6. However this may be, the psychological effect of Euwe's move is exactly as was intended – devastating.

23. ♕xh8 ♖c2!

One rook is sacrificed, the other joins the attack.

24. ♖c1?

Not being a computer, Geller is unable to push the Restart button and find his bearings in the totally new and unexpected situation that has arisen. Blocking the g2-b7 diagonal by 24.♘e4 is useless after 24...♗xe4, but 24.d5! would have thrown a spanner in the works. In the pre-computer era it took weeks of heated debate, full of arguments and counterarguments, to finally establish that White saves himself by the skin of his teeth, both after 24...♗xd5 25.♖d1! ♖xg2+ 26.♔f1 gxh6 27.♕xh6 and 24...♕b6+ 25.♔h1 ♕f2 26.♖g1 ♗xd5 27.♖e4.

24... ♖xg2+ 25. ♔f1

By playing 24.♖c1 White has prevented 25...♕c4+, but there are other roads to Rome...

25... ♕b3! 26. ♔e1 ♕f3

And White resigned.

After Zürich Euwe gradually withdrew from the chess arena, though he would never leave. He resigned his teaching job in 1956 to start working with computers: first in business, then at university. In 1970 Euwe was elected President of FIDE, by now the unquestioned world body for chess. He began promotional work for chess: travelling extensively, giving simultaneous exhibitions wherever he went, and convincing many new countries to join FIDE. His most visible triumph in this capacity was the organisation of the 'Match of the Century' between Fischer and Spassky in 1972, which we shall discuss in a later chapter. Without Euwe's unflagging and selfless commitment this match would never have happened.

Euwe was the author of more books, articles and game annotations than any other writer on chess before or after him. He always wrote with the 'ordinary club player' in mind, the amateur chess enthusiast who wants to know more about his favourite pastime and is in search of a good teacher. Euwe was that teacher, through and through. His explanations of strategy and tactics, of openings, middlegames and endgames were always crystal clear and are as relevant today as they were when he wrote them.

The Hague-Moscow 1948 –
A New Beginning

It goes without saying that international chess throughout Europe practically came to a standstill during World War II, but that doesn't mean that no chess was played. On the contrary, in many countries chess was a popular way of diverting people's minds from the day-to-day misery they had to endure. It should come as no surprise therefore that organised chess life quickly reformed itself after the surrender of Nazi Germany on May 7, 1945. But how different did the world look after over five years of war!

Europe was a shambles, the Soviet Union had emerged from the war as a new global superpower, controlling large parts of Eastern Europe, and the Cold War was on the horizon. The chess world followed suit: a radio match between WWII allies the USA and the USSR, held in September 1945, resulted in a truly staggering 4½-15½ defeat for the Americans, leaving the rest of the world in no doubt that in chess as well as in politics a new superpower had arisen. Lasker and Capablanca were dead, while Alekhine had come under fierce criticism for his collaboration with Nazi Germany and died in March 1946. What was to become of the World Championship?

Many people agreed that this was the moment for FIDE to take charge, but the reality was that in 1946 this "World Chess Federation" was still very much in its infancy. How realistic was it for this tiny organisation to take on real responsibilities such as organizing a World Championship? And what exactly did this involve? Was it just about organising one match and nothing else? More than anyone else, the chess world has Max Euwe to thank for the historic changes that eventually emerged from this chaos. At the FIDE Congress of 1946 it was he who proposed that the title of World Champion should be awarded by FIDE from now on. It was also he who, when talks between various national federations about his proposal had reached a seemingly hopeless dead end, managed to bring the adversaries back to the negotiating table. Again it was he who, at another chaotic FIDE Congress in 1947, immediately and unhesitatingly gave back the world title that had just been awarded to him 'ad interim', when the Soviet delegation, having appeared two days late, offered to organise a tournament for the title. Euwe's first and foremost concern was that all serious contenders should have the chance to take part. Fair play! And so the 1948 World Championship came to pass.

The participants were to be those of the famous AVRO tournament that had been held in the Netherlands in 1938, minus Capablanca and Alekhine who had died. The AVRO tournament should have been the first FIDE Candidates Tournament, intended to select a challenger for World Champion Alekhine. In the end it did not receive that official status following disagreements, but the impact and prestige of the tournament had been enormous nevertheless. Ten years later almost every participant in the AVRO event was still considered to be of world class.

The final standings of AVRO 1938 had been:

1/2.	Keres and Fine	8½ /14
3.	Botvinnik	7½
4/6.	Euwe, Alekhine and Reshevsky	7
7.	Capablanca	6
8.	Flohr	4½

Only Salo Flohr (1908-1983), one of the world's very best players in the early 1930s but perhaps past his prime ten years on – or at least considered to be so by the authorities of the Soviet Union, were he had fled from Nazi persecution just before the outbreak of war – was to be replaced. In his place came Vasily Smyslov (1921-2010) who had shown both in tournaments in the Soviet Union during the war and in Groningen 1946 that he too was now a member of the world's elite.

The tournament was thus to be a six player event, but in the end only five took part. Reuben Fine (1914-1993) declined his invitation for reasons that have never been fully clarified, although they were probably both of a personal and political nature. Together with Reshevsky and Keres, Fine had been one of the bright young stars of the 1930s, and a serious threat to the older generations from 1935 onwards. Between them they won many international tournaments, culminating in their supreme triumph at the AVRO tournament.

But the war had changed everything. Fine, a US citizen, didn't trust the Russians, nor FIDE, nor his own US Chess Federation that had failed to back him up in his struggle with the first two. This may sound as if he trusted no one at all, but it seems much more likely that he was simply right. His withdrawal reflected both the existing chaos in the chess world and the very real power politics of the Soviet Chess Federation, who regarded an individual simply as something to be annihilated if 'greater interests' were at stake. At any rate these struggles signalled the end of Fine's chess career. He still participated in a few relatively minor tournaments around 1950, but then withdrew completely, limiting his further chess activity to the writing of several books among which *Basic Chess Endings* is probably the most famous. Generations of chess students have learned their endgame skills from this book. For many of them Fine's fame as a writer has probably eclipsed his reputation as the world class player he once was.

The remaining five were Euwe, Botvinnik, Smyslov, Keres and Reshevsky. They faced each other five times, making a total of twenty games for every participant, a highly demanding and exhausting schedule! The first two cycles were played in The Hague, the remaining three in Moscow.

Botvinnik was generally considered the favorite. Like Keres, Fine and Reshevsky he had shown himself a force to be reckoned with during the 1930s, but being a Soviet citizen he had had fewer opportunities to demonstrate his chess powers than his Western contemporaries. Every time Botvinnik *did* get permission to play abroad though, he had made a very strong impression and his third place in the AVRO tournament in 1938 had probably been a slight disappointment to him rather than the huge success it really was. Two years earlier he had already shared first place in a supertournament (with Capablanca) in Nottingham and by 1938 he must have felt that his time had come.

Euwe and Keres were viewed as Botvinnik's most dangerous rivals: the former World Champion and the winner of the AVRO tournament who seemed destined to follow in Alekhine's footsteps with his dazzlingly brilliant attacking style. Unfortunately these were also the two players who had been hit hardest by the ten years that had passed since 1938.

For Euwe, who in 1938 was still in his heyday, the extra ten years counted heavily. Although not exactly an old man at 47, he was by far the oldest of the five competitors. In a gruelling contest such as this, energy was sure to be a telling factor.

Front row from left to right Euwe, Smyslov, Keres, Botvinnik and Reshevsky

For Keres, whose native Estonia had first been occupied by Nazi Germany, then by Soviet Russia, almost everything had changed. He was now, through no choice of his own, a Soviet citizen with all the limitations on his personal freedom that came with this status.

Keres had to start his chess career all over again in a new and completely different environment. Eventually he succeeded brilliantly, but the World Championship title would always elude him. He was a participant in every Candidates Tournament from 1950 to 1965, coming second in four of them. He won the Soviet Championship three times in an age when this title was considered almost as prestigious as the World Championship itself. He won or finished high up in almost every tournament he played up until his death in 1975. Until Viktor Korchnoi came along, Keres was universally named as 'the strongest player never to become World Champion'.

Smyslov, the youngest participant, was not expected to win – yet – mainly because in all tournaments where Botvinnik and he had played together prior to 1948, Botvinnik had always come out on top.

In the same way Samuel Reshevsky was also seen as a dangerous outsider rather than a top favorite. Like Morphy and Capablanca before him, Reshevsky (1911-1992) had begun his chess career as a child prodigy. He was born in Poland, and from a very young age his parents 'exploited' his chess talent by taking him on extensive tours, first in Europe and from 1920 onwards in America, where they eventually settled and acquired US citizenship. On one of these occasions he met Euwe for the first time, when he faced him in a simultaneous exhibition he (Reshevsky!) gave in Amsterdam in 1920 (Euwe won.) In 1924 Reshevsky gave up chess in order to complete his education. He started playing again in 1931, but never turned professional again, supporting himself instead with his work as an accountant. Nevertheless he became one of the best players in the world and for a long time was seen as the only Westerner who posed a real threat to Soviet hegemony, especially in the early 1950s. Reshevsky never won the right to challenge for the world title, but came very close to doing so a couple of times. He was also probably the first player in the history of chess to fully integrate a clever handling of the clock into his playing style, turning time trouble into a dangerous weapon. Being a notoriously slow starter Reshevsky would use oceans of time in the opening and early middlegame, leaving himself very little time on the clock for the later stages of the game. Yet whereas to most players this sounds like a horror scenario, for Reshevsky time trouble worked as a kind of concentration enhancing drug. Although he would occasionally lose on time, or lose because of a time trouble related blunder, the large majority of these games went well for him. Playing against such a 'time trouble junkie' is not so easy and Reshevsky always made the most of the intense pressure generated by this situation. Most of his opponents were afraid of the clock, Reshevsky regarded it as his best friend.

A tournament with so much at stake was bound to be fiercely contested and so it was. However the outcome was never in doubt, for Botvinnik was in superb form and completely dominated. He led from start to finish and managed to secure the title with three rounds to spare. Behind him Smyslov, Keres and Reshevsky battled it out for second place. Euwe was in dreadful shape and came last by a wide margin. The final standings were:

1.	Botvinnik	14/20
2.	Smyslov	11
3/4.	Keres and Reshevsky	10½
5.	Euwe	4

Player	Botvinnik	Smyslov	Keres	Reshevsky	Euwe	Points
Mikhail Botvinnik		½ ½ 1 ½ ½	1 1 1 1 0	1 ½ 0 1 1	1 ½ 1 ½ ½	14
Vasily Smyslov	½ ½ 0 ½ ½		0 0 ½ 1 ½	½ ½ 1 ½ ½	1 1 0 1 1	11
Paul Keres	0 0 0 0 1	1 1 ½ 0 ½		0 ½ 1 0 ½	1 ½ 1 1 1	10½
Samuel Reshevsky	0 ½ 1 0 0	½ ½ 0 ½ ½	1 ½ 0 1 ½		1 ½ ½ 1 1	10½
Max Euwe	0 ½ 0 ½ ½	0 0 1 0 0	0 ½ 0 0 0	0 ½ ½ 0 0		4

This tournament was the beginning of a new era. Firstly, FIDE was henceforth in charge: after so many years of anarchy, the chess world had its own governing body. Secondly, the World Championship was put on a solid organisational footing, designed to give every chess player, at least in principle, a fair chance.

A three-year World Championship cycle was set up, aiming to produce a challenger for the world title through a series of qualifying events. For this purpose the chess world was divided into geographical zones. The national federations within each zone were to provide a fixed number of participants for a *Zonal Tournament*, offering one or more qualifying spots for the next stage, the *Interzonal Tournament*, where at last the participants were determined for the final stage, the *Candidates Tournament*. The victor of the Candidates won the right to play a match for the World Championship.

It was a revolutionary, democratic renewal of the chess world. However although the absolute power of the World Champion had been broken, he still enjoyed a tremendous advantage over his challengers. Whereas they had to struggle through three intensely demanding qualifying stages, the World Champion could just relax and prepare for the next match at his leisure. To make matters worse – for the challenger – in the event of a tie the reigning World Champion would retain his title. And even if he lost, the new rules offered the right to a revenge match within a year!

These were tremendous advantages and Botvinnik was to make full use of them.

The Hague/Moscow 1948 also marked the beginning of the now legendary Soviet domination of the chess world, so strong that it even survived the Soviet Union itself. (Bobby Fischer managed to interrupt it in 1972, but his reign was short-lived.) Chess, or more accurately chess as a competitive sport, had enjoyed a privileged position in the Soviet Union ever since the 1920s, shortly after Alekhine had fled the country. Following the success of three major international tournaments in Moscow (1925, 1935 and 1936), and again when it became clear that the Soviet Union had a potential World Champion in its ranks in the person of Botvinnik, chess was given government support on an unprecedented scale. Although one cannot of course forget the state control that went with it. All over the country training facilities and a great number of tournaments were set up. Players and coaches were paid by the government and enjoyed tremendous prestige, giving them the necessary economic and moral support to devote themselves entirely to chess.

It worked. In a relatively short period of time the Soviet Union developed a chess culture the like of which the world had never seen before and is unlikely ever to see again. In stark contrast to the West, where chess players had to fend for themselves, all too often enjoying no income other than their chess earnings and with little or no social prestige, the Soviet Union produced one top player after another. All of them had coaches, seconds and other staff if required and enjoyed tremendous moral support from millions of their amateur chessplaying countrymen.

In short, whereas in the West chess remained what it had always been – an essentially amateur, individual lifestyle – in the Soviet Union chess became an ultra-professional sport, a matter of international prestige, and of interest to the highest levels of Soviet leadership.

Mikhail Moiseyevich Botvinnik

Mikhail Moiseyevich Botvinnik was born in 1911 in what was then the Russian Empire, but his formative years coincided largely with those of its successor, the Soviet Union. This young, idealistic and highly organised society fitted Botvinnik like a glove. His chess talent was recognised at an early age and when success came to him in the 1930s he became the ideal poster boy for his ambitious country. He owed much of his success to government support, but his government owed him a lot as well, for it was upon these early successes by Botvinnik that the foundation for the Soviet Union's chess supremacy in the decades to come was built. From a pioneer he became a champion, from a champion he became a shining example, from an exemplar he became a legend. Botvinnik's nickname in later life, the Patriarch, perfectly summarises his key position in Soviet chess history.

The period between 1946 and 1970, the year he retired, is sometimes called the *Botvinnik Era*. While this epithet is fully justified – for he *did* tower over this period – there is something strange about it nevertheless, because in reality his proud victory in the 1948 World Championship marked the *end* of his series of outstanding successes rather than the beginning of it. As a defending Champion Botvinnik would never win a match for the World Championship and he also won very few tournaments, while in the decade or so before 1948 he had been well-nigh unbeatable. Indeed, Botvinnik could have been World Champion as early as 1940 if there had been no World War II to make a match against Alekhine an impossibility.

This remarkable discrepancy, between his *position* as World Champion on the one hand and his rather
modest (for a World Champion) *results* on the other, is explained by
the fact that, no matter how professional his approach to chess, in reality he always remained an amateur.
Obviously, being an amateur in the
Soviet Union was entirely different
from being an amateur in the West.
However it is a fact that Botvinnik
was not only a chess player but also
an electrical engineer and later a
computer scientist, and that he was
as devoted to his 'work' as to his
'hobby'. Although he was never financially dependent on his job (as
for instance were Euwe and Reshevsky), Botvinnik always put a lot of
time and effort into his non-chess
work and after he became World
Champion in 1948 his engineering
and science work became his main
occupation. From then on Botvinnik

*Mikhail Botvinnik giving a simultaneous exhibi-
tion in 1973 (photo Jos Sutmuller)*

effectively limited his chess activities to defending his title every three years. He
rarely played a tournament, and if he did it was mainly for training purposes, as
preparation for a match.

This semi-retirement partly explains why Botvinnik's challengers never seemed to
be in any way inferior to him. He suffered from a chronic shortage of practice!
Botvinnik's first World Championship match, in 1951 against David Bronstein
(1924-2006) ended in a 12-12 tie, enough for Botvinnik to retain his title. Three
years later, in 1954, his first match against Smyslov also ended in a tie. Another
three years later he was beaten by Smyslov (9½-12½), but won the revenge match
(in 1958) 12½–10½ to take back his title. History repeated itself when Mikhail Tal
came along in the next cycle: Botvinnik lost the first match (12½-8½) in 1960, but
again exercised his right to a return match with great success a year later (13-8). It

Mikhail Botvinnik in 1936

wasn't until 1963, when beaten by Tigran Petrosian, that Botvinnik lost the title for good since by then FIDE had abolished the right to a return match.

Another factor of course was the fantastically high level, not just of his challengers, but of all those *they* had had to beat in order to climb to the top in the USSR. And in a way *they* owed this high level to *him*: without Botvinnik's inspiring and trailblazing career from the late 1920s onwards the Soviet School of Chess would never have become what it was. Botvinnik personified the standard every aspiring new star had to meet; he was always the man to beat. Looking at his achievements in this light it becomes truly impressive that he managed to stay on top of the chess world for as long as he did. It also explains why, after his defeat to Petrosian, Botvinnik decided not to make use of his right to a place in the next Candidates tournament; he had had enough. He still played the occasional tournament until finally retiring in 1970. After then Botvinnik devoted himself to coaching – Karpov, Kasparov and Kramnik were among his pupils – but most of his time went to the development of a chess engine and similar computer research. He died in 1995.

Botvinnik's contribution to chess can hardly be overestimated. As a young man he had already developed his own methods of study and preparation and even published those methods for all the world to see and copy, not restricting himself to publication in the Soviet Union alone either. Botvinnik's approach was both scientific and practical. He analysed his own games and those of his main rivals in great depth, drawing conclusions about his own strengths and weaknesses and theirs, which he then made use of in his preparation. He also prepared himself physically and mentally, making as sure as he could of being able to cope with the length and specific demands of each event. Botvinnik's attention to detail was legendary. He would simulate the expected playing conditions in training games, where – a non-smoker himself – he would ask his opponent to smoke – and blow the smoke in his face too! – or he would turn on the radio if he expected a noisy playing hall. Opening preparation by Botvinnik was both on a very high level and intensely practical. His repertoire was not large – at least not by present day standards – but deeply studied and understood. He preferred a complicated middlegame, but always strove to be strategically prepared for any type of middlegame that could arise from his openings.

Botvinnik was the first to adhere to – and force his entourage to follow – a strict routine and have iron discipline *during* a tournament, limiting distractions to a minimum. His commitment to the result was total, his willpower legendary. Even so, Botvinnik also received a lot of help, always working with a team of seconds and other helpers. This is where the power of the Soviet state made a huge difference. Until the late 1980s games were adjourned, normally after five hours and 40 moves of play. It stands to reason that a good second (or a whole team of seconds) was a great advantage when analysing the adjourned position during the break. Whereas Western players had to pay for their seconds, the Soviet Chess Federation always provided help, especially for an important event. The results of this teamwork could be truly astonishing. In the chapter on Euwe we have already seen a spectacular escape by Botvinnik from a seemingly hopeless position, yet his most famous 'adjournment triumph' was his draw against Bobby Fischer at the 1962 Olympiad in Varna. Curiously, it was the only time these two giants of the chessboard ever met over the board.

♟ Botvinnik, Mikhail
♟ Fischer, Robert James
🌏 Varna 1962

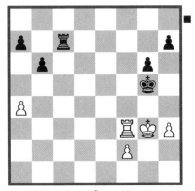

Position after: 45. a4

The game was adjourned in this position. For those readers who have never seen an adjourned game I will briefly explain the procedure. Precisely at the end of the scheduled playing time, traditionally five hours, the player whose move it was would – after due consideration – 'seal' their move. To seal a move meant that instead of playing the move on the board it would be written down on a piece of paper which was then put in an envelope, sealed and safeguarded by the arbiter. This was the 'sealed move', known only to the player who had sealed it.

We don't have the space to discuss this endgame in great detail, but every chess player who has had some experience with rook endings will see at a glance that White is in big trouble. He is a pawn down and he does not seem to have a lot of counterchances. Fischer thought so too, for he simply went to bed and slept like a log. Botvinnik, on the other hand, made his team (including himself) stay up and examine the position down to the last detail. If there was even the slightest chance of saving the game it *had* to be found. After all, it was not just a matter of personal success but of national prestige that was at stake.

Botvinnik has later described in some detail how the Russian team set to work. First they had to decide what the sealed move might be. They quickly dismissed 45...♖c4 as over-aggressive because of 46.a5! bxa5 47.♖f7 a6 48.h4+! ♔h6 49.♖d7 and Black cannot make any progress due to the passive position of his king. Waiting moves like 45...♔h6 were also found not to pose any major problems. The only really strong move was

45... ♖c5!

which, when the game was resumed the next morning, indeed turned out to be Fischer's sealed move. Black prepares both ♖c5-a5 and ♖c5-f5, safeguarding a route for his king towards the centre and the queenside via f6. Once Black's king is able to support his queenside pawn majority there is very little hope for White to save the game. So what should White do? 46. ♖f7 ♖a5 seems rather pointless nor does passive defence offer much hope. But in the dead of night the Soviet team – in his annotations Botvinnik credits Geller with the discovery – hit upon an astonishing idea. By the early hours of the morning team Botvinnik finally had everything worked out and under control.

46. ♖f7! ♖a5 47. ♖xh7!

Looking at this superficially, one might be forgiven for concluding that the simplest move is always the best. In reality this exchange of pawns works for White only because of a deeply hidden point, not revealed until five moves later.

47... ♖xa4

If all that White had achieved with his previous two moves was a simple race between Black's two connected passed pawns and his own two against one majority on the kingside, White would indeed be hopelessly lost. That is what Fischer must have thought when he went to sleep without a worry. The venom, however, is in concrete details.

48. h4+ ♔f5

To begin with, it turns out that Black not only *can*, but *must* use his king in order to start his queenside pawns moving. If he 'plays it safe' with 48...♔f6, protecting his pawn on g6, White has 49.♖b7! when it is Black's rook that will have to assist the pawns. This is such a slow process that White gains time to create counterplay on the kingside, i.e. 49...♖a5 50.♔g4 b5 51.f4, when the consistent 51...a6 planning 52...♖a4, 53...b4, 54...a5, 55...♖a3 etc. runs into 52.♖b6+ ♔f7 53.♖b7+ and Black cannot make further progress.

49. ♖f7+ ♔e5 50. ♖g7 ♖a1 51. ♔f3

Naturally, 51. ♖xg6?? would lose the rook to 51...♖g1+. However after the text Black has to lay his cards on the table. If he protects his g-pawn with 51...♔f6, White has 52.♖b7 and the situation is identical to the variation 48...♔f6, discussed above. Nor does 48...♔f5 49. ♖f7+ change anything. So ...

51... b5

But now we have...

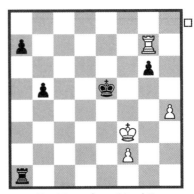

Position after: 51... b5

52. h5!!

Instead of taking another pawn White gives one away, or so it seems. That's why a move like this is so very difficult to foresee. In reality White is just exchanging his h-pawn for Black's all-important b-pawn, which of course changes everything. If instead 52. ♖xg6 b4, Black would comfortably win the pawn race.

52... ♖a3+ 53. ♔g2 gxh5 54. ♖g5+ ♔d6 55. ♖xb5

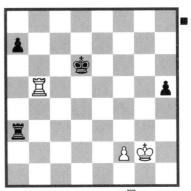

Position after: 55. ♖xb5

Time to take stock. The two pawns on f2 and a7 are equally strong, while Black's extra h-pawn can easily be stopped by White's king. By now it must have dawned on Fischer that a draw has become inevitable, but he kept on playing, perhaps to work off a sense of disillusionment.

After **55... h4 56. f4 ♔c6 57. ♖b8 h3+ 58. ♔h2 a5 59. f5 ♔c7 60. ♖b5 ♔d6 61. f6 ♔e6 62. ♖b6+ ♔f7 63. ♖a6** ("At this point Fischer should have offered a draw" was Botvinnik's rather severe comment) **63... ♔g6 64. ♖c6 a4 65. ♖a6 ♔f7 66. ♖c6 ♖d3 67. ♖a6 a3 68. ♔g1** "an ashen-faced Fischer shook hands with me and left the playing hall with tears in his eyes" (Botvinnik). Be that as it may, Botvinnik's version of events clearly betrays the enormous emotional impact on *both* players of the outcome of this adjournment. The 'post-mortem' continued for several years. After Botvinnik had published his notes to the game, Fischer tried to show that if he had played 51...♔d4 instead of 51...b5 he would have won. The difference between this line and the variation 52.♖xg6 b4 is marginal, but in the end it was established White's chances were just sufficient to earn a draw so we won't go into this debate.

By now, it should have become clear that Botvinnik was a great endgame expert so we will now turn to his opening and middlegame skills. Perhaps the following game can give the reader a feeling of just how frighteningly powerful Botvinnik's play could be.

 Botvinnik, Mikhail
 Capablanca, José Raúl
🌐 AVRO-tournament 1938

In 1938 Botvinnik was still a young man, but he already held a reputation for his beautiful style, a perfect marriage between strategy and tactics yet with the force of a bulldozer. To most in 1938 it still seemed incredible though that even the great Capablanca could be bulldozed.

1. d4 ♘f6 2. c4 e6 3. ♘c3 ♗b4

The Nimzo-Indian Defence, named after the great opening pioneer Aron Nimzowitsch, was still new and relatively unexplored in those days. Rather than attempting a 'refutation' Botvinnik treats the opening in a calm, purely strategical way. His moves all fit into a well thought out long-term plan.

4. e3 d5 5. a3 ♗xc3+ 6. bxc3 c5 7. cxd5 exd5 8. ♗d3

Only eight moves have been played, but the contours of the approaching middlegame are already visible. White's plan is to build a strong pawn centre with f2-f3 and e3-e4, when chances of a kingside attack are likely to materialise 'automatically'. For Black the situation is less clear. He will have to ward off White's attack with one hand while trying to cook up something on the queenside with the other.

8... 0-0 9. ♘e2 b6 10. 0-0 ♗a6

Proposing to exchange White's powerful light-squared bishop. If White avoids this with 11.♗c2 the bishop on a6 will be a force to be reckoned with. In his notes to this game, Botvinnik, with admirable objectivity, admits that it is impossible to say which option is best.

11. ♗xa6 ♘xa6 12. ♗b2

But this move he criticises, as he so often unmercifully criticised his own decisions. For Botvinnik the search for the truth always had priority over self-congratulations. The immediate 12. ♕d3, in order to provoke 12... ♕c8 before developing the bishop, would have been more accurate.

12... ♕d7!

Now 13.♕d3 can be met by 13...♕a4, blockading White's queenside.

13. a4 ♖fe8

Botvinnik calls this "a surprising mistake for someone of Capablanca's cali-

bre". It is of course a natural developing move, but Black should have been more ambitious, starting immediate counterplay along the c-file with the incisive 13... cxd4 14. cxd4 ♖fc8.

14. ♕d3

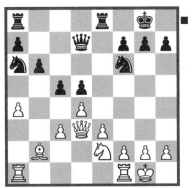

Position after: 14. ♕d3

14... c4

A difficult strategic decision, yet it is resolutely dismissed by Botvinnik, who calls it a serious positional blunder. He says Black should have played 14...♕b7, keeping the c-file open. It is clear that Capablanca's understanding of the position was completely different to Botvinnik's. Capablanca's plan is to attack and capture White's a-pawn, not overly worried about White's attacking chances on the other side of the board.

15. ♕c2 ♘b8 16. ♖ae1

White is concentrating all his forces behind his yet to be built pawn phalanx in the centre – deep strategy indeed! Yet even here Botvinnik is critical of his own play, saying 16.♘g3 would have been more accurate in order to prevent 16...♘h5.

16... ♘c6

16...♘h5 would have prepared 17...f5, stopping the e3-e4 advance. In this case White would probably have chosen a plan involving f2-f3, h2-h3 and g2-g4 in order to gain space on the kingside, before carrying on with the e4 plan. Capablanca however, sticks to his guns.

17. ♘g3 ♘a5 18. f3 ♘b3

Mikhail Botvinnik

This is the point of Black's play; the a4-pawn is doomed. However the price Black has to pay is very high – the knight on b3 is completely cut off from the battle about to break out in the centre and on the kingside.

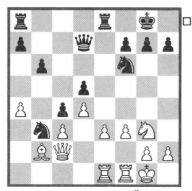

Position after: 18... ♘b3

19. e4 ♕xa4 20. e5 ♘d7 21. ♕f2!

An important move. Black was threatening to play 21...♘bc5! when, if he could bring a knight to d3, Black's chances would improve dramatically. After the text move White's threat is 22.♘f5.

21... g6 22. f4

The bulldozer starts rolling. White wants to play 23.f5.

22... f5 23. exf6 ♘xf6 24. f5

Every single move breathes consistency, with intimidatory effect.

24... ♖xe1 25. ♖xe1 ♖e8

By exchanging as many pieces as possible Capablanca is hoping to take the sting out of White's attack. This is sensible and could even be called instructive, yet it turns out be insufficient after a series of precise moves by Botvinnik. Was there anything better? Probably not. Botvinnik analyses 25...♖f8 and his conclusion is that Black's position would have been untenable after 26.♕f4!. He backs this up with the beautiful variation 26...♕a2 27.fxg6! ♕xb2 28.g7! ♔xg7 29.♘f5+ ♔h8 30.♕h6 ♖f7 31.♕xf6+! ♖xf6 32.♖e8+ and mate.

26. ♖e6!

Intensifying the pressure. Black cannot play 26...♘e4 because of 27.♘xe4 dxe4 28.fxg6!, nor does 26...♔g7 27.♖xf6! ♔xf6 28.fxg6+ offer any hope.

26... ♖xe6 27. fxe6 ♔g7

This looks like a good defence, but unfortunately White still has one extra attacking unit in reserve, his bishop.

28. ♕f4!

Threatening both the simple 29.♕c7+ as well as the treacherous 29.♘f5+! gxf5 30.♕g5+ and mate.

28... ♕e8

Defending against both threats and attacking e6; Black is hanging in there.

29. ♕e5

Naturally this move is intended to defend the pawn on e6, but it does much more than that. Black's knight is pinned and the pin almost completely paralyses Black's position. There are no immediate threats, but with moves like ♗b2-a3 or (if Black plays 29...♘a5) 30.♗c1 on the horizon White is about to increase the pressure to breaking point. Capablanca's reply is therefore, once again, perfectly logical...

29... ♕e7

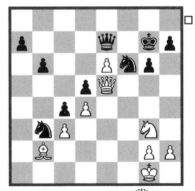

Position after: 29... ♕e7

30. ♗a3!!

...but insufficient. This brilliant combination is the beginning of the end.

30... ♕xa3

'Taking back' his previous move wouldn't save Black as after 30... ♕e8 31. ♕c7+ ♔g8 32. ♗e7 his position collapses.

31. ♘h5+!

The first point.

31... gxh5

Again, there is no sense in refusing the sacrifice. If, for example, 31... ♔h6 32. ♘xf6, Black has a few checks, but in the end he gets mated in view of 32... ♕c1+ 33. ♔f2 ♕d2+ 34. ♔g3 ♕xc3+ 35. ♔h4 ♕xd4+ 36. ♘g4+ etc.

32. ♕g5+ ♔f8 33. ♕xf6+ ♔g8

Now what? It looks like the game is about to end in perpetual check.

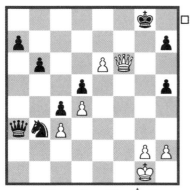

Position after: 33... ♔g8

34. e7!

The second and by far the most diffi-cult point of White's combination. Again everything hangs on accurate calculation. Black has plenty of checks, but White can bring his king to safety while Black's king remains doomed.

34... ♕c1+ 35. ♔f2 ♕c2+ 36. ♔g3 ♕d3+

After 36... ♕xc3+ 37. ♔h4 ♕e1+ the checks peter out quickly, e.g. 38. ♔h3 ♕e3+ 39. g3. Capablanca has spotted one last – and very clever – trap.

37. ♔h4 ♕e4+ 38. ♔xh5 ♕e2+ 39. ♔h4 ♕e4+ 40. g4!

If 40. ♔h3 Black saves himself by the skin of his teeth with 40... h5!. The mating threat on g4 in combination with the newly available escape square for Black's king on h7, make it impossi-ble for White to win.

40... ♕e1+ 41. ♔h5

Black resigned. This is perhaps Botvin-nik's most celebrated victory. IM Hans Bouwmeester, who was my coach when I was a junior, often told me that a real Grandmaster needs to be beaten three times in a single game: firstly in the opening, again in the middlegame and then *again* in the endgame. That is exactly what happened here.

An alert reader may have noted that so far I have not used the terms International Master and Grandmaster in this book, and this is not a coincidence. As an honorific the titles 'Master' and 'Grandmaster' had been used for many years, but they were not in any way official until 1950 when FIDE granted these titles to a small number of players. A few years later a system of formal conditions came into effect (since changed and added to many times) that allowed players to apply for one of these titles once they had fulfilled certain requirements. Broadly speaking a player has to score a Master or Grandmaster norm in two or three international tournaments. The norms – a given number of points to be scored in the tournament – are calculated so as to reflect the relative strength of one's opponents.

Although these titles are still highly prestigious, nowadays another method for calculating the relative strength of players, the Elo rating system introduced in 1970, has become at least as important. This system takes *all* world ranked games an individual plays into account, not just their best efforts (which may have been a long time ago). In so doing, an Elo rating reflects one's present day level rather than one's best ever performances.

The two systems have over time become intertwined, since the calculation of Master and Grandmaster norms is now based on the Elo ratings as well as the titles of a player's opponents.

Vasily Smyslov

Vasily Vasilyevich Smyslov was born in Moscow in 1921. He learnt chess from his father, a good player who owned a large collection of chess books. The chess level was high in Moscow (and competition accordingly tough), but when Smyslov started playing tournaments at the age of fourteen he immediately created a stir. Both his results and his fluent style, showing unusual depth and understanding, made a deep impression. His first major success was winning the Moscow Championship in 1938. Two years later he came third in the Soviet Championship, ahead of Botvinnik and Keres. After WW II, when international chess life picked up again, Smyslov immediately broke through to the top. In the radio match between the USA and the USSR in September 1945 he annihilated Reshevsky 2-0. Then in the first truly important post-war international tournament, Groningen 1946, he came third behind Botvinnik and Euwe. His second place in the 1948 World Championship Tournament was confirmation of his quickly acquired status, not a surprise.

Yet a match against Botvinnik would have to wait. This had nothing to do with Smyslov being ready for such a match or not, but was entirely due to the changed situation now that the World Championship was under FIDE control. Although under the new rules the road to a match for the World Championship had undoubtedly become fairer, it had also become much more difficult. Whereas in the old days – in theory – a bag of gold had been all that was needed, qualification now had to be earned by working one's way through an immensely testing series of tournaments. Precisely *because* this was fair and everybody had a chance, compe-

Smyslov at work against Darga in 1964 in Amsterdam (photo Jos Sutmuller).

tition was extremely tough and nowhere more so than in the Soviet Union where only a world class performance would suffice to get you through the *first* of these qualifiers.

In the first cycle using the new system, many countries found everything so new that they did not even manage to organise a Zonal Tournament. As a result several participants in the 1949 Interzonal Tournament had to be selected by FIDE. Nonetheless, the Interzonal was duly held and the cycle culminated according to plan with the Candidates Tournament of 1950, held in Budapest. Here two other Soviet stars stole the limelight: Isaac Boleslavsky (1919-1977) and the aforementioned David Bronstein. These two shared first place with a two point lead over Smyslov, who finished third, ahead of his fellow pre-tournament favorite Keres. Bronstein won the play-off against Boleslavsky and his match against Botvinnik resulted in a tie.

The second World Championship cycle under FIDE culminated in the legendary 1953 Candidates Tournament in Zürich and was won by Smyslov. With a score of 18/28 he finished two points ahead of his main rivals, Keres, Bronstein and Reshevsky, a superb achievement. Yet, like Bronstein three years before him, he was unable to wrest the title from Botvinnik. Again the match was tied at 12-12, enough for Botvinnik to remain World Champion. With truly impressive determination however, Smyslov also won the next Candidates Tournament, held in Amsterdam in 1956. A year later he *was* successful in arriving at what many had seen as his destiny: beating Botvinnik 12½–9½ to become World Champion.

Smyslov's World Championship reign was short-lived. Botvinnik made use of his right to a revenge match the following year and in this, the two rivals' third match within five years, Smyslov was unable to sustain the high level he had displayed throughout their first two matches. Botvinnik won 12½–10½ and regained 'his' title.

Smyslov was never to get another match for the title. On several more occasions he managed to qualify for Candidates Tournaments, which became Candidates *Matches* after 1965. However he could never win one again, although in 1983 he set an amazing record by reaching the final Candidates Match at the age of 62. He lost to Garry Kasparov, his junior by no less than 42 years!

Smyslov, with his wife Nadezhda, after winning the Candidates Tournament in 1956

Yet even though he was World Champion for only a year, Smyslov is generally regarded as one of the greatest players who ever lived. His unique talent and his equally unique gift of 'turning the talent into results' enabled him to spend almost an entire lifetime at the top of the game. Smyslov won or finished near the top in almost all the elite tournaments he played from around 1940 until well into the 1980s. Even after then he kept playing until deteriorating eyesight finally forced him to retire. He died in Moscow in 2010.

During his lifetime the name "Smyslov" became synonymous with a playing style that was unspectacular yet implacable and amazingly versatile. When Smyslov was seventeen he was already famous for his deep understanding of the opening, middlegame *and* endgame. His positional vison was legendary, yet he was also a great tactician and never afraid of sharp opening variations. He had the necessary patience for slowly realising even the tiniest of advantages, yet he could also be brutal, swift and decisive if that was what the position demanded. Smyslov made some important contributions to opening theory and a remarkable number of variations carry his name. Yet looking at his games you get the impression that he did not actually attach that much importance to the opening phase, preferring to spend his energy on the middlegame and endgame instead. Endgames were without doubt his forte. His knowledge, understanding and precision in handling every type of ending were perhaps unequalled. Even his great rival Botvinnik admitted that in this aspect of the game Smyslov surpassed him.

I think for Smyslov himself such distinctions hardly mattered. He always strove for 'harmony', a term of his own invention for what was essentially maximum cooperation between all of his pieces. It can't have been a coincidence that he was also very musical, an accomplished singer, often giving recitals during chess tournaments. For him chess, like music, perhaps even like life, was first and foremost an art.

As with many of the really great players, to make a selection of Smyslov's best games is well-nigh impossible as there are simply too many of them. I have chosen two personal favorites, which highlight his unique versatility. The first is one of Smyslov's most famous games, a resounding victory over Botvinnik.

♙ Botvinnik, Mikhail
♟ Smyslov, Vasily
🌐 14th game Moscow 1954

This match, the first of the three these two great rivals were to play, featured extremely tough fighting. At the time this game was played Botvinnik was leading 7-6 and only four games so far had ended in a draw.

1. d4 ♘f6 2. c4 g6 3. g3 ♗g7 4. ♗g2 0-0 5. ♘c3 d6

When playing with the black pieces Smyslov was always looking for active counterplay. His repertoire against 1.d4 included the Nimzo-Indian, the Grünfeld and the Slav, all of which he enriched with original and important new ideas. The King's Indian was never one of his main openings, but this game illustrates how smoothly and easily Smyslov was able to adapt to any given situation. For Botvinnik Smyslov's choice of opening must have come as a shock.

6. ♘f3 ♘bd7 7. 0-0 e5 8. e4 c6 9. ♗e3

Here Botvinnik deviates from the main line, 9.h3, perhaps intending to avoid his opponent's preparation. However Smyslov turns out to be well prepared even for 9. ♗e3, which until then had hardly ever been played.

9... ♘g4 10. ♗g5

White is hoping to provoke 10...f6, closing the diagonal of the all-important King's Indian bishop on g7 but Smyslov's counterplay is aggressive and well calculated.

10... ♕b6 11. h3

The attempt to win a pawn with 11. ♗e7 ♖e8 12. ♗xd6 would be futile after 12... exd4.

Position after: 11. h3

11... exd4!

In his annotations to the game Botvinnik is full of praise for his opponent's preparation against 9.♗e3, "a move I had never played before except in some training games". Black is relying on a piece sacrifice in order to create complications, but it quickly becomes apparent that there is more to it than that.

12. ♘a4 ♕a6 13. hxg4 b5

It is not very difficult to see that this wins back the piece. However to correctly evaluate the resulting position, with doubled pawns and several weaknesses on both sides, is a different matter.

14. ♘xd4

White had several alternative ways of winning material, but Black always has sufficient counterplay. Both players mention the variations 14. c5 dxc5 15. ♘xc5 ♘xc5 16. ♗e7 ♘e6 and 14. ♗e7 ♖e8 15. ♗xd6 bxa4 16. ♘xd4 ♘e5! with excellent chances for Black.

14... bxa4 15. ♘xc6!?

Possibly White should have been slightly more conservative here with 15. b3 ♘e5 16. ♗e7 ♗xg4 17. f3 ♖fe8 18. ♗xd6. Both Smyslov and Botvinnik assess the position after 18... ♖ad8 as "good for Black", but in a much later analysis Kasparov mentions 19.c5, calling the position 'unclear'.

15... ♕xc6 16. e5 ♕xc4 17. ♗xa8 ♘xe5

Position after: 17... ♘xe5

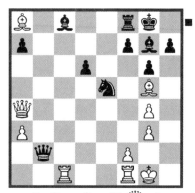

Position after: 20. ♕xa4

The first wave of complications has subsided, leaving a position which is very hard to judge. White is an exchange up, but with weak pawns on b2 and g4. All Black's pieces are on excellent squares so it hardly comes as a surprise that both players in their annotations to this game assess the position as better for Black. Kasparov is less pessimistic for White and considers chances to be about equal.

18. ♖c1 ♕b4 19. a3

Again White is facing a difficult choice. The text forces Black to immediately capture the weak b2-pawn, allowing White to eliminate Black's potentially dangerous pawn on a4. Kasparov focusses mainly on 19. ♗e7.

19... ♕xb2 20. ♕xa4

20... ♗b7!

The ability to clearly distinguish between what is important and what is not is the mark of the true champion. Instead of going for an uninspiring pawn grab (20... ♗xg4 21.♕xa7), Smyslov firmly keeps the initiative.

21. ♖b1?

The only real mistake of the game. Botvinnik describes how after 21. ♗xb7 ♕xb7 he spent a long time looking for a way to defend his king's position against the threat of 22...♘f3+, but failed to find the 'easy' solution 22. ♖c3!. Then after 22... ♘f3+ 23. ♖xf3 ♕xf3 24. ♗e7 ♖c8 25. ♗xd6 material balance is restored and, although Black is still marginally better, there are no realistic winning chances.
21. ♖b1 is very forcing; if Black doesn't find a good reply he can resign. But Smyslov is up to the task.

21... ♘f3+ 22. ♔h1

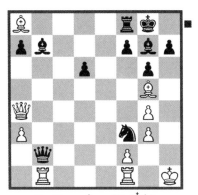

Position after: 22. ♔h1

22... ♗xa8!

The solution isn't so difficult: Black sacrifices his queen but immediately gains a rook and two minor pieces as compensation.

23. ♖xb2 ♘xg5+ 24. ♔h2 ♘f3+ 25. ♔h3 ♗xb2

In a strictly material sense the balance has not been disturbed – White has a queen against Black's three minor pieces. What is much more important though is the positional balance: White's king is hopelessly trapped. The almost nonchalant ease with which Smyslov turns this advantage into a full point is very impressive.

26. ♕xa7 ♗e4!

Now let us look at Smyslov the endgame virtuoso.

The depth of Smyslov's strategic thinking is revealed in his comments to this move. He points out that if White were able to force the exchange of rooks with ♖f1-b1-b8 his chances of a succesful defence would improve.

27. a4 ♔g7 28. ♖d1 ♗e5 29. ♕e7 ♖c8

White was hoping to achieve some counterplay through the exchange sacrifice 30.♖xd6. After the text move 30.♖xd6 is brutally crushed by 30...♖c1! when mate is inevitable.

30. a5 ♖c2 31. ♔g2

The only move, but now the decisive blow comes on the other side.

31... ♘d4+ 32. ♔f1 ♗f3 33. ♖b1 ♘c6

White resigned. Black's next move will be 34...♗d4 and White is busted. "A sublime game, which should make even these two great players proud" was Euwe's comment in his newspaper report on the match.

♙ Smyslov, Vasily
♟ Euwe, Max
🌏 The Hague/Moscow 1948

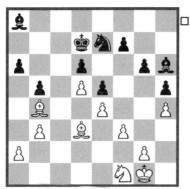

Position after: 40... ♘e7

This was the adjourned position. White is slightly better because his space advantage makes it easier for him to manoeuvre his pieces to target Black's weaknesses. Yet Black really has only one weakness, his pawn on d6. Does White have realistic winning chances or is his just a symbolic advantage? Smyslov demonstrates how to proceed in this type of position, i.e. step by step.

41. g4!

The sealed move, which immediately sets Black a difficult problem. The threat is 42.gxh5 gxh5 43.♘g3 winning a pawn. How should Black defend against this?

41... hxg4

It is almost impossible to prove, but in all probability 41... ♗f4 (to prevent ♘f1-g3) was a better chance. In his notes to this game Smsylov tells us how he was planning to proceed in that case. First he was going to fix the kingside pawn structure with 42.g5, then attack on the queenside, answering say, 42... ♘c8 with 43. ♗a5 ♗c1 44. a4! bxa4 45. bxa4 ♗b7 46. ♔g2 followed by ♘f1-d2-c4. Exchanging pawns on g4 gives White the option of creating a passed h-pawn, but the main drawback is that White's passive pawn on f3 disappears. This is a small, yet very important, structural improvement of White's position.

42. fxg4 ♗c1

A major alternative would have been to seek active counterplay at once with 42...f5. Both players give 43. g5! ♗g7 44. ♘e3!, smothering every further prospect of active play. After the text though, 43...f5 is a serious postional threat, because Black's king's bishop then remains active. Hence White's next move.

43. g5!

The option of creating a passed h-pawn is sacrificed for the more pressing task of eliminating Black's counterchances. Euwe, in his notes in the tournament book, points out that Black would have no problems at all if his king and knight could swap places: with a king on e7 and a knight on d7 Black has the prospect of playing ♘d7-c5 followed by ♗a8-b7-c8.

Considerations such as these are what positional chess is all about.

43... ♗b7 44. ♔f2 ♘c8

Yet even in an endgame, where strategical long-term thinking seems to be all that matters, concrete and very precise attention to detail is all-important. Black could have played 44...♘g8, planning to get some counterplay with 45...f6.

Smyslov then gives 45.♘g3! f6 46.♘e2!, forcing Black to play 46...♗b2, which allows 47.♔e3! followed by ♔e3-d2-c2. The unfortunate Black bishop then has to retreat to d4 where it is exchanged, leaving behind an even more unfortunate black pawn on d4, which will then be captured. An impressive demonstration of Smyslov's pinpoint accuracy!

45. ♘e3 ♔e7

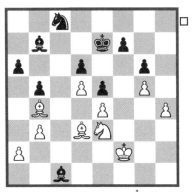

Position after: 45... ♔e7

46. ♗a5!

In preventing the manoeuvre ♘c8-b6-d7, as indicated by Euwe above, White takes away some of the pressure against d6. This is a question of judgment; which is the most important consideration?

46... ♗a3 47. ♔g3 ♗c5 48. ♗d2!

Games like this should either be studied deeply or not looked at at all. Playing through the moves superficially can't possibly reveal the deeper points and hidden subtleties which are an essential part of what is going on. For example, no *engine*, using its purely numerical evaluations would be able to help us understand this endgame.

By placing his bishop on c5 Black has reinforced the defence of his queenside, so Smyslov switches his attention to the other side of the board. If 48...♘b6 (the move Black is longing to play), Black's plan is thwarted by 49.h5!, when 49...gxh5 50.♘f5+ leaves Black's position in disarray (50...♔d7 51.♗e2). The intermediate exchange 49...♗xe3 does not help either, since after 50.♗xe3 the knight on b6 is under attack, making it impossible for Black to prevent the creation of a dangerous passed pawn via 51.h6.

48... ♔f8 49. ♘c2

Another subtle yet powerful move, directed against the regrouping 49...

♘e7 (followed by 50... ♗c8), which now fails to 50.♗a5 ♗c8 51.b4, when 52.♗c7 will win the d6-pawn. The constant oscillating of White's bishop between d2 and a5 is remarkable. Black is thus constantly prevented from improving his position. Strangely enough, this is not a passive strategy, because in so doing White is actually improving his own position as well.

49... ♔e7 50. ♗e2

This bishop is now free to position itself on the h3-c8 diagonal while also preparing h4-h5.

50... ♘a7

Euwe lets this moment pass without comment, but according to Smyslov 50... ♘a7 is a vital mistake and Black should have played 50... ♘b6!.

51. ♗a5! ♘c8

The difference between 50... ♘a7 and 50...♘b6 is that after 50...♘b6 there would have been no need for Black to 'take back' his previous move; Black could have played the much more constructive 51...♘d7. As we shall see, the loss of time involved gives White the opportunity for yet another sophisticated manoeuvre. The idea behind 51.♗a5 is to stop Black from playing 51... ♗c8 in view of 52. b4! ♗g1 53. ♔g2 ♗d4 54. ♘xd4 exd4 55. ♗b6 and the knight is trapped.

52. ♗g4!

Position after: 52. ♗g4!

Looking at the position superficially, it is almost impossible to imagine that Black is getting dangerously close to zugzwang. The moves he would *like* to play 52...♗b6? (53.♗xc8) and 52...♘b6? (53.b4 ♘c4 54. bxc5 ♘xa5 55.c6 ♗a8 56.♗c8), both lose on the spot, while the waiting move 52...♔e8 runs into 53.♗c7 ♔e7 54.♔g2! when it *is* zugzwang: both 54...♔e8 55.b4 ♗a7 56.♗xc8 ♗xc8 57.♗xd6 and 54...♘a7 55.b4 ♗d4 56.♘xd4 exd4 57.♗b6 drop a pawn. 54...♗a7 55.♘b4 followed by 56.♘c6+ only makes things worse.

Smyslov's laconic and succinct commentary was "The battle is over".

52... f6

This is now a stay of execution only.

53. ♗e6 fxg5 54. hxg5

Black has run out of options. Euwe chose to try to break out of his prison with **54... ♘b6 55. b4 ♘c4** which duly cost him a pawn after **56. bxc5 ♘xa5 57. cxd6+** (57. c6? would now be a mistake because of 57... ♗xc6!) **57... ♔xd6 58. ♗f7**. The remaining endgame still requires some precision from White, but Smylov was – of course –

more than up to the task. After **58... ♘c4 59. ♗xg6 a5 60. ♔g4 b4 61. ♗f5 ♔e7 62. ♗e6 ♘d6 63. ♘e3! ♘xe4 64. ♔f5 ♘d6+ 65. ♔xe5 ♘f7+ 66. ♔f4 ♘d8 67. ♘f5+ ♔f8 68. g6 ♘xe6+ 69. dxe6 a4 70. ♔e5** Euwe resigned. His generous final comment: "A beautiful endgame!".

What strikes me again and again in Smyslov's games are their freshness, the open-mindedness and the complete lack of prejudice that characterised his play – and the fearlessness of it! I remember vividly how astonished I was when in 1979, when Smyslov was 58, he refused to shy away from an ultrasharp variation of the Ruy Lopez against Jan Timman, already a world class player and no less than 30 years his junior.

♙ Timman, Jan
♟ Smyslov, Vasily
☽ Bad Lauterberg 1979

1. e4 e5 2. ♘f3 ♘c6 3. ♗b5 a6 4. ♗a4 ♘f6 5. 0-0 ♘xe4 6. d4 b5 7. ♗b3 d5 8. dxe5 ♗e6 9. ♘bd2 ♘c5 10. c3 d4 11. ♘g5!?

Position after: 11. ♘g5!?

Vasily Smyslov during the Interpolis Tournament in 1992 (photo Jos Sutmuller)

This spectacular move had been introduced by Karpov in 1978 during his
world championship match against
Korchnoi in Baguio City. After a long
think Korchnoi decided to avoid complications and played 11...dxc3. Smyslov however goes straight for the jugu-
lar.

11... ♕xg5 12. ♕f3 0-0-0

Black not only gives back the piece, but
effectively offers a piece himself, for
after the practically forced

13. ♗xe6+ fxe6 14. ♕xc6 ♕xe5 15. b4

 Black can only survive by playing

15... ♕d5

This forces some more exchanges,
but...

16. ♕xd5 exd5 17. bxc5 dxc3 18. ♘b3 d4

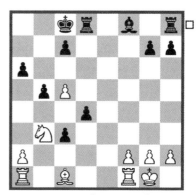

Position after: 18... d4

far from resolving the tension the exchanges have resulted in a tremendously complicated endgame. Who is
better? The game ended in a hard-
fought draw after 55 moves.

Smyslov was a modest, quiet and kindly man, not one to push himself forward.
This sometimes led people to wrongly assume that he must have been a modest
and kindly *chess player* as well. The absurdity of this notion was brought home to
me when as a junior I was called "a kind of Smyslov, but with considerably more
courage" by a well-meaning, but obviously ignorant journalist in a local Dutch
newspaper. When I read this I felt almost painfully embarrassed. More courage
than Smyslov! How *do* you come up with it? It is fortunate that Smyslov was unlikely to have read this newspaper report.

Mikhail Tal

To write about World Champions is almost by definition to write in superlatives. These chess players *are* superlative and only a non-chess player would be able to fail to see that and thus write about them in more sober terms. Even so, among these giants of the game there are some for whom even superlatives are not enough. Such a man was Mikhail Tal. Born in Riga in 1936, Tal held the title of World Champion for one year (1960-61) and died in Moscow in 1992 at the age of 55.

Tal was one of those very few chess players for whom chess is everything and more. Chess was his profession, his passion and the air that he breathed. Paradoxically however, he was also much more than just a chess player: he was a wizard. He mesmerised his fans *and* his opponents, not just by his play but by his whole personality. He was someone who was able to overawe people, yet he did so without a trace of aggression or arrogance. He beat opponents by looking into their eyes, by shaking their hands, by lighting a cigarette. Not all of them, of course, but the more faint-hearted ones were simply powerless against the force of his charisma. Tal was completely uninhibited by the usual conventions of society. Kind and affectionate in life, he turned into a monster at the chessboard. In a word he was *indescribable*. Let us therefore leave words aside for a moment and try to *feel* what it was like to face him at the chessboard.

♙   Tal, Mikhail
♟   Tolush, Alexander
🕐   Moscow 1957

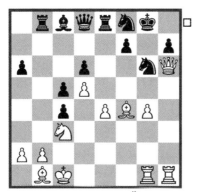

Position after: 28... ♘eg6

This game was played in the final round of an exceptionally strong USSR Championship. Tal, Tolush and Bronstein were leading with 13/20, so this was a game between two of the three leaders. The third, Bronstein, played Kholmov, who was on 12 points, together with Spassky. Keres was on 12½, so he still had a chance as well. The pressure must have been almost unbearable.

Alexander Tolush (1910-1969) was a dangerous attacking player and in this tournament he was at the top of his form. In his game against Tal, however he had been on the defensive right from the start. In the diagrammed position Black's kingside is showing the scars of having been heavily battered. Black's dark squared bishop is gone, there are some gaping holes in his pawn structure and White's major

pieces look like they are ready to move in for the kill. Even so, Black's position is reasonably solid, his weaknesses are covered and ...e5 is a potential stronghold for his pieces, for White's pawn structure too has been damaged.
How does White progress?

29. ♗g5

Straightforward enough. Black cannot allow ♗g5-f6, so his next move is forced.

29... f6

Now what does White want?

30. e5!

Opening the b1-h7 diagonal for the other bishop on b1 gets priority over saving the bishop on g5. Perfectly logical! Yet in a messy position like this most players find it very hard to *see* the logic underneath all the chaos. White is now threatening to play 31. ♗xg6, e.g. 30...fxg5 31.♗xg6 hxg6 32.♕h8+ ♔f7 33. ♖h7+! and White wins.

30... ♖xe5!

Tolush finds an ingenious defence.

31. ♗xg6 ♖b7!

Now h7 is protected, one of White's bishops will fall and the loss of an exchange after 32.♗f4 ♘xg6 is bearable. However Tal's ideas about the position are entirely different.

32. ♘e4!

Throwing his last reserves into battle.

32... fxg5 33. ♖f1!

And still White refuses to withdraw his bishop from g6! The threat is 34.♘f6+ so Black has no choice but to eliminate the knight.

33... ♖xe4 34. ♗xe4 ♖g7

Position after: 34... ♖g7

The storm is over and it is time to assess the damage. Materially, having won an exchange for two unimportant

pawns White has done well, but the really important factor is that he has managed to keep the initiative. Tal finishes the job with a steady hand.

35. ♖f6! ♗xg4 36. ♖hf1 ♘d7 37. ♖xd6 ♕e7

It looks as if Black is still hanging on, but after White's next move everything falls into place.

38. ♖xa6!

Parrying the threat 38...♕xe4 with a counterthreat 39.♖a8+.

38... ♔h8 39. ♗xh7

Another blow. 39. ♖a8+ ♖g8 would still have been defensible for Black, but after the text 39...♖xh7 40.♖a8+ is deadly. A check on e3 is also useless, e.g. 39...♕e3+ 40.♔b1.

39... ♘b8 40. ♗f5+ ♔g8 41. ♗e6+ ♗xe6 42. ♖xe6

Black resigned; his last line of defence has been annihilated. Tolush's comment after the game: "Today I have lost to a genius".

Mikhail Tal with characteristic cigarette (photo Jos Sutmuller)

Any normal human would have been immensely proud of this game, but Tal played like this every day. In fact he probably played like this many times a day, for he was a passionate blitz player and never missed an opportunity to indulge in this 'hobby' of his. In 1988 he won the first official Blitz World Championship and shortly before his death in 1992 he left his hospital bed for a few hours in order to compete in a blitz tournament in Moscow, where he beat Kasparov.
In and out of hospital is Tal's story in a nutshell, for he suffered from bad health throughout his life. He underwent several operations, was a heavy smoker, a heavy drinker, and was briefly addicted to morphine. In between all the health drama he played chess.

The above game against Tolush brought Tal his first Soviet Championship since Bronstein could only draw against Kholmov. Tal was only twenty years old; never before had anyone won this coveted title at such a young age. The next year Tal won again – a rare achievement in itself – and qualified for the Interzonal Tournament in Portoroz in 1958, which he also won. A year later he won the Candidates Tournament in Bled/Zagreb/Belgrade.

Tal's style never varied: boldness, swagger, sacrifices (both correct and incorrect), adventure, action and stubbornness, again and again. He seemed to be making fun of 'correct' chess – serious, rational, scientific – which Botvinnik was teaching. Tals' play was visionary, impulsive, risky, always prepared to sacrifice. He himself called it his "hooligan style" and that describes it well. The chess world was in shock. How could anyone play like this *and* be tremendously successful? But the crowd loved it.

A year later Tal overcame Botvinnik as well; it seemed inevitable for the human hurricane that Tal was. Already called the Magician of Riga, now he was World Champion as well.

Botvinnik didn't play badly in his 1960 match against Tal, but the latter's indomitable energy and sometimes shocking moves must have placed Botvinnik under great pressure and probably exhausted him both mentally and physically. Tal himself wrote a marvellous book about the match. In a witty, highly personal, yet wonderfully objective way he discusses all 21 games – the score was 12½–8½ in Tal's favour – in great depth. Here, I will just give a few examples of the blows with which Botvinnik had to deal.

♙ Tal, Mikhail
♟ Botvinnik, Mikhail
🌐 3rd game Moscow 1960

Position after: 4... ♗xf3

5. gxf3!?

The move of a hooligan! No player in his right mind would consider anything other than the 'normal' 5.♕xf3. Yet Tal spots an opportunity for unsettling his opponent and takes it – without being in the least embarrassed, one may add. The audience reacted with confusion and disbelief. Botvinnik, who of course saw his opening preparation circumvented, reacted stoically. He achieved an advantage, but the game was eventually drawn by perpetual check.

♙ Botvinnik, Mikhail
♟ Tal, Mikhail
🌐 6th game Moscow 1960

Position after: 21. ♖a1

21... ♘f4!

A visionary move! All of Black's pieces are optimally placed, except for the bishop on g7. Now should Black let himself be pushed onto the defensive by the threat of 22.g4? Of course not! "If this sacrifice is bad, my position is bad," was Tal's simple motivation.

21... ♘f4 had the effect of an explosion. What had been a fairly steady positional game suddenly turned into an enormously complicated battle. Tal won in 47 moves.

♙ Tal, Mikhail
♟ Botvinnik, Mikhail
🌐 9th game Moscow 1960

Position after: 10... ♗d6

11. ♘xe6!?

"A speculative sacrifice" is the rational term commentators are fond of when trying to 'tame' a move like this, making it look understandable and to a certain extent even logical. But what Tal does here is exactly the opposite; he wants to take the game away from logic and understandability. He wants to fight on his own terms.

Tal was never that interested in opening theory as most people understand it – no important variations have been named after him. He was always trying to get a *type* of position he liked, rather than outwitting his opponent in a well-known line.

Botvinnik accepted the sacrifice, defended very carefully, and won after a tough fight in 58 moves.

In between games like these Tal also played beautifully logical, strategical games, patiently defended himself when in trouble, and showed great endgame prowess. Thus it was hardly surprising that Botvinnik could not deal with this highly unusual opponent: a hooligan and a magician at the same time.

Winning the World Championship was the crowning achievement in Tal's unparalleled string of successes. By 1961 he was beginning to suffer from serious kidney problems and lost the return match to Botvinnik 13-8. Tal's health would remain frail until his death and although he played with great vigour between his periods of bad health it was almost impossible for

Mikhail Tal (photo Jos Sutmuller)

him to be successful at the highest level over a longer period of time. Tal was forced to withdraw from the Candidates Tournament in Curaçao in 1962 because of health issues, but in the next World Championship cycle he made it to the final where he was beaten by Spassky. As late as 1985 he only just missed out on qualifying for the Candidates matches. Tal nonetheless enjoyed two very succesful periods, one in 1972-73 and one in 1979, again winning some very strong tournaments, but by now playing in a more mature style which combined genius with experience.

A good example of his later style is the following game from 1973.

♙ Spassky, Boris
♟ Tal, Mikhail
🌐 Tallinn 1973

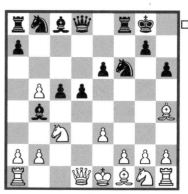

Position after: 9... 0-0

Two former World Champions meet. For Spassky 'former' was a very recent change of status, having lost his title to Fischer only half a year earlier. Tallinn 1973 was a first step on the long and arduous road of adjusting to the new situation and trying to regain his former strength. Tal on the other hand was in one of his best periods ever and bursting with energy. The difference soon becomes apparent.

1. d4 ♘f6 2. c4 e6 3. ♘c3 ♗b4 4. ♗g5

A sharp variation which Spassky played often in his youth. Tal accepts the challenge without hesitation.

4... h6 5. ♗h4 c5 6. d5 b5!?

Sacrificing a pawn in order to break down White's central pawn chain. A logical plan, but one that requires great courage.

7. dxe6 fxe6 8. cxb5 d5 9. e3 0-0

Time for a first assessment. White is a solid pawn up, but Black has a small lead in development and his central pawns look threatening; already a d5-d4 push is looming large over White's

position. However so long as White has the reply a2-a3, he does not need to worry yet, i.e. 9...d4 10.exd4 cxd4 11.a3 ♗a5 12.b4.

10. ♘f3

This move has been criticised by Tal and other commentators because White still does not *have* to stop 10..d4. Spassky probably agreed, since in a later game he preferred 10.♗d3, keeping the option open of developing his knight to e2, in order to support c3 which after the text soon turns out to be a weakness.

10... ♕a5

Tal immediately puts his finger on the weak spot. Not only is 11... ♗xc3+ now a threat, 11... ♘e4 would also be quite disastrous.

11. ♗xf6 ♖xf6 12. ♕d2

Again Spassky choses a move which is logical enough but is condemned by Tal in his notes. Tal recommends 12. ♕c1 instead, keeping the queen's rook protected so that a future a2-a3 will be more powerful.

12... a6!

Getting rid of the pawn on b5, which hinders Black's piece deployment.

13. bxa6

White is still playing as if the world is in perfect order. It would have been more sober to return the extra pawn with 13.b6 or 13. ♗e2 axb5 14. 0-0 in order to complete development. However this would have been tantamount to admitting that White's opening play had been a failure, so Spassky sticks to his guns.

13... ♘c6!

Black's pressure is becoming tangible with the threat of d5-d4 renewed. Taking back the pawn on a6 is not a priority.

14. ♗e2

Again Spassky choses the bravest move, but again this is the sort of courage that borders on foolhardiness. Tal advocates 14.♕c1 even here, again in order to meet 14...d4 with 15.a3, but Spassky chooses to weather the storm.

Position after: 14. ♗e2

14... d4!

The start of a deep and complicated attack, which had to be perfectly calculated. Typical Tal!

15. exd4 ♖xf3 16. ♗xf3 cxd4 17. 0-0

17. ♗xc6 would have lost on the spot to 17... dxc3, while Tal was intending to counter 17. ♖c1 (planning to meet 17... dxc3 18. bxc3 ♗a3 with 18. ♗xc6) with 17... ♗xa6! 18. ♗xc6 ♖d8. Black would be a full rook down but the attack against the white king, unable to escape, is deadly.

17... dxc3 18. bxc3 ♗xc3 19. ♕d6

This move saves White from further material losses since 19... ♗xa1 20. ♕xc6 would be very bad for Black.

19... ♖xa6! 20. ♗xc6 ♗b4!

Forcing the white queen to abandon the bishop. Other moves such as 20...

♗xa1 21. ♖xa1 or 20... ♗e5 21. ♕e7! are insufficient.

21. ♕b8 ♖xc6 22. ♖ac1

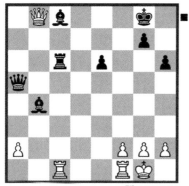

Position after: 22. ♖ac1

It still seems very unclear which of the players is in charge of the situation. With two bishops against a rook Black has a material advantage, but the pin on his c8 bishop might well tip the balance in White's favour. When he played 14...d4 Tal must have foreseen this problem, for if he had had nothing better than 22... ♖xc1 23. ♖xc1 the whole idea would have been a fiasco.

22... ♗c5!

This not only solves the problem of the pin, it puts the finger on a very unexpected, yet highly relevant weakness in White's position as well, the f2 pawn.

23. ♖c2

Consistent, yet it soon turns out that by continuing to try to exploit his chances

along the c-file White is seriously endangering himself.

23... ♕a4!

This must have been painful for White. 24. ♖fc1 fails to 24... ♗xf2+! 25. ♔xf2 ♖xc2+ so White has to put the brakes on.

24. ♕b3 ♕f4

Exchanging queens would have taken all the power away from Black's position but the choice between 24...♕e4 and 24...♕f4 must have been a difficult one. In his notes Tal gives the spectacular variation 24... ♕e4 25. ♖fc1 ♗b7! 26. ♕xb7 ♗xf2+! 27. ♔f1 (27. ♔xf2 ♖xc2+ loses the queen) 27... ♕d3+! 28. ♔xf2 ♖xc2+ 29. ♖xc2 ♕xc2+ followed by 30... ♕xa2, when Black is a pawn up in a queen ending with very reasonable winning chances. Many players would have jumped at this opportunity, having already survived so many dangers. Tal, however, senses that there is more to be gained by refusing to release the tension yet.

25. ♕g3

Tal recommends 25. ♕f3 instead, forcing Black to retreat his queen to d6 or c7 if he still refuses to exchange queens. After the text Black is able to keep his sights trained on the f2 pawn.

25... ♕f5! 26. ♖fc1 ♗b7!

This very important move is made possible by the variation 27.♕b8+ ♔h7 28.♕xb7 ♗xf2+!.

27. ♕f3 ♕g5

Now that his rook on c6 is protected, Black can afford to keep his queen in an aggressive position. Should White try for a repetition of moves with 28.♕g3, he gets hit in his Achilles' heel again, i.e. 28...♗xf2+!, when both 29.♕xf2 ♕xc1+! and 29.♔xf2 ♖xc2+ 30.♖xc2 ♕f5+ lose on the spot.

28. ♕b3 ♖c7! 29. g3

If instead 29. ♕xe6+ ♖f7 30. g3, ♗xf2+ is a straightforward win for Black.

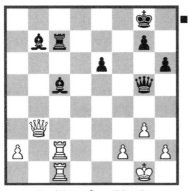

Position after: 29. g3

29... ♗xf2+!

Now that White has further weakened his kingside defences by opening the long diagonal his position is ready for demolition.

30. ♔xf2 ♕f6+ 31. ♔e1 ♕e5+ 32. ♔f1 ♗a6+ 33. ♔g1 ♕d4+ 34. ♔g2 ♕e4+ 35. ♔g1

There is no escape. If 35. ♔h3, Black would have played 35... ♖xc2 36. ♕xc2 ♗f1+!, winning the queen.

35... ♗b7

Tal in his element.

36. h4 ♕h1+ 37. ♔f2 ♖f7+ 38. ♔e2 ♕e4+

White resigned.

Perhaps a game like this is even more 'magical' than the brute force the *young* Tal used to crush his opponents. There is no provocation, no open declaration of war, no chaos. Everything is common sense, almost inconspicuously so. Yet each and every move is strong and to the point, not one of them is superfluous or less than accurate. A game like this is pure poetry – poetry on a chessboard.

Tigran Petrosian

In a way it must have been a relief for the chess world when in 1961 Tal's run of incomprehensible successes finally came to an end. Order was restored. Botvinnik was World Champion again and magic no longer seemed to determine the outcome of major tournaments. Of course Tal would continue to astonish and enchant his admirers, he would continue to remain one of the world's very best, but he was *the* best no longer; the hurricane had exhausted itself. This short period of relative calm at the top of the chess world allowed someone else to come to the fore, someone who had also been one of the best for some time but had not yet been able to establish himself as *the* best: Tigran Petrosian.

Tigran Vartanovich Petrosian was born to Armenian parents in 1929 in Tbilisi, the Georgian capital. He certainly showed talent as a youth, but it wasn't until he moved to Moscow in 1949 that his chess career really took off. From then on, Petrosian's rise to the top was very fast. He shared second place with Keres in the 1951 Soviet Championship, which was also a qualifying event for the 1952 Interzonal Tournament in Stockholm.

He again shared second place in Stockholm, which meant that he qualified for his first Candidates Tournament: Zürich 1953. In this legendary event Petrosian came fifth, behind Smyslov, Keres, Bronstein and Reshevsky. Although perhaps not quite as sensational as Tal's meteoric rise to the top only a few years later, fifth place was a tremendous achievement all the same.

From that time onwards, Petrosian was firmly established as one of the very best players in the Soviet Union, which of course meant he was also one of the best in the world. He participated in the Candidates Tournaments of 1956 and 1959, won the Soviet Championship in 1959 and 1961, but it wasn't until 1962 that he was able to make that last, tiny – yet enormous – step to the top by winning the Curaçao Candidates Tournament, half a point ahead of Geller and Keres. Finally, he had achieved what only Bronstein, Smyslov and Tal had managed to achieve before him: a match for the World Championship against Botvinnik.

Tigran Petrosian

The title match was held in Moscow in 1963 and Petrosian's victory (12½-9½) did not come as a great surprise. At the age of 52 few expected Botvinnik to be able to withstand another challenger who was his junior by a generation. This time Botvinnik's defeat was final since FIDE had abolished the right to a return match. Botvinnik did receive a place in the next Candidates Tournament, but he decided that enough was enough and declined. It was the end of an era: Botvinnik's time was finally over.

Petrosian was to retain the title for six years. He defeated Boris Spassy in 1966 (12½-11½), thus becoming the first reigning World Champion to win a title match since Alekhine had beaten Bogoljubov in 1934! In tournaments however Petrosian never truly dominated during the six years of his reign. It was just not part of his character to try to demonstrate his superiority everywhere and always. Petrosian held the world title and that was enough for him. His method of ruling the chess world was to be the *primus inter pares*, the first among equals. It is characteristic of him that the three tournaments which he won as World Champion were all shared victories: in Los Angeles 1963 and Buenos Aires 1964, both tied with Keres, and the 1968 Moscow Championship, equal with Bronstein. In every other tournament that Petrosian played during these six years, he finished behind the winners: second, shared second, third, fourth, and once even shared ninth, scoring 8½/17 in Moscow 1967, 2½ points adrift of the winner, Leonid Stein.

Where Petrosian *did* show his immense strength was at Chess Olympiads. In Havana 1966 he scored ten wins and conceded only three draws on top board, a phenomenal result which he almost equalled two years later in Lugano. Perhaps he felt under less pressure in team events. Of course these performances also say something about the cavernous difference in strength between the Soviet Union and the rest of the world. In those days the World Champion had almost no serious rivals except in his own country, where there were many.

Three years after their first match Spassky again challenged Petrosian and this time he was successful, winning with a score of 12½-10½ after a gruelling fight. As a former World Champion ("This at least is a title nobody can take away from you," he used to joke – but was it a joke?) Petrosian remained active and kept having excellent results. He won two more Soviet championships (in 1969 and 1975) and he was a participant in the qualification cycles for the World Championship several more times. However he never again obtained the right to challenge the reigning World Champion – and probably didn't regret it. Petrosian's last tournament was Niksic 1983. He died a year later at the age of 55 after a long illness.

Yet it may have been Petrosian's playing style rather than his results, tremendous as they were, that made him one of the most remarkable kings of the game. If Tal was the champion of attack, Petrosian was the undisputed king of defence.
For this he has been both admired and vilified. It goes without saying that *all* great champions are great defenders, who even under tremendous pressure find ways to make life as difficult as possible for their opponents, but Petrosian had a unique talent for spotting danger earlier than any of his (attacking) adversaries. In Petrosian's games these dangers never seemed to materialise, thanks to his ability to nip them in the bud, giving his play an aura of invulnerablity which was magical in the eyes of admirers but boring in the eyes of critics.

It is true that his drawing percentage was always high, but it wasn't fear that motivated him, nor inclination to avoid a full scale battle. What guided him was simply an unusually highly developed sense of danger. Petrosian's top priority was indeed to avoid losing, but the way in which he managed to do so had the mark of a genius and certainly had nothing in common with the play of a coward or a boring player, who never plays an interesting move simply because he can't think of one. In Petrosian's hands defence was an art form.

One of the qualities for which Petrosian was most famous was his mastery of the purely positional exchange sacrifice, based not (just) on calculation but on long-term positional thinking. The classic example is:

♙ Reshevsky, Samuel
♟ Petrosian, Tigran
🕤 Zürich 1953

Position after: 25. ♖fe1

White's position looks threatening and it is not easy to see how Black can find counterplay. Things would be different if Black had a knight on d5, but how to get there?

25... ♖e6!

So simple, so logical, yet this idea is so hard to find – and one has to have the courage to sacrifice material! The dangerous e-pawn is stopped and all of a sudden the path for Black's knight to d5 is clear. The only problem with 25... ♖e6 is that it costs the exchange. But what is an exchange? A rook for a knight. Is a rook always the more valuable piece? Not here!

26. a4

Reshevsky must have felt that his initiative was slipping away so with 26. a4 he hopes to tempt Black into playing the seemingly logical 26...b4, after which 27.d5! ♖xd5 28.♗xe6 followed by 29.♕xc4 leads to a much more open type of position, where White's material advantage *is* a major factor. However Petrosian does not allow himself to be sidetracked.

26... ♘e7!

Iron logic indeed. The threat of 27...♞d5 forces White to retreat.

27. ♗xe6 fxe6 28. ♕f1

Reshevsky also senses danger. The more active 28. ♕f2 ♞d5 29. ♖f3 would have allowed 29... b4!, which under changed circumstances becomes a strong move.

28... ♞d5 29. ♖f3 ♗d3 30. ♖xd3 cxd3 31. ♕xd3 b4!

The final chain in a series of fearless defensive moves. 31...bxa4 32.c4 would have given White the advantage thanks to his strong pawn centre, but after the text 32. c4 ♞b6 33. ♖c1 ♞xa4 would be very risky for White.

32. cxb4 axb4 33. a5

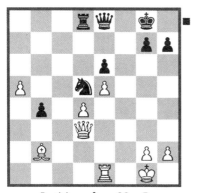

Position after: 33. a5

White has an extra pawn and a passed a-pawn to boot, but with the beautiful knight on d5, against a very passive bishop on b2, Black has ample posi-

tional compensation. The game continued **33... ♖a8 34. ♖a1 ♕c6 35. ♗c1 ♕c7 36. a6 ♕b6 37. ♗d2 b3 38. ♕c4 h6 39. h3 b2 40. ♖b1 ♔h8** and was adjourned in this position. The players agreed to a draw without further play since neither can improve their position. If, for example 41. ♗c3?, 41... ♕xa6 42. ♕xa6 ♖xa6 43. ♗xb2 ♖b6 would follow, when the pin against the bishop far outweighs the loss of a pawn.

Sacrifices such as these often took the opponent completely unawares, for example in the following game, against the champion of attack *himself*:

♙   Tal, Mikhail
♟   Petrosian, Tigran
♟   Riga 1958

Position after: 31. ♕g4

In this game Petrosian *has* allowed his opponent more attacking chances than he would have desired. Indeed, with his pressure against Black's kingside –

based on the half-open f-file and the threatening h5-pawn plus Black's pieces being tied to the defence of c5 – it seems as if Black can only wait for White to find a way forward. In his notes to the game, Tal, who was on the verge of his meteoric rise to the top, describes how he felt confident of winning. But then Petrosian uncorked

31... ♖f4!

and suddenly everything had changed. Black offers White the choice of winning an exchange or a pawn, but in both cases the situation on the board is utterly changed: White's kingside attack disappears and Black's pieces spring to life.

In the game Tal took the exchange with **32. ♗xf4 exf4 33. ♘d2** (Tal later preferred 32. ♖xf4 exf4 33. ♗xf4, but here too Black definitely has enough counterplay), but after the reply **33... ♘e5** he decided to return some of the material to avoid being pushed onto the defensive: **34. ♕xf4 ♘xc4 35. e5 ♘xe5 36. ♘e4.** Petrosian countered this new wave of aggression with the cool defensive move **36... h6!** and within just a few moves (**37. ♖ae1 ♗b8 38. ♖d1 c4 39. d6 ♘d3**) he had taken over the initiative. The game lasted 73 moves and White only just managed to make a draw.

Interestingly, this setback did not stop Tal from winning the tournament – Petrosian finished second.

Petrosian is one of those great players from whom you can learn that tactical genius and positional mastery are not mutually exclusive. On the contrary, they complement each other to perfection; the above examples already prove this. In both cases there is a strategic decision which is then implemented by tactical means. But Petrosian could also do this when *he* was the attacker. Here is a famous fragment of a game from his first World Championship match against Spassky:

♙   Petrosian, Tigran
♟   Spassky, Boris
⬙   10th game Moscow 1966

19... f4!

In this game Petrosian was pushed onto the defensive right from the start – but that is where he liked to be!

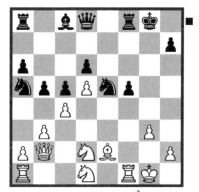

Position after: 19. ♗e2

20. gxf4 ♗h3?

Spassky has played the opening and the early stages of the middlegame very powerfully. This may explain why he now begins to overreach. The simple 20... ♘g6, or alternatively the more forceful 20... ♖xf4, would have won back the pawn and firmly held on to the initiative. The text is designed to force 21. ♖f2 before playing either of the above moves (21. fxe5 is impossible due to 21... ♕g5+). Spassky must have underestimated Petrosian's reply.

21. ♘e3!

An exchange sacrifice. That should not have come as a surprise to his opponent!

21... ♗xf1 22. ♖xf1 ♘g6

Unwilling to admit he has made a mistake, Spassky refuses to change course and keeps on playing for the attack. Isaac Boleslavsky, who was Petrosian's second in this match, claims that 22... ♘d7 23. ♗g4 ♘f6 would have been more solid.

23. ♗g4! ♘xf4?

Spassky perseveres in his error. Boleslavsky points out that 23... ♕f6 should have been played, even though by now White has a clear advantage, e.g. 24. ♗e6+ ♔h8 25. ♕xf6+ ♖xf6 26. f5.

24. ♖xf4!

Another exchange sacrifice, although to call it a sacrifice is really irrelevant. In a single smooth motion White takes over the attack.

24... ♖xf4 25. ♗e6+ ♖f7 26. ♘e4!

Taking on f7 is not urgent. With his knight hopelessly out of play on ...a5, Black is absolutely powerless against the assault.

Position after: 26. ♘e4!

26... ♕h4 27. ♘xd6 ♕g5+

The alternative 27... ♕e1+ is also met by a knight sacrifice: 28. ♔g2! ♕xe3 29. ♗xf7+ ♔f8 30. ♕h8+ ♔e7 31. ♘f5+! ♔xf7 32. ♕g7+ followed by 33. ♘xe3, winning the queen.

28. ♔h1! ♖aa7

If instead 28... ♕xe3 White wins as in the previous variation.

Position after: 28... ♖aa7

Now what? One more blow! But which one?

29. ♗xf7+ ♖xf7 30. ♕h8+!

Black resigned. Games like this not only erase the difference between strategy and tactics, but between attack and defence as well. They are one smooth, logical movement

Remarkably, Petrosian had already played almost the exact final combination ten years earlier (and arguably in an even more brilliant version).

♙ Petrosian, Tigran
♟ Simagin, Vladimir
🌏 Play-off match for the Moscow Championship 1956, game 5

44. ♕a8+ ♔g7 45. ♗xe5+! ♕xe5 46. ♕h8+! ♔xh8 47. ♘xf7+ Supreme elegance! Black resigned.

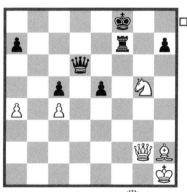

Position after: 43... ♕xd6

But however beautiful his combinations, it is undeniable that Petrosian's core business was the slow suffocation of helpless victims. Somehow he always managed to make it look like he was on the defensive in these games. Perhaps that impression was gained by the almost exaggerated care he gave to the prevention of every possible (and impossible!) counterchance in a position where he already had his opponents in an iron grip. The strangling process would then evolve automatically, sometimes imperceptibly. This unique ability has earned him the nickname *boa constrictor*.

Petrosian, Tal and Geller during the Candidates Tournament in Curaçao 1962
(Source: Max Euwe Centrum)

♙ Petrosian, Tigran
♟ Pilnik, Herman
🌐 Candidates Tournament Amsterdam 1956

---

1. d4 ♘f6 2. c4 c5 3. d5 e5 4. ♘c3 d6 5. e4 g6 6. ♘f3 ♗g7 7. ♗g5 ♘a6

If Black wants to challenge White's bishop the best moment would have been here or the next move. After the immediate 7...h6, for instance, exchanging on f6 would have been pointless, 8. ♗e3 could have been met by 8... ♘g4, and if 8. ♗h4 the aggressive 8...g5 9. ♗g3 ♘h5 was a realistic option.

8. ♗e2 ♘c7 9. ♘d2!

This takes the sting out of 9...h6, since both 10. ♗e3 and 10. ♗h4 can now be played without any drawbacks.

9... ♗d7 10. a4 b6 11. ♘b5

The Argentinian Grandmaster Herman Pilnik, who at the time was one of the best players in the world outside the Soviet Union, often played this Czech Benoni opening. Perhaps he felt invulnerable in a closed position where everything seems to hinge on long-term strategic decisions alone. However with 11. ♘b5 Petrosian poses an unexpectedly concrete problem...

11... ♗xb5?

...and Pilnik fails to cope. Giving up the light squared bishop will be the cause of some serious (long-term!) problems for Black. He should have played either 11... ♘xb5 or 11... ♗c8.

12. cxb5!

Possibly Pilnik underestimated this unorthodox recapture. Routinely recapturing 'towards the centre' with 12.axb5 would have allowed Black an equally routine method of creating counterplay: 12...0-0 followed by 13...a6.
After the text c4 becomes a beautiful square for White's knight. This changes the character of the position completely.

12... 0-0

Position after: 12... 0-0

13. b4!

White immediately puts pressure on his opponent's queenside. Black is now facing a difficult and unpleasant choice. Capturing on b4 gives White command of the open c-file (13... cxb4 14. ♕b3 a5 15. bxa6 ♘xa6 16. ♗xa6 ♖xa6 17. ♕xb4), with the long-term prospect of installing a rook at c6. On the other hand, leaving White the option to take on c5, with a White knight supreme on c4, is equally unattractive. Pilnik decides to go for the first of these possibilities, but in an improved version.

13... h6

Should White now unthinkingly retreat his bishop to e3, Black has 13...cxb4 followed by 15... ♘d7, which will allow him to put a knight on c5 and reinforce his queenside.

14. ♗xf6!

Remarkably, Petrosian commits exactly the same positional 'mortal sin' as did Pilnik on move 11, exchanging his good bishop for a knight. Yet, whereas Pilnik's 11... ♗xb5 really was a positional mistake, Petrosian's 14. ♗xf6 is a demonstration of deep insight. It soon becomes clear that White's remaining 'bad' bishop is actually doing a very important job, while Black's is no more than an onlooker.

14... ♕xf6 15. 0-0

White delays the exchange on c5 and keeps the tension since Black capturing on b4 is still nothing to worry about. Thus Black is left with a lot of uncertainty as to his oppponent's plans.

15... ♖fd8 16. ♘c4 ♗f8 17. g3!

Black's last two moves were clearly intended as preparation for meeting the expected b4xc5 with d6xc5. By playing 17.g3 White opens up a new possibility to start an attack on the kingside with f2-f4. Should Black be forced to concede his entire central pawn structure (e.g. after 18.bxc5 dxc5 19.f4 exf4 20.gxf4) his position would become very precarious indeed. In order to prevent this Pilnik now changes tack and decides to take on b4 after all.

17... cxb4 18. ♕b3 ♔g7 19. ♖fc1

Again Petrosian shows emphatically that he is not in a hurry, but there is also a concrete tactical reason for delaying the recapture: 19. ♕xb4 ♘e6! 20. dxe6 d5 would give Black counterplay.

19... h5 20. ♘e3!

A truly remarkable move, for there were no less than two ways of winning material in this position. Firstly White could have played 20. ♕xb4 in order to meet 20... ♘e6 21. dxe6 d5 with 22. ♕b2 dxc4 23. exf7 winning a pawn, and secondly he could have played 20.

♘xb6, which leaves White either a pawn or an exchange ahead, the latter if Black plays 20... ♘xb5 21. ♘xa8 ♘d4 22. ♕d3 ♖xa8.

Petrosian must have considered these moves, but he does not let himself get sidetracked. A characteristic detail: in his notes to this game he does not even mention 20. ♕xb4 or 20. ♘xb6. Although Petrosian's play looks unhurried, perhaps even a trifle slow, in actual fact none of his moves is superfluous and every little *zwischenzug* fits seamlessly into the whole plan. I call this a work of art.

20... ♘e8 21. ♕xb4 ♖dc8 22. ♖c6

Strategically, the battle is over. Taking on c6 is not an option for Black, so all he can do is wait and see where White will strike the decisive blow.

22... ♕d8 23. ♖ac1 ♘f6

The knight is heading for c5, but Petrosian wouldn't be Petrosian if he were to allow this.

24. ♗f1!

A white bishop appears on h3 at precisely the right moment. Should Black now persist in his plan he will have to pay a high price: 24... ♘d7 25. ♗h3 ♘c5 costs the exchange, while 25... ♖xc6 26. dxc6 ♘c5 27. ♘d5 ruins Black's position completely. Pilnik again decides for a change of plan.

24... 罝cb8 25. 奧h3 a6

Position after: 25... a6

26. 罝e1!

At first sight this is just incomprehensible. Wasn't this rook excellently placed on c1 and what possible purpose does it serve on e1? Petrosian was clearly proud of this move and takes great care in his notes to explain that in his view it is not just a good move, but 'the only one'. "By playing 25...a6 Black has weakened his pawn on b6. In order to attack this weakness White has to put his knight on c4. For this purpose the pawn on e4 must be protected. But how? Retreating the bishop from h3 (奧h3-g2) would be like taking a step backwards, while 26.f3 constitutes an unpleasant weakening of White's pawn structure which allows counterplay by means of 26...axb5 27.axb5 h4. The only remaining option is to play 26.罝e1" (Petrosian). That is what logical thinking looks like!

26... axb5 27. axb5 ⑬h7 28. ⑬c4 罝a2

Superficially it seems that Black has created some counterplay, with moves like 豐d8-f6 and ⑬h7-g5 in the air. However, a couple more subtle defensive moves by Petrosian suffice to neutralise these dangers without – and this is of vital importance! – weakening White's attacking power on the queenside in the slightest.

29. 奧g2 豐f6 30. 罝f1 ⑬g5 31. 豐b3 罝ba8

The pawn on b6 could no longer be saved.

32. h4 ⑬h7 33. 罝xb6 罝a1 34. 罝c6 罝8a2 35. 豐e3

Everything stays under control.

35... 豐d8 36. 罝xa1

Petrosian admitted that 36.b6 would have been a quicker win. In time trouble and with the win practically in his pocket his play loses some of its edge.

36... 罝xa1+ 37. 曾h2 ⑬f6 38. f3

Under the changed circumstances Petrosian doesn't want to part with his bishop any more, for this piece is now an important defender of White's kingside, so he now prefers this pawn move over 38. 奧h3. He considers the weakening of his second rank not to be a serious problem.

38... ♛b8 39. ♕b3 ♘d7 40. b6 ♘c5 41. ♕b2 ♖a4 42. ♕b5 ♖a2 43. ♖c7

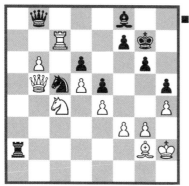

Position after: 43. ♖c7

43... g5

A last attempt at creating confusion. It is not clear what Black had in mind against the natural (and materialistic) 44.hxg5, but Petrosian follows his own train of thought. Now that Black has left a hole in his pawn structure on f5, ideal for a white knight, Petrosian switches to a direct kingside attack.

44. ♘e3

"The simplest" he calls this.

44... gxh4 45. ♘f5+ ♚g8 46. gxh4 ♖a6 47. b7 ♖a7 48. ♖c8 ♕xb7 49. ♕e8 ♘d7 50. ♘xd6

Black resigned. His fortress, which once looked impregnable, has been razed to the ground.

Boris Spassky

Boris Spassky, the man who beat the unbeatable Petrosian in 1969, was perhaps the most tragic of all World Champions. No matter how great and wonderful a player he was, his defeat by Bobby Fischer in the "Match of the Century" in 1972 has caused him to go down in history as "that Russian guy who lost to that American. What's his name?". This image was made worse by the many publications and movies about the match (or about Fischer) in which he was portrayed as a bad guy, a loser or a downright idiot, depending on what sort of character was needed to make the winner of the match look like the desired kind of hero. Needless to say, these distortions of his character bear little resemblance to the great player Spassky really was.

Boris Vasilievich Spassky was born in 1937 in Leningrad (renamed Saint Petersburg in 1991). He is the first 'king of the chessboard' who is still alive at the time of writing. He is also the first in the long line of Soviet World Champions whose life witnessed the downsides of being a Soviet citizen as clearly as the benefits.
It started like a fairy tale. Little Boris learned chess at the age of five and soon turned out to be extremely talented. He rose through the ranks in record time and when he qualified for his first Candidates Tournament (at the Göteborg Interzonal in 1955) he was only 18 years old. For this he was awarded the Grandmaster title. Never before had a chess player risen to such rarefied heights at such a young age. (Ominously, perhaps, the record was broken three years later by ... Bobby Fischer.)

In that Candidates Tournament, a year later in Amsterdam, Spassky finished equal third, behind Smyslov and Keres. For a 19-year-old this achievement was stunning, and would have been even today, in an age of totally changed age-performance expectations.

Yet from that moment on Spassky's career began to stagnate. First he, like everybody else, had to allow Comet Tal to pass him by. It was Tal who inflicted a painful defeat upon Spassky in the final round of the 1958 Soviet Championship, resulting in Tal winning the title and Spassky missing out on a qualifying place for the next Interzonal. This was all the more heartbreaking since Spassky had been in sole first place only a few rounds before the end of the tournament.

It was a difficult period for Spassky and for some years he alternated excellent results with occasions where he failed conspicuously at crucial moments. He lost a game to William Lombardy of the USA at the World Student Team Championship in Leningrad in 1960, which resulted in the USA winning the tournament, not the Soviet Union. This of course was not what was expected from a representative of the ideal communist state and Spassky was punished for it, temporarily being banned from going (and playing) abroad.

Experiences such as these must have undermined his peace of mind and consequently his self-confidence as a player. This was made worse by the divorce from his first wife *and* the breakup with his long-time coach Alexander Tolush, who had supported him during his first run of successes. When in 1961 Spassky again failed to qualify for the Interzonal (again due to a last round loss, this time to Leonid Stein), his future – and probably his present as well – must have looked very bleak indeed.

However in that same year his fortunes finally changed for the better. In Igor Bondarevsky (1913-1979) Spassky found a new coach who stimulated him to work hard again, as a result of which he regained his confidence. From now on Spassky would play with great concentration and tremendous focus, no matter how high the odds or the tension in a particular game. Towards the end of 1961 Spassky won the Soviet Championship. His ban on travelling was lifted, allowing him to resume his fine play in tournaments abroad. The new World Championship cycle, starting with the Zonal tournaments of 1963/64, saw a rejuvenated Spassky. He fought his way through two immensely tough qualification rounds ("The

Boris Spassky World Champion
(Source: Max Euwe Centre)

Amsterdam 1964 Interzonal was the hardest tournament I ever played") and in the Candidates Matches (which had replaced the old Candidates *Tournament*) he first beat Keres, then Geller and finally Tal, a stellar performance. Finally, Spassky had arrived where he had been expected for years, on the threshold of the World Championship. As we have seen in the previous chapter Spassky didn't win that first match against Petrosian, but he wasn't discouraged and calmly waited for the next cycle, where as the previous challenger, he was seeded directly into the Candidates Matches. This time he *was* successful. After beating Geller (again), Larsen and Korchnoi in the Candidates Spassky now beat Petrosian as well, 12½-10½. World Champion at last!

The story of a true champion? Most definitely. If a documentary or film about Spassky's life had been made in, say, 1970, it would have been a heroic tale of the overcoming of setbacks, of personal growth and of success. A good closing scene would have been his legendary win over Fischer at the 1970 Siegen Olympiad, a game that attracted thousands of fans and which was Spassky's crowning effort in a tremendously succesful tournament, where he won the gold medal for the best performance on board one.

♙ Spassky, Boris
♟ Fischer, Robert James
🌐 Olympiad Siegen 1970

We will take a closer look at Bobby Fischer in the next chapter, but for a proper understanding of the situation it is essential to know that at the time this game was played Fischer had just had a fantastic run of successes and was already seen by many as *de facto* the best player in the world. FIDE ratings had just recently been introduced and Fischer was the number one by a colossal margin, with Spassky only second even though he was World Champion. It would be an understatement to say that this game was eagerly anticipated. The playing hall and the commentary room were filled to overflowing by chess fans from around the world. Hotels were fully booked within a range of some 50 kilometres. As a prelude to what was to happen two years later in Reykjavik, this game fully deserves to be called "the Game of the Century".

1. d4 ♞f6 2. c4 g6 3. ♞c3 d5

The Grünfeld Defence, one of Bobby's favorite openings. It is sharp, uncompromising and just a touch risky.

4. cxd5 ♞xd5 5. e4 ♞xc3 6. bxc3 ♗g7 7. ♗c4

This was the Grünfeld's main line in those days. White builds a strong pawn centre and concentrates his attacking forces on the kingside. The two combatants had contested this variation once already, in Santa Monica 1966, a game that was also won by Spassky.

7... c5 8. ♞e2 ♞c6 9. ♗e3 0-0 10. 0-0 ♛c7 11. ♖c1 ♖d8 12. h3

Spassky almost always included f2-f4 in his plans for this type of position. In 1966 he had been successful with 12. ♛e1 e6 13. f4, but later analysis had convinced him that Black could (and should) have gone for an exchange of queens with 12...♛a5 13.f4 cxd4. With the text he 'sacrifices' a tempo in order to prevent a possible ♗c8-g4. The immediate 12.f4 ♗g4 has always been considered good for Black.

12... b6 13. f4 e6 14. ♕e1 ♘a5 15. ♗d3 f5!

Stopping White from advancing his f-pawn and increasing the pressure on White's central pawn phalanx.

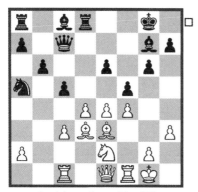

Position after: 15... f5!

16. g4!

Spassky replies in spirit. Neither player wishes to let go of the initiative.

16... fxe4 17. ♗xe4 ♗b7 18. ♘g3 ♘c4 19. ♗xb7 ♕xb7 20. ♗f2 ♕c6 21. ♕e2 cxd4 22. cxd4 b5

The situation is beginning to look bad for White. His d-pawn is at least as vulnerable as Black's e-pawn and Black's knight on c4 is looking very powerful.

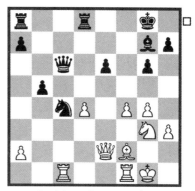

Position after: 22... b5

23. ♘e4!

Again Spassky refuses to be driven backwards. Rather than give his d-pawn some extra protection with 23. ♖fd1, he activates his knight.

23... ♗xd4!?

A characteristic moment. Spassky liked sacrificing pawns, Fischer liked to take them. Who is right? Spassky himself recommended 23... ♖f8 24. ♘c5 ♖ae8 here, claiming that Black would have been better. However most commentators find this view too pessimistic and point out variations like 25. a4! a6 26. ♘xa6 ♕xa6 27. axb5 ♕xb5 28. ♕xc4 ♕xc4 29. ♖xc4 ♖xf4 when the position becomes drawish. Did Fischer want more? Undoubtedly he was playing for a win (as was Spassky), but even someone as objective and unemotional as a computer engine would find it hard to decide which was the better choice.

Boris Spassky (right) in a game against Planinc in 1973.

24. ♘g5!

Superficially 24. ♗xd4 ♖xd4 25. ♘f6+ ♔g7 26. g5 looks good, but after 26... ♖ad8 White finds it hard to strengthen his attack and Black is threatening 27...♖d2.

24... ♗xf2+?!

Psychologically this may have been the turning point in the game. "Fischer is playing for a win, otherwise he would have retreated his bishop to f6", explained Spassky. However Fischer is a pawn up and he is not going to relinquish a material advantage for no reason.

25. ♖xf2 ♖d6 26. ♖e1 ♕b6 27. ♘e4!

Taking the pawn with 27. ♘xe6 would have caused White trouble after 27... ♖e8 28. f5 ♖d2, but after the text it becomes clear that White's initiative is becoming dangerous. What is Black to do? If he decides to protect his extra pawn 27...♖c6 is the only available option, yet in that case he would relinquish his chances of active play along the d-file. It also has the drawback that after (27...♖c6) 28.♖d1 the position is just very unclear. Fischer wants clarity, he wants the initiative *and* he wants the extra pawn. Does he want too much? His next move can also be interpreted as an 'ordinary' oversight. But is there really such a thing?

27... ♖d4?! 28. ♘f6+ ♔h8

If Black was playing for an exchange of queens 28... ♔g7 would have been more logical, but Fischer has other plans.

29. ♕xe6!

Position after: 29. ♕xe6!

Perhaps Fischer had thought this capture was impossible, for it now seems as if Black is winning on the spot with the powerful 29...♖d1.

And even if you realise that White then has the very nasty reply 30.♕f7!!, it is extremely difficult to see (and believe!) that after 30...♖xe1+ 31.♔g2, not only is White not getting mated, but Black doesn't even have a perpetual check. After 31...♕c6+ 32.♔g3, neither 32...♖e3+ 33.♔h4 ♖xh3+ 34.♔xh3 ♕h1+ 35.♖h2 nor 32...♖g1+ 33.♔h4 ♖xg4+ 34. ♔xg4 ♘e3+ 35.♔g5 ♕c5+

36.f5 achieve anything. Instead of this, 31...♘e3+ is more testing, yet after 32.♔f3! ♕c6+ 33.♔g3 ♖g1+ 34.♔h4 ♖xg4+ 35.hxg4 ♕h1+ 36.♔g5, although Black has managed to protect h7 (even retaining his extra pawn!), he is powerless against White's all-out attack. There is the simple threat of 37.♖e2 while Black's only active move 36...♖c8 is refuted brilliantly with 37.♖d2! (threatening 38.♖d7) 37...♘xg4 (or 37...♖c5+ 38.f5) 38. ♖c2! ♖d8 39.♖e2! winning.

With this possibility ruled out, Black needs to completely reorientate himself to the new situation. Even for the very great, such an enormous mental turnaround may be a bridge too far.

29... ♖d6 30. ♕e4 ♖f8?

This extra attack on the f6-knight was unnecessary and suggests that at this point Fischer lacked a clear vision of the position's requirements. It would have been better to play 30... ♖ad8, keeping both rooks active *and* protected. If then 31. g5, both 31... ♖d2 and 31... ♖d3 would have offered Black better chances than the game.

31. g5 ♖d2 32. ♖ef1

Position after: 32. ♖ef1

32... ♕c7?

Fischer loses his composure. In preventing White from playing 33.♕e7, he takes his queen off the a7-g1 diagonal, thereby allowing White's initiative to become stronger. He could have put up more of a fight with 32... ♘d6, or by offering an exchange of queens via 32... ♖xf2 33. ♖xf2 ♕e3.

33. ♖xd2! ♘xd2 34. ♕d4!

Spassky seizes his chance. He now threatens 35.♘e8+, the reason why he does not have to worry about 34...♘xf1. Black is left with a choice between 34...♕b6, going into an endgame that is worse than the one he avoided earlier in the game and 34...♖d8, which although more in line with the aggression he showed earlier on is obviously asking for trouble. Fischer choses the latter, hoping against hope...

34... ♖d8?! 35. ♘d5+ ♔g8

If 35... ♕g7 White can simply take on d2. After the text 36.♕xd2 can still be met by 36...♕c5+.

36. ♖f2! ♘c4 37. ♖e2

White's rook joins the attack and this is decisive. The threat is 38.♖e7.

37... ♖d6

Clutching at straws. 38.♖e7 is now (more or less) neutralised by 38...♕b6. With the rook still on d8 this wouldn't work, e.g. 37... ♕b6 38. ♖e8+! ♖xe8 39. ♘xb6 or 38...♔f7 39.♕xb6 ♘xb6 40.♖xd8.

38. ♖e8+ ♔f7

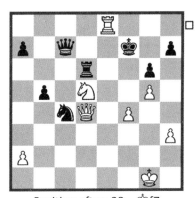

Position after: 38... ♔f7

39. ♖f8+!

An elegant finishing touch. If 39...♔xf8 40.♕h8+ wins the house. Black resigned.

This must have been a glorious moment for Spassky. Thunderous applause broke out in the playing hall. The Soviet ambassador embraced and kissed his champion. If only the movie could have stopped here ...

Alas, in real life movies cannot be stopped. Life always goes on, and in this case it went on with Fischer's triumphal procession through the Interzonal Tournament, the Candidates Matches, with the final stage being "Reykjavik 1972" where Fischer exacted a terrible revenge.

For a Westerner it is perhaps impossible to truly appreciate the immensity of the impact the 1972 title match must have had on Spassky: the colossal pressure that was put on his shoulders, the reprisals afterwards. Chess was politics in the Soviet Union. Winning was obligatory and if, for whatever reason, there happened to be a failure the 'guilty' party had to be punished. But for a loss of this size, losing what was in the eyes of the Soviets perhaps the most prestigious of all sporting World Championships – to an American no less, and with the whole world watching to boot – there were perhaps no reprisals severe enough since the days of Lenin and Stalin were over. Spassky fell into disgrace, of course, and life became much more difficult and unpleasant for him, but he was allowed to continue to play chess. Spassky never regained the full strength of his prime years but he remained one of the best players in the world for a considerable period of time. At first he behaved like a loyal Soviet citizen, winning amongst other tournaments an exceptionally strong Soviet Championship in 1973. However in 1976 Spassky had had enough of life in the USSR and together with his third wife emigrated to France where, following in Alekhine's footsteps, he later acquired French citizenship. He continued to participate in several cycles for the World Championship, his best result being to reach the final of the Candidates Matches in 1978, where he lost to Korchnoi. Spassky also won a number of elite tournaments (e.g. Bugojno 1978 and Linares 1983), but gradually his ambition and his willingness to put everything else aside for chess dwindled. He began agreeing to many short draws, often without a fight. He also started accepting invitations for tournaments that were far below his level in order not to have to exert himself too much. In short, he began to slowly fade into the background of the chess world.

Then in 1992 Spassky suddenly made one last and final reentry into the limelight in what has been called the "Revenge Match of the Century". This was a contest, organised and financed by a Serbian multimillionaire, completely in accordance with Fischer's every wish. The Fischer-Spassky rematch "for the World Championship" was held in the middle of the civil war that followed the breakup of Yugoslavia in 1991-1992.

Spassky (right) in his second match against Fischer in Sveti Stefan 1992.

It was a bizarre event, to which we will briefly return in the next chapter. For Spassky it must have been the last great chess stimulus of his life, even though he did lose to Fischer again.

Since that match Spassky hasn't played much and by now he is fully retired. He suffered a stroke in 2006 and again in 2010. He returned to Russia in 2012 and now lives in relative seclusion in Moscow.

Spassky's style is often described as universal. It is the highest praise a chess player can get. He felt at home in all positions, was able to adapt to different opponents, remained calm under all circumstances and rarely found himself in time trouble. A king of the chess board, literally.

Although Spassky was a classical player, always sound and logical, he wasn't afraid of stretching that logic and soundness almost to breaking point if necessary. A few examples:

♙ Averbakh, Yuri
♟ Spassky, Boris
♘ Leningrad 1956

This game was played in a three-way play-off for the Soviet Championship.

Position after: 16. ♘f3

Black has been completely outplayed in the opening. White has a commanding grip on the kingside and there is no counterplay in sight. All the same, almost no one would even consider, let alone actually take, the radical decision that Spassky now ventures.

16... ♘c6!?

Question marks, exclamation marks, they are powerless to express an evaluation of this move (but I give a couple of them all the same). Objectively Black's chances are even worse after 17.dxc6 bxc6 than before, but psychologically Spassky's knight sacrifice has the effect of an earthquake. Gone is the pleasant prospect of expanding the

positional advantage at his leisure, suddenly Averbakh is faced with a Black knight manoeuvring via e6 to d4, counterplay along the b-file, a potential pawn avalanche in the centre. Chaos! Add to that the insult of it all, the shamelessness of such a move!

The subsequent course of the game justified Spassky's decision completely: Averbakh lost the thread, returned some of his material advantage and only just managed to save half a point after a struggle that took 73 moves.

Ironically, neither of the two players were successful in this three-way play-off. It was the third man, Mark Taimanov (1926-2016) who took the title.

♙ Spassky, Boris
♟ Bronstein, David
♘ Leningrad 1960

1. e4 e5 2. f4

Spassky was one of the very few world class 20th century players who had the courage (and the inclination) to occasionally venture the King's Gambit in between the 'normal' 2.♘f3 games. His direct predecessor in this respect was … Bronstein.

2... exf4 3. ♘f3 d5

Bronstein chooses a modern variation, more or less ignoring White's gambit intentions and striving instead for simple and sound piece development. The truly wild and romantic 19th century lines start with 3...g5.

4. exd5 ♗d6

Yet he chooses to do so in his own way! The main line is 4... ♘f6, intending to take back on d5 with the knight and thus avoiding the loss of tempo which would result from 4... ♛xd5 5. ♘c3. Bronstein does not hurry to recapture the pawn, a rather provocative plan.

5. ♘c3 ♘e7 6. d4 0-0 7. ♗d3 ♘d7 8. 0-0 h6?

Surely this is a little bit *too* subtle. Moves like 8... ♘f6 or 8... ♘g6 would have been perfectly sound. Did Bronstein want to prevent a possible ♘f3-g5? Whatever concrete variation he may have had in mind is rather unclear.

9. ♘e4!

White takes the initiative. Perhaps Bronstein had underestimated this move, which simply gives away the pawn on d5.

9... ♘xd5 10. c4

An unorthodox way of developing the queen's bishop!

10... ♘e3 11. ♗xe3 fxe3

Now what? Was it Spassky's intention to regain his pawn with a move such as 12. ♖e1?

12. c5!

By no means. Spassky's planning is on a much grander and more ambitious scale.

12... ♗e7 13. ♗c2!

Preparing to form the battery ♗c2 and ♛d3. If Black blocks the b1-h7 diagonal by playing f7-f5 or g7-g6 at some point, his move h7-h6 will be shown to be an unpleasant weakening of his kingside pawn structure.

13... ♖e8 14. ♛d3 e2

An attempt to improve slightly on 14... ♘f8 or is Black just trying to induce an element of chaos? After 14... ♘f8 White would follow up with 15. ♖ae1 and round up the e3-pawn smoothly, leaving his queen and king's rook on their optimal squares. Admittedly, if White now simply replies 15. ♖f2, the 'damage' caused by 14...e2 would hardly have been noticeable, but instead...

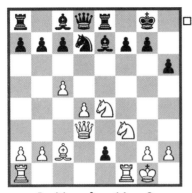

Position after: 14... e2

15. ♘d6!!

Just as with 16...♘c6 in the previous example, it is impossible to categorise this move in terms of ! or ?. If one judges on genius and courage, then surely !! is right, yet objectively the sober 15. ♖f2 would probably have been the better move.

15... ♘f8?

Bronstein, who was already in time trouble here, does not manage to keep a clear head. That he doesn't take the rook is a surprise of course, but not as strange as it looks since after 15... ♘f8 it is too late for White to go back on his chosen path because 16.♖f2 loses to 16...cxd6. Nor is it strange that Bronstein wishes to prevent ♕d3-h7+ – who wouldn't?.

Yet, if he would have had the time (and the clarity of mind) to accurately calculate variations, Bronstein would have realised that his only chance lies precisely here. Despite furious efforts by

many commentators no win has ever been found for White after 15... exf1=♕+ 16. ♖xf1 ♗xd6 17. ♕h7+ ♔f8. A plausible follow-up would be 18. cxd6 cxd6 19. ♕h8+ ♔e7 20. ♖e1+ ♘e5 21. ♕xg7 ♖g8 22. ♕xh6 ♕b6 23. ♔h1 ♗e6 24. dxe5 d5. White has a pawn for the exchange and Black's king has not managed to reach safety, but there is no mate. A human finds the position "unclear". An engine coolly declares it to be "0.0" and comes up with long variations ending in perpetual check.

16. ♘xf7!!

There is no doubt about the evaluation of *this* move. White is winning in all variations.

16... exf1=♕+ 17. ♖xf1 ♗f5

A resourceful defence, which at least saves Black from getting mated, yet the resulting position is simply too good for White.

The most beautiful variation would have been 17... ♔xf7 18. ♘e5+ ♔g8 19. ♕h7+! ♘xh7 20. ♗b3+ ♔h8 21. ♘g6 mate!

Instead 17...♕d7 18.♘3e5 followed by 19.♗b3 just loses, while 17... ♕d5 18. ♗b3 ♕xf7 19. ♗xf7+ ♔xf7, although slightly more stubborn, is almost equally hopeless after 20. ♕c4+ ♔g6 21. ♕g8!.

18. ♕xf5 ♕d7

At the cost of a bishop Black has managed to regroup, but his king's position has been damaged beyond repair. Spassky finishes off smoothly.

19. ♕f4 ♗f6 20. ♘3e5 ♕e7

The continuing vulnerability of Black's king is illuminated by the variation 20... ♗xe5 21. ♘xe5 ♕e7 22. ♕e4! when Black is defenceless against the threat of 23. ♖xf8+.

21. ♗b3 ♗xe5

The sort of move you play when you have no time left to resign.

22. ♘xe5+ ♔h7 23. ♕e4+

Black resigned. This is perhaps Spassky's most famous game, not just because of the unique double piece sacrifice it contains, but also because the finish was used in the 1963 James Bond film *From Russia with Love*.

Yet it would be a misunderstanding to think that Spassky's style was characterised by sacrifices and other such violence. Spassky was feared for his 'silent' moves, nondescript quiet moves which at first don't seem to change anything, but on closer inspection turn out to have made all the difference.

♙ Spassky, Boris
♟ Korchnoi, Viktor
🌐 Kiev 1968

This position arose in the seventh game of the Candidates Matches Final.

Position after: 25... ♘c7

With his more actively placed pieces and better pawn structure, the advantage clearly lies with White. But how to proceed? All of Black's potentially vulnerable pawns are protected and Black is threatening to considerably lessen the pressure on his position with 26...♕e6. 26.♘d5 is a move that leaps to the eye, yet after the sober 26...♕e6 White has not achieved anything.

26. ♕b6!

Hard to find, elegant and very strong. The point is that 26...♕e6 now loses a pawn to 27.♗xc5, but Black's real problem is that it is not easy to come up with anything else. Perhaps 26...c4

would have been Black's best chance. Korchnoi played **26... ♔g7**, giving White the chance to finally play **27. ♘d5!**, winning a pawn. The game continued **27... ♕e6 28. ♗xc5 ♗xc5 29. ♕xc5 ♘b5 30. ♕e3 ♕c6+ 31. ♔b1 ♘d4 32. ♖c1 ♕b5 33. ♘c7! ♕e2? 34. ♘e6+ ♔h7** and now White has another elegant queen move to finish the game... *(see diagram)*
35. ♕h6+! and Black resigned.

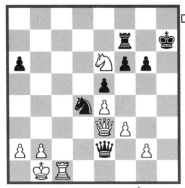
Position after: 34... ♔h7

Finally, in any overview of Spassky's most memorable games the following fragment cannot be left out.

♙ Larsen, Bent
♟ Spassky, Boris
🌐 Belgrade 1970

In 1970 a match was organised by FIDE between the Soviet Union and the 'Rest of the World'. Media interest in this prestigious event was huge with the encounter between Spassky and Fischer, expected on board one, eagerly anticipated. To the astonishment of all, this encounter never materialised.

Danish Grandmaster Bent Larsen (1935-2010) claimed top board for the 'Rest of the World' and to the surprise of all and sundry Fischer agreed to this, going on to beat Petrosian 3-1 on board two. The Soviet team won by the slightest of margins 20½-19½. With hindsight this was quite an impressive victory by the Soviets, but at the time it

was viewed rather as a sign of weakness. Soviet hegemony was still alive, but perhaps beginning to crumble.

Position after: 12. h3

It is obvious that Black has the better chances in this position, primarily because of his significant lead in development. Yet the total annihilation that now follows must have come as a great surprise; not just to the audience, but to the players themselves.

12... h4!

Boris Spassky (photo Cathy Rogers)

Tearing open White's kingside.

13. hxg4

Exchanging bishops makes no difference: 13. ♗xg4 ♗xg4 14. hxg4 hxg3 15. ♖g1 has the same fatal consequences as the game continuation.

13... hxg3 14. ♖g1

It is clear that after 14. ♖xh8 ♖xh8 White loses on the spot but the text seems to hold White's position together. Or does it?

14... ♖h1!!

This is the stuff of which fairytales are made.

15. ♖xh1 g2

Already resignation is called for. Larsen must have been in a state of shock – never having been hit by an earthquake before – for he played **16. ♖f1** (One would expect 16. ♖g1, although this too loses quickly after 16... ♕h4+ 17.♔d1 ♕f2 or even 17... ♕h1.) and only resigned after the further moves **16... ♕h4+ 17. ♔d1 gxf1=♕+**. A unique game.

Robert James Fischer

No one who features in this book is anything less than a great champion. Every 'king of the chessboard' was (and is) exactly what the title says: a king. Yet, if one of them has to be singled out as larger than life, larger than 'just' a World Chess Champion, then surely that person must be Robert James Fischer, the man who beat 'the Russians' in an era where this was world news, the Cold War.

Robert, who was mostly called Bobby, was born an American citizen in 1943 and died an Icelander in 2008. These are just about the only non chess-related bio-graphical facts in his life which are not in dispute. Applauded and condemned throughout his life (and afterwards), he was Mr. Controversial if ever there was one. Not just in the eyes of the general public but within the chess community as well, the words 'mad' and 'genius' are probably most often used to describe him. A genius he certainly was. Mad? Well, I suppose this depends on your perspective on madness.

No doubt there were many factors that moulded Fischer's life and chess career, but at the root of his complex personality must have been a difficult childhood. Fischer was born in Chicago in 1943 into a single parent family consisting of his mother and a half-sister. There was no father, although his birth certificate men-tioned the name of a German scientist his mother had married during a long stay in Moscow in the 1930s, but who had not accompanied her when she left the Soviet Union in 1938. It wasn't until 2002, when his mother's FBI file was made public – she had been suspected of communist sympathies in the 1950s – that it dawned on the world that Fischer's real father must have been somebody else.

The family lived in modest circumstances and moved around a lot until they settled in Brooklyn, New York City, in 1949, the year Bobby learnt to play chess. When
he accidentally came upon a chess book he became obsessed with the game,
causing his mother concern. In the US, unlike the Soviet Union, there were no Pioneer Palaces where, under the watchful eyes of a small army of coaches, children could play their first tournaments and hone their talents. What was a US
parent to do with such a hugely talented chess kid?

However, Bobby's unique talent simply could not be hidden. He participated in a
simultaneous exhibition when he was seven and here he was 'discovered' by
some discerning chess enthusiasts who recognised his talent and adopted him into their circle. There followed some quiet years where Bobby was surrounded by
good, some even very good, players in an atmosphere were he could study the
game at his leisure and play as much as he liked. This must have been a decisive
period in his life. On the one hand he was able to completely devote himself to his
overriding passion, on the other he could simply close the door to the outside
world, where he felt considerably less at ease. These habits would stay with him

for life. In 1956 Fischer entered the American tournament arena. The speed with which he came, saw and conquered was breathtaking. At only thirteen years of age he won the US Junior Championship by a large margin and in the strongest open tournaments America had to offer he also scored well. However it was the quality of his play that really caused a sensation. The following game, played towards the end of 1956 against one of the best players in the US, was published all over the world and was received with stunned disbelief.

♙ Byrne, Donald
♟ Fischer, Robert James
♘ New York 1956

The Byrne brothers, Donald (1930-1976) and Robert (1928-2013), were part of a generation that started to dominate US chess in the early 1950s and continued to do so for many years. It must have been an unsettling experience for them, young and strong as they were, to be surpassed by someone younger and stronger still.

Position after: 11. ♗g5

At first glance the position seems a quiet one, where battle is yet to get underway. With his next move Fischer

completely destroys this all-too-placid view of the situation. The battle is not about to start, it is already almost over! The execution is about to begin.

11... ♘a4!

Lightning strikes! If White accepts the sacrifice with 12.♘xa4, he finds himself on the verge of defeat after 12...♘xe4: both 13.♕xe7 ♕xe7 14.♗xe7 ♖fe8 and 13.♗xe7 ♘xc5 14.♗xd8 ♘xa4 leave White at least a pawn down in a bad position.

12. ♕a3 ♘xc3 13. bxc3

If Black had nothing special here, White would escape relatively unscathed. But 13-year-old Bobby *does* have something up his sleeve.

13... ♘xe4!

An exchange sacrifice in order to gain the initiative.

14. ♗xe7 ♕b6

If now 15.♗xf8 ♗xf8 16.♕b3 ♘xc3! Black would have more than enough compensation for the exchange. It is understandable that Byrne is looking for alternatives yet, as is so often the case, in doing so he only makes matters worse.

15. ♗c4

Hoping to escape with an inferior but playable position after 15...♖fe8 16. 0-0.

15... ♘xc3!

This required some very deep and accurate calculation. The first point is that 16.♕xc3 ♖fe8 leaves White a pawn down in a bad position, but the key to the combination is far more difficult to see.

16. ♗c5 ♖fe8+ 17. ♔f1

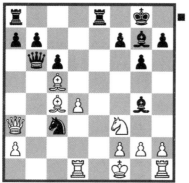

Position after: 17. ♔f1

It looks as if Black has made a miscalculation. If he moves his queen, he will be a piece down after 18.♕xc3.

17... ♗e6!!

Brilliant, truly brilliant! It is hard enough to spot this idea at all, especially when calculating several moves in advance, but Black also had to avoid falling into a devilish trap. If 17... ♘b5, a move that *seems* to consolidate both Black's material and positional advantage, White has the devastating blow 18. ♗xf7+! winning material in all variations, e.g. 18... ♔xf7 19. ♕b3+ ♗e6 20. ♘g5+ ♔g8 21. ♘xe6 ♘xd4 22. ♘xd4+ ♕xb3 23. ♘xb3.

18. ♗xb6

If White withdraws his bishop from c4 (18. ♗d3), 18... ♘b5! is now very strong. There are several other variations, but they are all in Black's favour: 18. ♕xc3 runs into 18... ♕xc5!, while 18. ♗xe6 even allows mate after 18... ♕b5+ 19. ♔g1 ♘e2+ 20. ♔f1 ♘g3+! 21. ♔g1 ♕f1+! 22. ♖xf1 ♘e2 mate! White has no alternative other than to accept the queen sacrifice.

18... ♗xc4+ 19. ♔g1 ♘e2+ 20. ♔f1 ♘xd4+ 21. ♔g1 ♘e2+ 22. ♔f1 ♘c3+ 23. ♔g1 axb6

It must have been maddening for White. Five forced moves and all the while losing material.

24. ♕b4 ♖a4!

Remorseless. Byrne now played **25. ♕xb6 ♘xd1 26. h3**, which is hopeless, but continued the unequal contest until he was mated on move 41.

"The Game of the Century" was the jubilant headline in the American press. A nice compliment of course, but it also shows how much pressure was put – enthusiastically yet mercilessly – on 13-year-old Bobby's shoulders.

Fischer's results continued to impress. He was invited to take part in the US Championship (1957/58) which he won, a point ahead of Reshevsky. This was a sensation. Not only was he – at fourteen! – the youngest US Champion ever, the victory also earned him a place in the 1958 Interzonal in Portoroz, Yugoslavia. And here Fischer was successful again. Without any international experience to speak of and still only fifteen, he held his own against world class opposition, finishing equal fifth and sixth in a very strong field (scoring 12/20), enough to qualify for the Candidates Tournament the following year. It was an achievement unparalleled in chess history.

From then on, all eyes in the chess world were focussed on Fischer. His incredible results, his mature play *and* his unusual personality and behaviour filled chess columns and magazines around the world. More importantly, he was beginning to be seen as a prospective threat to Soviet hegemony even outside the world of chess. The Cold War was taken very seriously indeed in those days and anything (or anyone) that could be used to humiliate the Soviet Union was sure to receive a lot of attention in the West, especially in America. The 'enemy camp', too, perceived Bobby as a potentially dangerous threat. No matter how many World Champions they could boast, the Soviets were acutely aware of the fact that one talented player – although he would of course have to be *super* talented – would be enough to break their hegemony.

However these possibilities were still in the future. At the Candidates Tournament in Bled/Zagreb/Belgrade 1959 Fischer was still a little too young to overcome the very best Soviet Grandmasters. With a score of 12½/28 he finished equal fifth/sixth with Yugoslavian star Gligoric, behind the four Soviet representatives Tal, Keres, Petrosian and Smyslov, but ahead of his Western 'colleagues' Olafsson and Benko. The latter had fled his native Hungary a year before and was about to become an American citizen himself.

Fischer himself felt no doubt whatsoever that he already was, or was about to become, the best player in the world. Muhammad Ali's battle cry "I am the greatest!" might have been his. Ever since his first confrontation with the Soviets in 1958 he was completely focussed on beating all of their top players and on breaking down the powers that 'stopped him' from doing so. These to Fischer were FIDE, the US Chess Federation (who did not give him the support he felt he needed), but most of all 'the Communists', with the Soviet Union topping that list.

Fischer became a fierce anti-communist and since he was both extremely vocal and utterly undiplomatic he caused quite a stir even away from the chessboard. Precisely the character traits that made him successful as a chess player left him ill-equipped for 'normal' social behaviour. A monomaniac, ambitious and tenacious, Fischer was also egocentric, stubborn and completely unable to see anyone else's point of view. The meaning of the word compromise remained unknown to him throughout his life, which must have made him lonely and suspicious. It was also the cause of his many conflicts, especially with chess organisers. Perhaps this was the only instrument nature had provided him for dealing with the outside world. He left school at the age of sixteen and severed relations with his mother. No compromises! And

so he went out into the world, still only a boy but already a man at the chessboard, a battle-hardened warrior. A lone cowboy against that all-powerful Soviet state.

In the years that followed Fischer's star rose rapidly and inexorably. In the ten years between 1957 and 1967 he played the US Championship eight times. He won them all, once – in 1963/64 – with a score of 100%: 11 out of 11! Internationally he was also nearing the very top of the game. In 1960 he won a tournament in Mar del Plata together with Boris Spassky, to whom he lost. From this time on Spassky was to be not only a rival but also a friend. Later that year Fischer came second at a supertournament in Bled, behind Tal but ahead of Petrosian and an impressive array of other top players. Fischer was the only undefeated player in this field and – even more importantly – he beat both Tal *and* Petrosian in their individual encounters. After that, his fantastic win of the 1962 Stockholm Interzonal, 2½ points ahead of the runner-up, came as no surprise. By now Bobby was expected to finish on top in almost any tournament.

However, the Candidates Tournament in Curaçao, also in 1962, was a disappointment. Behind Petrosian, Geller and Keres, Bobby 'only' came fourth. It caused him to openly accuse his Soviet opponents of cheating. Were they? It is true that it was later revealed that Geller, Keres and Petrosian *had* made an agreement to play short draws against each other, which in an extremely tough tournament such as this saves a lot of energy. But that is all. Fischer's protest did, however, lead to a change in the format of the Candidates from a tournament into a set of matches where collusion is impossible. Bobby's statements were taken seriously indeed!

In fact Fischer's complaints attracted much attention, not just within the chess world but from the mainstream media as well. In America, *Life Magazine* and *Sports Illustrated* featured extensive portraits of him, a ground-breaking moment not just for Fischer himself but for US chess as a whole. Yet there were things he said and did that already presaged the 'diagnosis' of paranoia or a related mental illness that was suggested (but never officially diagnosed) in later years. For instance his accusation levelled against Viktor Korchnoi, the fourth Soviet representative in Curaçao, of throwing games to his compatriots, although impossible to prove or disprove, certainly sounds absurd if you know Korchnoi.

In short, even Fischer had to find out the hard way that the final steps to the summit are the most difficult. One even wonders whether he really wanted to take those last steps – whether it wasn't sufficient for him to *know* he was the best without having to prove it to the world – for at times his behaviour was downright harmful to his own interests. To begin, Fischer refused to participate in the next Interzonal Tournament (held in Amsterdam in 1964). This echoed his stubborn behaviour in a match against Reshevsky in 1961, which he abandoned after 11 games (24 had been planned) following an argument with the organiser. Two years later Fischer had not forgiven this particular organiser, evidenced by his refusing an invitation to a very prestigious tournament in Los Angeles. This gave him a reputation of being difficult and of making absurdly high demands. Though understandable, this was actually very unfair for it was never vulgar self-interest that drove him. Fischer always made his demands on behalf of *all* chess players, or perhaps we should say on behalf of chess itself. He always demanded perfect conditions *for all players* in a tournament, both financially and organisationally. It was always organisers with whom he had conflicts. They were the ones who made him feel threatened and hard done by, never his fellow chess players with whom he mostly enjoyed good relations.

In fact Fischer has contributed hugely towards the emancipation and professionalisation of chess. The fact that this contribution was often mired in conflicts, sometimes bizarre demands, a lot of verbal violence and (in the end) a huge media circus, has obscured its value, yet later generations have profited enormously from all the fuss he made.

In the next World Championship cycle Fischer took this self-destructive behaviour to an even higher level. After ten rounds of the Interzonal Tournament in Sousse in 1967, when leading with 8½ points, he came into conflict with the organisers.

What did Fischer do? He packed his bags and left. "If that's the way they organise this World Championship qualification tournament, I can't be bothered". It must have been hugely frustrating both for his fans and for all those who simply wanted to see him play for the World Championship. The aura of 'a mad genius' began increasingly to make him a worldwide celebrity.

A few years passed and Fischer barely played. He did however publish a book, *My 60 Memorable Games*. It was an instant bestseller and to this day it remains one of the most fervently praised books in chess history. Yet it was also an ominous sign: writing, not playing. Was this book intended as a farewell to  the chess world? In 1969 Fischer again refused to take part in the US Championship, which doubled as the next Zonal Tournament, again because of a disagreement with the organiser. This time even the US Chess Federation was beginning to get desperate and took the highly unusual step of asking Pal Benko, now a US citizen, to give up his place in the 1970 Interzonal in order to give Fischer a chance of becoming World Champion. Benko agreed, FIDE agreed and – most importantly – Fischer agreed as well.

Fischer makes his way through the crowd on his way to a game in Reykjavik

Thus began the final act of Bobby Fischer's almost surrealistic chess career. He journeyed to Europe for the Interzonal Tournament due to be held in Palma de Mallorca in the autumn of 1970, warmed up a little by playing in some smaller events (very successfully, although he did lose that famous game to Spassky at the Siegen Olympiad) and passed the test with flying colours. He outclassed his opponents at the Interzonal, winning with a score of 18½ from 23, a full 3½ points ahead of his nearest 'rivals' Larsen, Geller and Hübner. It was the beginning of a triumphal procession, not just because he won everything, but because of the unprecedented margins. In three consecutive Candidates Matches he beat – no, crushed – first Taimanov 6-0, then Larsen, again 6-0, and finally Petrosian with the slightly more human but almost equally sensational score of 6½–2½. All of a sudden he was a mere step away from his ultimate goal. Only one man stood in his way: defending champion Boris Spassky.

Of course, Fischer would not have been Fischer if he hadn't fought tooth and nail against the fulfilment of his own wishes. The honour of organising this match, which the whole world awaited with bated breath, was given to the Icelandic capi-

Spassky and Fischer at the board in their world title match in 1972

tal Reykjavik. Chess is very popular in Iceland, so as far as local interest and competence was concerned FIDE couldn't have made a better choice. However... the aeroplane wasn't good, the money was insufficient, etcetera, etcetera. There was no end to Fischer's list of complaints, demands and threats that all seemed to say " Come on, disqualify me if you dare".

Fischer's antics must have demanded all the patience and flexibility FIDE President Max Euwe, chief arbiter Lothar Schmid and the organisers could muster to finally coax Fischer to the chess board. Perhaps even that would not have been enough if Spassky himself had not shown himself surprisingly indulgent. In the end probably no one, not even the mighty Soviet Union, wanted to be held responsible in the eyes of the world for the collapse of this more than eagerly awaited match. The whole world was watching. It had become more, much more than just a match between two chess players. This match simply couldn't be cancelled.

In the end Fischer came to Reyjavik, the match started – a week later than planned – and then this happened...

♙ Spassky, Boris
♟ Fischer, Robert James
🌍 1st game Reykjavik 1972

Position after: 29. b5

29... ♗xh2?

It is ironic that it had to be Fischer, praised over and over again for his crystal clear play, who on this occasion plays one of the murkiest moves in chess history. In a totally drawn position he allows his bishop to be ensnared and captured. Why? Was he playing for a win? Was it a blunder? Had he perhaps overlooked that after 30. g3 h5 31. ♔e2 h4 32. ♔f3 h3 33. ♔g4 ♗g1 34. ♔xh3 ♗xf2 the sneaky 35. ♗d2! keeps the bishop trapped? Was it overconfidence? Did he think that he would be able to draw anyway? Or did he do it on purpose? Was it part of a plan to unsettle Spassky? Fischer never gave a satisfactory explanation for this move, but almost every other chess 'expert' did. Whatever the truth, even after Fischer lost his bishop the remaining ending is still very difficult to win. Perhaps it *was* a draw, but Spassky managed to win in 56 moves.

What happened next is even more incredible. In truth there is just nothing sensible to be said about it except that it was the craziest thing that *could* have happened. Fischer didn't show up for the second game and was forfeited: 2-0. This was shocking! Again there are those who suspect that it was all part of a master plan, intended to upset Spassky. This is possible of course, but it does sound extremely unlikely. At this point surely the arbiter, FIDE or another responsible party must have been a whisker away from declaring the entire match forfeited. It was probably Spassky – again! – who saved the match (and Fischer with it): he decided to comply with yet another Fischer demand, to play in a room without camera's, something he could easily have refused. (Spassky was later condemned by the Soviet authorities for his noble action.)
This was the turning point in the match. Suddenly Fischer was completely focussed and in tremendous shape. He won the third game, stood his ground under enormous pressure in the fourth, and went on to win games five *and* six in impressive style. Spassky must have felt as if he had been knocked down by a truck. Where did this come from?

Fischer never relinquished his advantage. Mercilessly exploiting his chances whenever they appeared and defending tenaciously when on the back foot, he gradually increased his lead, clinching the match, which was scheduled for 24 games, after just 21 with a score of 12½-8½. The mission upon which he had embarked fifteen years earlier was accomplished. Fischer was World Champion at last.

And that was it. End of story. Though by now world famous, Fischer never again accepted a tournament invitation and little by little began to disappear from public view. This process of withdrawal culminated in 1975, when he was scheduled to defend his title against a new challenger but refused to play under any conditions except his own. In fact FIDE went a surprisingly long way towards accommodating

FIDE-president Max Euwe, having just awarded the wreath to the newly crowned World Champion.

him, but in the end he made one demand too many and was forfeited. Anatoly Karpov, the challenger, was declared World Champion.

No revolution broke out among the masses. Perhaps the general mood at the time can be described as sad but resigned. By now FIDE was firmly in charge of the chess world and besides, after not playing a single game for three years, hadn't Fischer sidelined himself more efficiently and more emphatically than any action FIDE could have taken? Nevertheless, many chess players were convinced that Karpov wouldn't have stood a chance against Fischer in 1975.

At first it was hoped that Fischer would one day come back, but as the years went by these hopes dwindled.

When he finally *did* return, precisely twenty years after the Reykjavik match, it was in the bizarre setting of Sveti Stefan 1992. Playing a match in a war-torn country against the very same Spassky (who of course had also aged twenty years) only served to demonstrate that is was too late to turn back the years. Kasparov, who had succeeded Karpov in 1985, remained the legitimate World Champion in the eyes of all but one, and Fischer, although still a surprisingly good player, made headlines for his disturbing (and disturbed) behaviour rather than his chess. He ranted and raved and never returned to the US after the match, afraid of being arrested for violating US economic sanctions against Yugoslavia. From then on Fischer was essentially homeless. At first he stayed in various countries in Europe and Asia, but when he publicly and enthusiastically approved of the 9/11 attacks in 2001, the US government went all out to have him arrested and his world became a small one indeed. Making friends was one thing Fischer had never learned properly. But he did have some! When he was arrested in Japan in 2004 for travelling with a revoked passport and deportation to America threatened, Iceland came to his rescue. The country where he had made history in 1972 offered him Icelandic nationality and with it safe haven. He spent his final years in Reykjavik in relative peace and died there in 2008 at the age of 64.

Will Fischer be remembered for what he *said* during the second half of his life or for what he *did* when he was young? Fortunately, it is a characteristic of chess games that they simply cannot disappear. Chess lovers from all over the world will always be able to enjoy works of art like this one:

♙ Byrne, Robert
♟ Fischer, Robert James
♔ New York 1963

This game was played in the third round of that legendary US Championship that Fischer went on to win with a score of 11/11. Almost all the top US players took part: Reshevsky, Evans, Benko, Bisguier, and the Byrne brothers. We have seen how Donald Byrne lost 'his' immortal game to Fischer seven years earlier. This time it was his brother Robert's turn.

1. d4 ♘f6 2. c4 g6 3. g3 c6 4. ♗g2 d5 5. cxd5 cxd5

Fischer has chosen a line that is without exception described as 'solid', not a weapon to play for a win with the black pieces. But Fischer cared nothing for 'statistical' information like this. He *always* played to win, yet never expected his openings to do the work for him.

6. ♘c3 ♗g7 7. e3

7. ♘f3 is the main line.

7... 0-0 8. ♘ge2 ♘c6 9. 0-0 b6 10. b3 ♗a6 11. ♗a3 ♖e8 12. ♕d2

So far so good. With his next move Fischer disturbs the quiet of the position.

Position after: 12. ♕d2

12... e5!

How many players would have had the courage to play this? Fischer was of course aware of the risks he was tak-

ing, as is shown by his comment in *My 60 Memorable Games*: "I was a bit worried about weakening my queen's pawn, but felt that the tremendous activity obtained by my minor pieces would permit White no time to exploit it. 12...e6 would probably lead to a draw." 12...e6 is indeed what nine out of ten players would have played.

13. dxe5 ♘xe5 14. ♖fd1?

According to Fischer this is already a decisive mistake. White should have played the other rook to d1, i.e. 14. ♖ad1. In his annotations Fischer shows signs of surprise when he feels forced to admit that it is not so easy for Black to even maintain equality here. Yet what this comment betrays more than anything else is Fischer's fervent optimism. After all, what could be more natural than a small edge for White if White hasn't made a single mistake yet? Nevertheless, Fischer claims that "Black keeps the initiative with 14... ♕c8". Later commentators, e.g. the famous German Grandmaster and researcher Robert Hübner, broadly confirm this diagnosis (although their assessment of the position is roughly equal rather than in Black's favour), with the alternative 14... ♕d7 also getting the seal of approval.

14... ♘d3!

A beautiful and logical move, yet during the game many people thought

Black was being overconfident and getting himself into trouble.

15. ♕c2?

No other move could have highlighted the difference between 14.♖ad1 and 14. ♖fd1 better. After 14.♖ad1 ♘d3, 15.♕c2 would have refuted Black's aggression, whereas in the game it allows a devastating combination. Yet even after a more solid move like 15. ♘d4 Black is already clearly better after 15... ♘e4 16. ♘xe4 dxe4.

Position after: 15. ♕c2?

15... ♘xf2!!

In hindsight judgment may be crystal clear: this is a brilliant knight sacrifice. Black completely throws the enemy position off balance and heads straight for victory. However it is not at all strange that *during* the game this move was seen merely as an attempt to muddy the waters, not just by some of the spectators but by Fischer's opponent as well.

16. ♔xf2 ♘g4+ 17. ♔g1 ♘xe3 18. ♕d2

Now if Black would have nothing better than to win back an exchange with 18...♘xd1 19.♖xd1, White would indeed have a large advantage.

18... ♘xg2!

It is becoming evident that Fischer understands the position more deeply and in a more dynamic sense than those fixated on material. He presides over the whole board and everything on it, with a special interest in White's king.

19. ♔xg2 d4! 20. ♘xd4 ♗b7+ 21. ♔f1

If 21. ♔g1, Black has 21... ♗xd4+ 22. ♕xd4 ♖e1+ with a decisive material advantage, while 21. ♔f2 is obviously asking for trouble due to 21... ♕d7 followed by 22...♕h3. Yet the text seems solid enough. What can Black do?

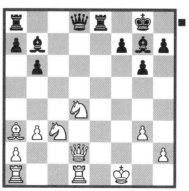

Position after: 21. ♔f1

21... ♛d7!

Simple, relaxed, deadly. White is free to defend himself against the threat of 22...♛h3+ any way he likes ... except there *is* no defence. To see this once 21...♛d7 has been played is difficult enough in itself – at this point two Grandmasters were discussing the game in front of an audience and were of the opinion that Black was lost! To see this in advance when playing 15...♞xf2 is almost superhuman.

"This is not chess, this is magic" was just one of many flabbergasted comments.

By resigning in this position Byrne made his most impressive move of the game. He saw that the only plausible defence 22.♛f2 ♛h3+ 23.♚g1 fails to 23...♜e1+!! 24.♜xe1 ♝xd4 and mate on g2 is is unavoidable. Fischer was "bitterly disappointed". He had hoped to be allowed to actually play these moves.

Fischer's optimism, so richly rewarded in this game, combined with a tremendous stubbornness, may have been the root cause of his success. He knew no fear and thus, unencumbered with a major 'normal' human handicap, he was able to push his boundaries beyond those of his fellow humans. This is illustrated by the next example, taken from one of his lesser-known games.

♙   Korchnoi, Viktor
♟   Fischer, Robert James
🌐 Interzonal Sousse 1967

Position after: 21. ♜xb8

Nothing could be more 'normal' in this position than to play 21...♜xb8, when

after 22.♚xd1 material is equal but Black has a positional advantage. Yet what does Fischer do? He plays **21... ♝xa4!? 22. ♜xf8+** (22. ♜xb7? ♝c6) **22... ♚xf8**. Black is an exchange down, but has an extra pawn, two bishops and a latent pawn avalanche on the queenside.

Now if the alternative to 21... ♝xa4 had been an inferior or even a dead drawn position, perhaps (some) other players would have made the same choice, or at least considered doing so. But with the excellent position resulting from 21...♜xb8 as the alternative? Fischer must have thought only of his winning chances and judged them to be higher after 21...♝xa4. Losing chances? Objectively they are definitely higher as well. But does Fischer care about that? Obviously not. The game was eventually drawn after a tough struggle (where it was Fischer who had to defend very carefully in the end!).

This shows how Fischer always played to win, fearlessly and regardless of the strength of the opponent. He radiated that attitude and most if not all of his opponents felt this. A game against him must have been an intimidating, even scary experience. "It was the terrible feeling of playing against a machine that would never make a mistake, which broke my mental resistance," is how Taimanov looked back on his disastrous 1971 Candidates Match against Fischer. This enormous mental 'power' (for lack of a better word), combined of course with an exceptional talent, made Bobby Fischer the chess player and the man he was. *For better or worse*, he was one of our greatest champions.

Not only as a player, but also as a reformer of the game, Fischer has gained a special place in the history of chess. Lasker and Capablanca had tried to change the game in order to future-proof it, to little avail. Yet Fischer really achieved something!

Worried by the ever-increasing importance and depth of opening preparation in the 1990s Fischer proposed a new starting position, or rather a game where the starting position is not fixed but determined by a random factor, almost ruling out opening preparation and making games much more exciting. Although Fischer Random Chess, or Chess960 (so called after the number of possible starting positions) has not (yet) superseded classical chess, ever since its introduction in 1996 it has been popular as an alternative, more relaxed way of playing the game, usually in combination with a faster time limit.

In 1988 Fischer also introduced a new type of chess clock, enabling a completely new method of allocating thinking time to the players. Whereas the classical method had always been to provide a fixed time for a fixed number of moves, the idea behind 'increment' is to give each player a little extra time with every move they make. Thus a player will always have at least *some* time for every move, since even in the worst time trouble they always get extra time, even if in tiny increments. This and the abolition of adjourned games, which also took place during the 1990s, has radically changed the game. When first introduced these changes met with considerable resistance, but nowadays playing with the Fischer clock (or the Fischer tempo) has become the most natural thing in the world.

Anatoly Karpov

The "Match of the Century" in 1972 with its worldwide media resonance had been a highlight in the history of chess. No one could have foreseen that for the glorious winner it would turn out to be the end of his career as well. Even less could anyone have predicted that in 1972 Fischer's successor was already waiting for the curtain to rise on the main act of *his* career. He was a worthy successor as well, destined to rule the chess world for ten long years with an iron fist. He would also bring back the chess crown to the country where it belonged – at least in the opinion of that country, the Soviet Union.

Yet to think that after Fischer the chess world returned to normal and everything continued where it had left off before Fischer's arrival is a mistake. The world was beginning to change. Cracks were appearing in the walls that communist Eastern Europe had built to isolate itself after World War II. In the West, growing prosperity and the huge shock waves generated by the publicity from the 1972 match brought about some lasting changes in the chess world. So complete was the break with the past that we can safely take the year 1972 as the beginning of a new era in chess. This rupture with the past is perhaps best symbolised by the truly bizarre fact that Fischer never played a single game against his successor, a unique occurrence in the history of chess unless we go as far back as Morphy and Steinitz, over a century before.

And it was not just Karpov. The whole generation after Fischer, with very few exceptions, has never played against or even met him.

In 1975 the young Russian Anatoly Yevgenyevich Karpov, born
in 1951, was proclaimed World
Chess Champion by FIDE President Max Euwe after long and
arduous talks failed to deter
Fischer from dictating every
single condition for a match
against his challenger, showing
no willingness to compromise.
Naturally, a Championship win
on forfeit was not the most
glorious way for Karpov to
start his reign, but the decision
that Karpov be awarded the
chess crown was almost unan-
imously viewed as right and
unavoidable – and fully deserved! In the years leading up
to his coronation Karpov had
emphatically taken up the role
of bright young star, outshining
all others. The chess world de-
plored the disappearance of

Anatoly Karpov in 1967

Fischer and was very sorry to miss out on a Fischer-Karpov match, but they did not
begrudge the new Champion his title.

Karpov's rise to the top was swift. He first made a name for himself in junior
events: in 1967/68 he won the (then unofficial) European Junior Championship
and in 1969 in Stockholm he became World Junior Champion. Two years later he
reached the very top of the chess world by winning the tremendously strong Moscow 1971 tournament, ahead of almost all the best Soviet players of the time.
Undefeated, with a score of 11/17, Karpov finished ahead of World Champion
Spassky and ex-World Champions Petrosian, Smyslov and Tal. The only player who
managed to stay level with him was Leonid Stein (1934-1973), one of the un-
crowned kings of the chess board. Stein was fantastically successful throughout
the 1960s *except* in the qualifying cycles for the World Championship, where he
always failed by the narrowest of margins.

Anatoly Karpov during the Interpolis tournament in Tilburg 1989 (photo Jos Sutmuller)

From then onwards, Karpov became unstoppable. In the 1973 Interzonal Tournament in Leningrad, which he won together with Korchnoi, he qualified for the 1974 Candidates Matches. There, in spite of his youth, Karpov was already widely viewed as favourite and didn't disappoint. He won matches against Lev Polugaevsky and Boris Spassky convincingly and then in the final won a war of attrition against Korchnoi by just 12½-11½, almost squandering a three point lead.

As World Champion Karpov did everything he could to prove he was worthy of the title. In this he was helped by the surging economic tide in the chess world. Ever since Fischer had started demanding truly professional prize money and had also generated the publicity needed to attract commercial sponsorship, there had been a noticeable upsurge in supertournaments all over the world. To attract the necessary sponsorship it was of the utmost importance to assemble as strong a field as possible, with the World Champion always being top of the list of invited players. Thus started a dynamic of ever stronger tournaments, with ever increasing prize money, which is still very much in evidence today. Generations of Western chess players have reaped the benefits of this trend, which gave them the opportunity to make chess their profession. With much more money in the game and chess more popular than it had ever been, the gap in playing strength be-

tween the Soviet Union and the West diminished, though it did not disappear entirely.

For Karpov this meant that he received many more invitations to foreign tournaments than his predecessors. Not only did he gladly accept them, he also received
the approval of the Soviet authorities to do so, for they too liked Western curren-
cy and welcomed the chance to lay their hands on some. Even more importantly,
with his phenomenal string of successes Karpov completely restored the prestige
of Soviet chess, which of course had suffered badly in the Fischer years. In fact,
until Kasparov defeated him in 1985 Karpov was clearly the most dominant of the
post-World War II World Champions. There was only one short moment when his
throne was seriously endangered – the closing stages of his 1978 match in Baguio
City in the Philippines, against Viktor Korchnoi.

The name Korchnoi has already come up several times in this book. This is not a
coincidence as he was twenty years older than Karpov and had already had a
splendid career before he played his first official World Championship match in
1978. Born in Leningrad in 1931, Korchnoi's rise to the top was slightly slower
than those of his peers Petrosian, Spassky and Tal, yet by the end of the 1950s he
too was firmly established as a world class player. He made it to the final of the
Candidates Matches in 1968 and again in 1974, but after his loss to Karpov in the
1974 match Korchnoi's grievances against the Soviet authorities (who had a
marked preference for Karpov and showed it) reached a point where he decided
that leaving the USSR was the only chance to save his chess career. Korchnoi de-
fected in 1976, staying behind in Amsterdam after a tournament there and eventually settling in Switzerland later the same year. (He was given Swiss nationality
some years later.) In retaliation the Soviet Union then launched a monstrous anti-
Korchnoi offensive, consisting of a smear campaign, pressure on FIDE to have him
thrown out of the World Championship cycle, a boycott of tournaments that
dared send Korchnoi an invitation, and the taking of his wife and son as hostages.
This blatant abuse of power led to a counter-campaign (of sorts) in the West,
which reached a climax during the match in Baguio City. (FIDE President Max Euwe had not yielded to the Soviet pressure.)

In a very different way from the 1972 'Match of the Century', the 1978 match was
the Soviet Union versus the rest of the world all over again. Moral support from
the West for Korchnoi was huge and the pressure put on Karpov by his own Soviet
authorities must have been enormous. Flooded by worldwide media interest,
constantly interrupted by incidents, and in a general atmosphere of extreme hostility between the two camps, the match went well for Karpov at first – after 27
games he had won five and lost only two. The winner of the match would be the

first player to win six games. Then Korchnoi won three of the next four games and all of a sudden the match was wide open at 5-5! With tension at boiling point the 32nd game was almost an anti-climax. Karpov won and the match was over.

This wasn't the end of Korchnoi's World Championship ambitions though, for in 1980 he won the Candidates Matches again. Even after he lost to Karpov once again in 1981 in Merano – this time very clearly 6-2 with 10 draws – he remained at the top of the game for many more years. Korchnoi died in 2016 at the age of 85 and even though he never won the world title he is generally regarded as one of the most famous and celebrated chess players in the history of the game.

Karpov's supremacy wasn't threatened again until Garry Kasparov, twelve years his junior, broke through to reach the top in startling fashion in the early 1980s. It was the start of a rivalry which even in chess history, so richly endowed with great rivalries, is unparalleled. No matter how hugely talented the young Kasparov was, Karpov was still at the height of his powers and the last thing he wanted was to lose his chess crown. Between 1984 and 1990 the two battled it out in no less than five (!) matches for the World Championship, each of them fiercely contested, very close and with the outcome in the balance practically until the last move. The first match was abandoned without a winner after 48 games with the score 5-3 in favour of Karpov (and 40 draws). The second was won by Kasparov (thus claiming the title) as was the third while the fourth was a blood-curdling 12-12 draw (enough for Kasparov to keep the title). Finally Kasparov won the fifth match as well. In total they played 144 World Championship games with the overall score 21-19 in Kasparov's favour with 104 draws. Not even the legendary match (or series of matches) between La Bourdonnais and McDonnell in 1834 bears comparison to this titanic struggle.

What is more, in between all these matches Karpov and Kasparov also faced each other in many tournaments. Here too they played a great number of fierce and fascinating games, for neither man was willing to yield even the slightest prize to the other. It is no exaggeration to say that Karpov and Kasparov inspired (and forced) each other to levels they would not have achieved on their own.

One of these tournaments in fact brought Karpov arguably his greatest triumph. In Linares 1994, one of the strongest tournaments ever held, he came first with an incredible score of 11/13, a huge 2½ points ahead of Kasparov and Shirov.

In 1993 Karpov again became World Champion and retained the title until 1999, but unlike his reign from 1975 to 1985, Karpov's second period as World Champion not only requires some explanation but depends to a large extent on your point of view. Earlier that year English Grandmaster Nigel Short (1965) had quali-

КАСПАРОВ   КАРПОВ

fied for a World Championship match against Kasparov. This was to be the first title match since 1972 without Karpov, who had lost to Short in the semi-final of the Candidates Matches. However, during the pre-match negotiations Kasparov and Short could not come to an agreement with FIDE president Florencio Campomanes, whom they accused of corruption and incompetence. In the end they decided to take the drastic step of breaking away from FIDE and set up their own organisation. It was the beginning of a historic split within the chess world that was to last until 2006. FIDE reacted heavy-handedly to what they perceived to be the hijacking of the World Championship (which by now carried not only prestige but a large amount of money, for FIDE as well). FIDE stripped Kasparov of his title, removed both players from the FIDE rating list and organised a World Championship match of their own between Karpov and Dutchman Jan Timman (1951), who had lost the final of the Candidates Matches to Short. Karpov won and was thus crowned World Champion again. He retained the title until 1999, when he refused to defend the title because of (yet another) FIDE-related conflict. FIDE had now turned 'their' World Championship into a 100 player knock-out event and Karpov didn't accept that.

So who was the 'real' World Champion between 1993 and 2006? Was it Kasparov and after him his successor Kramnik, or was it Karpov and his line of successors consisting of Khalifman, Anand, Ponomariov, Kasimdzhanov and Topalov? This is of course a very tricky question, comparable to asking who was the real Pope when there were two people priding themselves on that title, both with the support of their own backers.

If you prefer to look at it from a legal point of view, then perhaps you will be inclined to say it was the champions of FIDE, the official world chess organisation, who were the real titleholders. However, if you are primarily interested in who was the strongest player in the world (and who was the one to beat him in a classical match) you will probably be a supporter of Kasparov and his successor Kramnik. A diplomatic solution, first suggested in 2004 and often preferred on websites and in books, is to call Karpov and his successors the "FIDE Champions" and Kasparov and Kramnik the "classical World Champions" of the period.

For me, Kasparov simply remained World Champion in 1993. He was so clearly the best player then and for many years to come, until he lost – totally unexpectedly – to Vladimir Kramnik in 2000, that to call someone else World Champion sounds absurd. Of course, ever since 1948 FIDE has been responsible for holding (and awarding) the World Championship, but "1993" plus later developments have lost them if not the legal authority then surely the moral authority to dictate to the world. Not many chess players would want to return to the days before World War II when there was no global organisation to speak of. However, the period between 1993 and 2006 is undeniably a shameful one in the history of FIDE, and I think it is reasonable to simply pass over it in a book like this. Naturally though, opinions will always remain divided on this and many other related subjects.

World Champion or not, Karpov remained a very strong and successful player until, in the closing years of the 20th century, he shifted his attention to his business interests and his career in Russian (and FIDE!) politics. He still occasionally plays a small tournament or even a match, usually with a fast time control and almost always in the nature of an exhibition event. The rough and tumble of the elite tournament world no longer concerns him.

As for his playing style, Karpov is usually classified alongside Capablanca, Smyslov and Petrosian, the champions whose delicate positional touch and intuitive understanding of chess made them well-nigh invincible. In his youth, Karpov was admired for his cool, businesslike play, mercilessly exploiting slight positional advantages while never allowing the opponent serious winning chances, a style which was considered unnaturally adult in one so young. After he gained the ne-

Anatoly Karpov in the Fontys tournament in Tilburg 1996 (photo Jos Sutmuller)

cessary self-confidence to also use his tactical skills, Karpov's play became more universal. He had an almost uncanny knack for keeping the game 'under control' even in the most difficult circumstances. His mentality was exemplary: ambitious, focussed, accurate, calm and decisive in critical moments, always wanting to be the best. It was the mentality of a winner *pur sang*.

Karpov also enjoyed all the advantages the Soviet state had to offer. He had the best trainers, coaches, seconds and any other assistance he required. His openings were always prepared for him at the highest level. His competitiveness and his fast reflexes made him an excellent blitz player, a talent which stood him in good stead when chess sped up in the 1990s and blitz skills were imperative for tiebreaks.

The following game was a pivotal moment in Karpov's remarkably easy assent to the summit, his first win against the man who, in the absence of Fischer, served as Karpov's touchstone for his understanding of the game.

⬜ Karpov, Anatoly
⬛ Spassky, Boris
🌐 Moscow 1973

This game was played in a training tournament consisting of three teams: USSR-1, USSR-2 and a team of the country's best young players. Just how strong these young players already were is illustrated by the final standings: the USSR A-team won, but 'team B', led by Taimanov, could only come third.

1. e4 e5 2. ♘f3 ♘c6 3. ♗b5 a6 4. ♗a4 ♘f6 5. 0-0 ♗e7 6. ♖e1 b5 7. ♗b3 d6 8. c3 0-0 9. h3 ♘b8

The Breyer Variation, a Spassky speciality. Later that year, in the Soviet Championship (which he won), he would play the classical 9... ♘a5 against Karpov. That game was drawn after a fierce struggle.

10. d3 ♗b7 11. ♘bd2 ♘bd7 12. ♘f1 ♘c5 13. ♗c2 ♖e8 14. ♘g3 ♗f8 15. b4 ♘cd7 16. d4

A slow build-up to the approaching middlegame battle. Still, the strategic tension is palpable already. Both sides are waiting for the right moment to make a move in the centre. Neither wants to be too early (in that case his initiative might be easily neutralised and possibly backfire), nor too late (for that might result in permanent passivi-

ty). Black would like to play d6-d5 or c7-c5, possibly preceded by e5xd4. White is thinking of a2-a4 or c3-c4, possibly preceded by d4xe5.

16... h6 17. ♗d2 ♘b6 18. ♗d3 g6 19. ♕c2 ♘fd7 20. ♖ad1 ♗g7

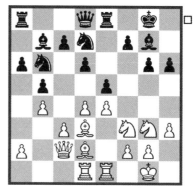

Position after: 20... ♗g7

21. dxe5

After a long think, Karpov is the first to take action. It quickly becomes clear that he has chosen precisely the right moment.

21... dxe5 22. c4 bxc4 23. ♗xc4

Now Black faces a difficult choice. The obvious move would be to eliminate the enemy bishop dangerously pointing at f7 with 23...♘xc4. However after 24.♕xc4 it is clear that White has won the opening battle. Black cannot play 24...♕e7 because that would leave the c7-pawn unprotected, so he must remain passive. Although White's advantage is not huge, the situation is not pleasant for Black. Spassky prefers a more 'beautiful', more ambitious, but also more risky move.

23... ♛e7

Now White is unable to stop the liberating advance c7-c5. Yet with his next two moves Karpov makes it clear that he retains the initiative.

24. ♝b3! c5

If now 25.bxc5 ♛xc5 Black's plan would work to perfection. However….

25. a4!

Wonderful! White intends to meet 25...cxb4 with 26.a5 when Black is in serious trouble, e.g. 26...♜ac8 27.♛a2 ♞a8 28. ♝xb4! winning.

25... c4!?

Again Spassky prefers counterattack to passive defence. The alternative 25... ♜ac8 26. a5 ♞a8 limits the damage, but after 27. ♛a2 White is clearly better.

26. ♝a2 ♝c6

A necessary follow-up to his previous move. Black cannot allow his opponent to just play 27.a5 and win the c4-pawn. Now, if White would have nothing better than 27.♝xc4 ♞xc4 28.♛xc4

♝xa4, Black's play would be justified. Karpov is not impressed.

27. a5!

An exchange sacrifice, requiring both courage and accurate calculation.

27... ♝a4 28. ♛c1 ♞c8 29. ♝xh6 ♝xd1 30. ♜xd1 ♞d6?

The critical move, yet it turns out to be the decisive mistake. It is understandable that Black doesn't want to give up his pawn on c4 without a struggle, since after the simple 30... ♞f8 31. ♝xg7 ♚xg7 32. ♛xc4 White, with two extra pawns and well-placed pieces, has excellent compensation for the exchange. In fact the text move is based on a beautiful tactical point and *seemingly* refutes White's play starting with 25.a4. Unfortunately for Spassky, the position contains a refutation of his refutation which is as simple as it is surprising.

31. ♝xg7 ♚xg7

(see diagram next page)

32. ♛g5!!

At first glance 30...♞d6 is refuted by 32.♛d2, which seems to win a piece, but actually loses at once because Black then has 32...♜ad8 33.♛xd6 ♞f6, exploiting the unprotected rook

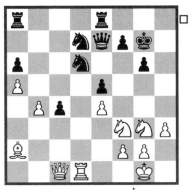

Position after: 31... ♔xg7

on d1. The textmove is a silent killer, not only because an offer to exchange queens is the last thing you would expect from someone who has just sacrificed the exchange, but also because it is so powerful. Up to this point the struggle has evolved on the queenside and in the centre of the board. Now suddenly Black's kingside is on the verge of collapse.

32... f6

Spassky doesn't want to give up his knight on d6 without a fight. If 32... ♖ac8 33. ♖xd6 ♕xg5 34. ♘xg5 ♘f6 35. ♘e2 the endgame is hopeless.

33. ♕g4

But now it turns out that Black has only made things worse. The threat is 34. ♖xd6 followed by 35. ♘f5+.

33... ♔h7 34. ♘h4

The speed of White's attack is amazing. Both 34...♖g8 35.♖xd6 ♕xd6 36.♘hf5! and 34...♘f8 35.♘xg6! ♘xg6 36.♕h5+ ♔g7 37.♖xd6 leave Black with little more than a smouldering ruin. The struggle is over. Spassky resigned.

It is this fearless willingness to sacrifice material, not in order to create chaos but as an efficient means of realising logical, strategic aims, that turns many of Karpov's best games into works of art.

♙   Karpov, Anatoly
♟   Sax, Gyula
🌐   Linares 1983

The contours of a razor-sharp Sicilian are still visible with White threatening to launch an attack with 14.g5.

14... ♘xe4!?

Hungarian Grandmaster Gyula Sax

Position after: 14. 0-0-0

(1951-2004) was an attacking player, who didn't like defence. Here he sacrifices a piece in order to take over the initiative.

15. ♘xe4 d5 16. ♕b3!

Karpov reacts in style. He would rather give up a pawn than lose the initiative.

16... dxe4 17. ♗c4 ♖f8

Black cannot castle kingside, because after 17... 0-0 18.g5 White's attack would be crushing, but his king does not seem to be in any danger on e8. If 18.g5 he just blocks the pawn with 18...hxg5 19.hxg5 g6, while 18.♗d5, (to eliminate the vital defender on c6) can be met by 18...♕b4, forcing the exchange of queens. Still, neither of these options are bad for White and many a player would have been more than happy with a slight endgame advantage after 18.g5 hxg5 19.hxg5 g6 20.♗d5 ♕b4 21.♗xc6+ bxc6 22.♕xb4 ♗xb4 23.♖g4. But not Karpov.

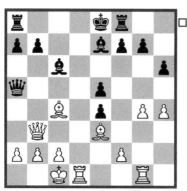

Position after: 17... ♖f8

18. ♖d5!

A purely positional exchange sacrifice, increasing the pressure on Black's position. To begin with, Black needs to make a difficult decision: should he accept the sacrifice or not?

18... ♗xd5

18...♕b4 is now weaker because of 19.♕xb4 ♗xb4 20.♖xe5+ while the problem with 18... ♕c7 is that it does nothing to alleviate the pressure. White simply continues 19. ♖gd1 or 19. ♗b5 to further strengthen his position. Accepting the sacrifice at least gives Black some material compensation for his positional problems.

19. ♗xd5 ♖d8

19... ♕b4 is again a possibility, but it is no longer the perfect solution since after 20. ♕xb4 ♗xb4 21. ♗xb7 ♖b8 22. ♗c6+ ♔e7 23. ♗xa7 ♖bc8 24. ♗xe4 White keeps a clear advantage.
The text move allows Black to meet 20.♗xb7 with 20...♗c5! 21.♗c6+ ♔e7 when White's attack comes to a halt.

20. ♗c4!

Outwardly this is just a tiny move, yet there is a terrible force behind it. Black is prevented from playing the active 20...♗c5 (since either 21.♗b5+ or 21.♕b5+ wins a piece), while the double threats of 21.♗b5+ and 21.♕xb7 pose huge problems for Black. Sax manages to find a clever defence, but it does not solve all his problems.

20... ♗b4! 21. c3 b5! 22. ♗e2 ♗d6

By giving away his b-pawn not on b7 but on b5, Black creates some vital space for his king. Compare for instance the position that would now arise after 23. ♗xb5+ ♔e7 with the one that would have arisen after 20...♗d6 21.♕xb7 ♕c7 22.♕xe4. In the latter case White's queen remains much more active. However, Karpov again comes up with a superior move.

23. ♕d5!

Not only does this move not (yet) accept the pawn offered, it also allows the seemingly powerful 23...♕xc3+. The point is that after the simple 24.♔b1! (not 24.bxc3 ♗a3+) Black has only aggravated his problems.
What Black *should* do is moot. If 23...a6, protecting his b-pawn, he will be completely tied up after 24. ♕c6+ ♔e7 25.♖d1 (when 25...♕c7 fails to 26.♖xd6!). According to Karpov 23...♕c7 would have been best. White then plays 24.♗xb5+ ♔e7 25.♕xe4, maintaining the pressure, but a straightforward win is not in sight.

23... ♔e7?

It seems logical to connect the rooks.

24. ♗c5!

Sax must have overlooked this move. In a single blow Black's king's protection is destroyed (24...f6 loses to 25.♗c4!) and White's attack is decisively reinforced.

24... ♗xc5 25. ♕xe5+ ♔d7 26. ♕xc5 ♕c7 27. ♕f5+!

Unrelenting accuracy. Black's king is prevented from reaching safety.

27... ♔e7 28. ♕xe4+ ♔d7 29. ♕f5+ ♔e7 30. ♖e1! ♖d6 31. ♗c4+! ♔d8 32. ♗xb5

Finally the storm has settled. It is clear that Black's position is damaged beyond repair. White has two pawns for the exchange, Black's king remains trapped and Black's rook on f8 is unable to make itself useful. Karpov finishes the game quickly and elegantly.

32... a6 33. ♗a4 g6 34. ♕f3 ♔c8

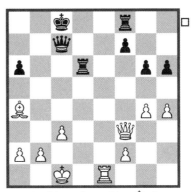

Position after: 34... ♔c8

35. ♖e7!

Now 35...♕xe7 fails to 36.♕a8+ ♔c7 37.♕a7+ ♔d8 38.♕b8 mate.

35... ♖d1+

Desperation, but 35... ♕b8 36. ♕e4

would be equally hopeless.

36. ♔xd1 ♕xe7 37. ♕a8+ ♔c7 38. ♕a7+ ♔d6 39. ♕b6+

Back resigned. If 39...♔e5 the simple 40.♕d4+ ♔e6 41.♗b3 is mate.

Based on these two games the conclusion could be drawn that Karpov was a great tactician rather than the dry positional player that he is always made out to be. And he was! If a combination was functional, Karpov would find it. Like Capablanca, his eye for *petites combinaisons* was phenomenal.

♙ Karpov, Anatoly
♟ Topalov, Veselin
🌐 Dos Hermanas 1994

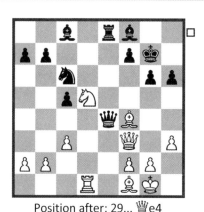

Position after: 29... ♕e4

30. ♘f6! ♔xf6

There is no choice: 30... ♕xf3 31. ♘xe8+ loses a whole rook.

31. ♗e5+! ♔xe5

Black's king is drawn forward as if by a magnet. Now the sober point of White's combination reveals itself.

32. ♕xe4+ ♔xe4 33. ♖e1+ ♔f5 34. ♖xe8

Attacking both bishops on the back rank White wins back the sacrificed material with interest. Topalov tried **34... ♗e6**, but after **35. ♖xf8 ♗xa2 36. ♖c8** he resigned.

Garry Kasparov

So dominant was Karpov in the years of his reign that it seemed his name and the term 'World Champion' had become inseparable – one was simply not complete without the other. It should come as no surprise then that Karpov's conqueror was none other than the man who has been called 'the greatest chess player who ever lived' more often than anyone else. It should also be no surprise that this transition took place by way of the greatest duel the chess world has ever witnessed.

Garry Kimovich Kasparov was born in 1963 in Baku in Azerbaijan, then a part of the Soviet Union, as Garik Weinstein. At some time during the early stages of his career both his first and surname changed, the former somehow without anyone noticing it much, the latter when he adopted his Armenian mother's (Russified) surname after his father had died. Kasparov learned to play chess at the age of five and made progress very rapidly. In this he was helped by several coaches, including former World Champion Botvinnik. His breakthrough came in a strong tournament in Minsk in 1978, when he was fifteen. He won and later said of this achievement that it gave him the feeling that he could one day be World Champion. After this first major success Kasparov's career developed like a dream. Just a few months later, he became the youngest player ever to qualify for the Soviet Championship. In this championship he came third, still only sixteen years of age. It was a fantastic achievement, but already people had come to expect so much of him that hardly anyone was surprised. Later that year (1979) he played his first major event abroad – a tournament in the Yugoslav spa town of Banja Luka which he won easily.

It wasn't just Kasparov's results that created a huge impression. His dynamic playing style and unusually deep opening preparation were widely admired (and feared). Ever greater triumphs in ever stronger tournaments made Kasparov the logical next challenger for World Champion Karpov before he was twenty years old. When he managed to beat Beliavsky, Korchnoi and Smyslov in the Candidates Matches of 1983 his ambitions were realised: Karpov versus Kasparov. The world of chess held its breath.

The match took place in Moscow under the format whereby the first player to win six games wins the match, with no maximum number of games. Ironically it was at Fischer's demand that FIDE had gone back to this ancient format in 1975. Eventually

(photo Jos Sutmuller)

Fischer refused to play even though this was one of his demands that had been accepted, but the format remained and was used in the Karpov-Korchnoi title matches in 1978 and 1981.

Karpov completely dominated the first part of the match – after only nine games he was already leading 4-0. Then the match took a bizarre turn. Kasparov dug his heels in and a series of 17 draws followed until Karpov won another game, leaving him just one win away from an overwhelming victory. Four draws later Kasparov won his first game. Another series of draws followed, 14 this time. Then all of a sudden Kasparov won two games in a row. At this critical moment panic must have broken out somewhere, whether in the Karpov camp, in FIDE, among the organisers (the match had of course already far exceeded its scheduled duration), but most probably somewhere at a high political level, where both players had their influential 'protectors'. The truth of this matter is unlikely ever to be fully revealed, but whatever happened behind the scenes, FIDE President Florencio Cam-

(photo Jos Sutmuller)

pomanes ended the match – without a winner being declared – 'on medical grounds'. Both players were said to be on the brink of exhaustion. That may or may not have been true (both Karpov and Kasparov vehemently denied it), but the fact remains that to abandon a World Championship match, whatever the reason, was unprecedented. There was to be a new match, this time in the more modern 'best of 24 games' format.

In hindsight, one may say that the 48 games of this first match, lasting from September 1984 until February 1985, taught Kasparov everything he still needed to know to beat Karpov. The second match (later in 1985) was fiercely contested and was only decided in the blood-curdling time trouble phase of the very last game. Kasparov won and thus at the age of 22 became the youngest World Champion in history (if we don't count Morphy).

The game of the match and perhaps *the* most famous game they ever played, was game 16. The score was level at that point: 7½-7½.

♟ Karpov, Anatoly
♟ Kasparov, Garry
🌐 Moscow 1985

---

1. e4

In a match of this calibre the choice of opening is a battlefield in itself. Both players had their teams of seconds, who were continually trying to find weak spots in the opponent's armoury. For the spectators and indeed for the players themselves the opening phase of every new game was an exciting one. What have they found? In game 12 Kasparov had surprised Karpov with a sensational novelty in a popular variation of the Sicilian Defence. Karpov had not managed to achieve any advantage whatsoever in that game, but it was clear that the last word on this matter was yet to be spoken.

1... c5

Kasparov always replied 1...c5 to Karpov's 1.e4 in this match. His plan clearly was to aim for as sharp and as dynamic a middlegame as possible.

2. ♘f3 e6 3. d4 cxd4 4. ♘xd4 ♘c6 5. ♘b5

It was in this variation that Kasparov had uncorked his novelty in game 12. In game 14 Karpov avoided a continuation of the theoretical battle, going for the sound alternative 5. ♘c3 instead.

With a few more days of preparation by his seconds under his belt, he apparently now felt sufficiently confident to take on Kasparov's new idea in earnest.

5... d6 6. c4 ♘f6 7. ♘1c3 a6 8. ♘a3 d5!?

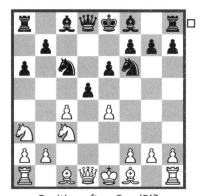

Position after: 8... d5!?

With this amazing new move Kasparov radically changed the face of this age-old variation. Over many decades countless games had been played along a well-established pattern of slow manoeuvring with the pawn structure remaining as it is for a long time. Now, with one stroke of brilliance, Kasparov sets the board on fire.

9. cxd5 exd5 10. exd5 ♘b4 11. ♗e2

In game 12 Karpov had gone for the obvious 11. ♗c4, firmly protecting his extra pawn on d5. However, the powerful reply 11... ♗g4! had convinced him that it would be unwise to attempt an outright refutation of Kasparov's new idea since the ambitious 12. f3 would leave Black's piece placement far superior to White's after 12... ♗f5 13. 0-0 ♗c5+ 14. ♔h1 0-0. Instead Karpov had played 12.♗e2, returning the pawn after all and obtaining no advantage after 12...♗xe2 13.♕xe2+ ♕e7 14.♗e3 ♘bxd5. The text is a more subtle move. White makes no attempt to hang on to d5 and focusses on good, fast piece development. If 11...♘bxd5 12. 0-0 for instance, he can be very happy with the outcome of the opening. However, Kasparov immediately makes it clear that his plans are very different.

11... ♗c5!?

An exclamation mark for the grandiose positional concept to just play around White's pawn on d5, a question mark because it turns out there is something wrong with it after all. When Karpov faced this position again, a year later against Dutch Grandmaster John van der Wiel in a tournament in Brussels, he had the refutation ready: 12.♗e3! ♗xe3 13.♕a4+! and White remains a pawn up without any counterplay to speak of (although the game was eventually drawn).

12. 0-0 0-0 13. ♗f3 ♗f5

White is beginning to feel the pressure. The knight on a3 is badly placed and cannot be easily rerouted because 14.♘c4 fails to 14...♗d3. Still, it is hard

to believe that Black really should have sufficient compensation for a pawn, let alone that he should already be better. After all, White has no weaknesses and apart from the knight on a3 all his pieces can be freely developed.

14. ♗g5 ♖e8 15. ♕d2 b5

Making it even more difficult for White to revive his a3 knight and introducing the latent threat of b5-b4.

16. ♖ad1 ♘d3!

Position after: 16... ♘d3!

Although only supported by the bishop on f5, this knight turns out to be amazingly difficult for White to dislodge. If 17.♗e2?, the powerful 17...♘xf2! 18.♖xf2 b4 wins.

17. ♘ab1?

According to Kasparov this move, logical though it is, is the only real mistake in the entire game. His recommendation is to be much more dynamic and play 17.d6! with murky complications. But that was precisely what Karpov always tried to avoid! His top priority was to keep things 'under control'. That a perfectly normal-looking move such as 17.♘ab1 is no longer able to achieve this, is amazing. In fact, it is one of the reasons this game is so very, very special.

17... h6 18. ♗h4 b4 19. ♘a4 ♗d6 20. ♗g3 ♖c8 21. b3

At last the moment seems to have arrived for dislodging Black's knight from d3, where it so completely blockades White's entire army – the manoeuvre ♘a4-b2 is coming.

Position after: 21. b3

21... g5!

Giving his opponent no time to breathe. 22.♘b2 loses a piece to 22...♘xb2 23.♕xb2 g4.

22. ♗xd6 ♕xd6 23. g3

Even under pressure Karpov's play remains logical through and through. By creating an escape square for his bishop he again 'threatens' 24.♘b2.

23... ♘d7!

Introducing two new and dangerous threats: ...♘d7-e5 and ...♕d6-f6. For example, if now 24.♘b2 ♕f6! 25.♘xd3 ♗xd3 26.♕xd3 ♘e5 Black is winning.

24. ♗g2 ♕f6! 25. a3 a5 26. axb4 axb4 27. ♕a2 ♗g6!

It is impressive to watch Kasparov consistently aiming to prevent even the slightest improvement of White's position. 28.♘d2 is now met by 28...♖e2!, winning.

28. d6

White's extra d-pawn has played no part in the proceedings whatsoever. Karpov now offers to return it, hoping that at least 28...♕xd6 will give him the opportunity to play 29. ♘d2. But Kasparov doesn't let go that easily.

28... g4! 29. ♕d2 ♔g7 30. f3

A risky attempt to free himself from Black's vice-like grip on his position. Yet what else was there?

30... ♕xd6 31. fxg4 ♕d4+ 32. ♔h1 ♘f6 33. ♖f4

Garry Kasparov (photo Cathy Rogers)

The game has entered a critical phase. Kasparov seizes every chance he gets.

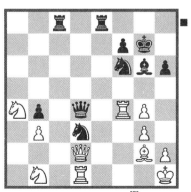

Position after: 33. ♖f4

33... ♘e4! 34. ♕xd3 ♘f2+ 35. ♖xf2 ♗xd3 36. ♖fd2

If White were able to consolidate his position he would still be in with a chance, but Kasparov remains relentless until the end.

36... ♕e3! 37. ♖xd3 ♖c1! 38. ♘b2 ♕f2! 39. ♘d2 ♖xd1+ 40. ♘xd1 ♖e1+

White resigned. Games like this earn the winner more than just a point, they gain a place among the Immortals.

But the end of the saga was not yet in sight. Part of the agreement in abandoning the first match was that Karpov, should he lose the second match, would be entitled to a revenge match, their third. And so the two rivals (more likely enemies by now) met again, less than a year after Kasparov had become World Champion. And although this time Kasparov was the clear favorite (he actually announced that he was going to "destroy" Karpov) it was a very close match again. The first half of the match took place in London and resulted in a 6½-5½ lead for Kasparov. The second half, which was played in Leningrad, at first went all Kasparov's way. When a truly magnificent win in game 16 had given him a 9½-6½ lead, the match seemed to be over. But then the incredible happened: Kasparov lost three games in a row! Suddenly the outcome of the match had become totally unpredictable. The decision came in game 22.

♙ Kasparov, Garry
♟ Karpov, Anatoly
🕑 London/Leningrad 1986

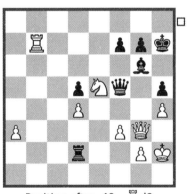

Position after: 40... ♖d2

In this position the game was adjourned. Karpov had been under heavy pressure from the start, but the general view of commentators and spectators alike was that he had managed to save himself. The pawn on d4 is attacked and if White has nothing better than to protect it with 41.♖b4, Black

forces a transition into an inferior, but tenable rook endgame with 41...f6 (42.♘xg6 ♕xg6 43.♕xg6+ ♔xg6). The problem is that White *does* have something better....

41. ♘d7!!

The sealed move. Kasparov had calculated everything through to the end. White is winning by force.

41... ♖xd4

If Black doesn't play this, 42.♘f8+ ♔h6 43.♖b8, threatening 44.♘xg6 followed by 45.♖h8+ will be lethal.

42. ♘f8+ ♔h6 43. ♖b4!!

This prevents the liberating queen exchange 43... ♕f4, thus keeping the stranglehold on Black's position intact. If 43... ♖xb4 44. axb4 Black has no move except 44... d4. In this case he actually promotes his pawn first, yet is still completely powerless after 45.b5 d3 46.b6 d2 47.b7 d1=♕ 48. b8=♕, for instance 48... ♕c1 49. ♘xg6 ♕xg6 50. ♕h8+ ♕h7 51. ♕gxg7 mate!

43... ♖c4

Other rook moves, e.g. 43... ♖d1, lose to 44. ♖b8 followed by 45.♘xg6.

44. ♖xc4 dxc4 45. ♕d6!

Threatening 46.♕d2+.

45... c3 46. ♕d4

Black resigned. He could still have played 46...♗h7 followed by 47...g5, but this is so utterly hopeless that Karpov decided not to bother.

Again Kasparov had a break of just one year before he had to face Karpov in their next World Championship match. The latter had to play only one short match against the winner of the new qualification cycle, the young Russian Andrei Sokolov (1963), to get there. It was the last remaining privilege for him from the chaos of the abandoned first match. On the one hand this was decidedly unfair to Sokolov (who had had to work his way through an immensely tough trajectory of qualification tournaments and matches), on the other hand Kasparov and Karpov were still considered so far above the rest of the world's best players, that a match for the World Championship without either of them would hardly have been taken seriously.

The match took place in Seville, Spain. Many people thought that this time Kasparov would really finish Karpov once and for all. Yet the opposite almost happened! It was a tremendously exciting and very close match. Three times Karpov took a one point lead, culminating in a win in the penultimate (23rd) game. With the score 12-11 in Karpov's favour, Kasparov *had* to win the last game in order to draw the match and retain his title, something no other World Champion had managed to do since Lasker against Schlechter in 1910. And so he did! In the first session, which was unusually tense, Kasparov kept his opponent under pressure, brilliantly sacrificed a pawn, survived a nervous time scramble and adjourned in an advantageous, but not clearly winning position. When the game resumed it quickly became clear that Karpov had exhausted himself. In time trouble he had missed a golden opportunity to make a draw and clinch the match and now lacked the necessary strength for a long drawn-out defence. Kasparov won, the match was drawn and Kasparov remained World Champion. He had survived what was perhaps his most difficult moment from the entire series of matches.

The match in 2000 between Kasparov and Kramnik (photo Cathy Rogers)

The last of the "K-K matches", as they were now called, was played in 1990, in New York and Lyon. Again Kasparov announced that this time he was going to crush his opponent, again he failed in this particular ambition, yet again he did eventually come out on top, 12½-11½. It was a fitting finale to a unique series of matches that were extremely tense and hard-fought and gave us a fantastic number of outstanding games.

Meanwhile, the world kept changing. It was not a coincidence that the first two of the K-K matches were played in Moscow (as was traditional when two Soviet players were involved) while the last three took place, partly or entirely, in the West. The Soviet Union had started to crumble, power vacuums were beginning to appear and somehow Karpov and Kasparov were able to take the liberty of selling their matches to the highest bidder, in the 'best' tradition of Western capitalism. Kasparov must have felt at home in these changing circumstances and before long he showed signs of wanting to decide for himself where and how matches for

Linares 2005 (photo Cathy Rogers)

the World Championship were to be played. In doing so he challenged the authority both of FIDE and of his own Soviet government.

Things came to a head in 1993 when Kasparov and his new challenger Nigel Short
broke free from FIDE. They organised their match for the World Championship
themselves in London and formed a new organisation, the PCA (Professional
Chess Association), a players association. Kasparov easily won the match (12½-7½)
and then organised a complete qualification cycle for the next World Championship match (which attracted almost all the same players who had participated in
the 'official' FIDE cycle).

The PCA cycle was won by Viswanathan Anand, a new star from India, who was
universally seen as a legitimate challenger and potentially a worthy successor to
Kasparov's throne. The Kasparov-Anand match, which was played in New York in
1995, proved much more difficult for Kasparov than the match against Short. They
started with eight draws before Anand drew first blood. However Kasparov hit

back immediately and in the end scored a resounding victory – 10½-7½ in the best of 20 match.

Soon afterwards the PCA lost their sponsorship and the organisation collapsed. This of course did nothing to improve the chaos which by now completely surrounded the World Chess Championship. While FIDE was desperately trying to make 'their' World Championship a success by radically changing the format (in 1997 a FIDE World Championship was played in a knock-out format for the first time), Kasparov was challenged with the task of creating a new organisation and of organising a new match for *his* title. In the first of these tasks he failed dismally, in the second he had to wait until 2000. True, he had chosen his own 'challenger' rather then giving everybody a fair chance to qualify, but since he had chosen Vladimir Kramnik, a new supertalent from Russia, the chess world was not too critical of the legitimacy of their match (apart from FIDE of course). Like Anand five years earlier, Kramnik was widely considered to be a worthy successor to the chess throne should he win. Between all these World Championship troubles Kasparov kept playing *and* winning tournaments, which cemented the legitimacy of his continuing claim to the highest title in chess, no matter what FIDE said or did to promote their own cause.

But to the great surprise of most chess fans, Kasparov did lose to Kramnik! Astonishingly, he didn't manage to win a single game, lost two and so had to concede defeat after 15 games (of 16 planned): 8½-6½. Kasparov remained number one on the rating list (a position that was slowly but surely becoming more and more prestigious), a status he was to maintain until he publicly announced his retirement from chess in Linares in March 2005, right after he had won his last tournament there. After some thirty years of competitive chess at the highest imaginable level he decided to end a career which is unlikely ever to be surpassed.

During his years as World Champion Kasparov turned into a global superstar, for whom the world was far larger than a chessboard. In fact his chess career has served as the perfect stepping stone for his current existence as a global citizen.

After his retirement Kasparov began to write books – books about himself, about his predecessors as World Champion, and also about entirely different subjects such as philosophy and politics. He also gave lectures, but above all he devoted himself to politics. Within just a few years he managed to become one of the most prominent critics of Russia's President Putin. He now lives in New York and has obtained Croatian citizenship.

(photo Cathy Rogers)

Kasparov remains a legendary figure in the chess world. He often shows up at prestigious events: he is involved with educational and propaganda efforts and he occasionally still plays in small but high level rapid or blitz tournaments. In this way he remains what he has in effect been throughout his life: a perfect ambassador for chess.

Kasparov's main legacy to chess is of course a treasure trove of beautiful games, that will continue to entrance and captivate chess players for as long as the game is played. The best of these he has further enriched with his own commentary, admirably thorough and objective, in a series of books that ought to be compulsory study material for each and every serious chess student. His work ethic in this is of the highest level. He never allows himself to make a superficial comment like "also interesting is..." or "another possibility might be...", but always strives for thoroughness, objectivity and truth.

Ultimate truth. That is what Kasparov has always aspired to: in his games, in his analyses and above all – and perhaps this is his greatest contribution to the game – in his opening preparation. It is no exaggeration to say that Kasparov has completely rewritten the theory of openings as he found it when he first opened a chess book. Always on the lookout for possible improvements, for new weapons that could be used to defeat his opponents before they even reached the middlegame, he modernised and changed existing theory beyond recognition. In this respect he has truly opened up a whole new era in chess.

Kasparov was one of the first to make use of computer help. The tirelessness, objectivity, thoroughness and accuracy that are by definition characteristics of a computer, form a natural extension to the way he himself worked. He was also fascinated by the growth in playing strength of computer engines during the 1990s and was not afraid to test his own strength against them in public, something most top players had already begun to shy away from. This culminated in two short, but highly publicised matches against the supercomputer Deep Blue in 1996 and 1997. Kasparov won the first match 4-2, but lost the second 2½-3½. His defeat in 1997 marked what might be termed as the capitulation of human intelligence to the artificial intelligence of computers and as such was widely perceived as a historic moment in the history of mankind.

Deep Blue, in the 'Computer History Museum' in Mountain View, California.

Let us now try to form an impression of the depth and accuracy of Kasparov's opening preparation and what this actually meant for his opponents. One of his most famous opening triumphs was the crucial tenth game from his match against Anand in 1995.

♙ Kasparov, Garry
♟ Anand, Viswanathan
🌐 New York 1995

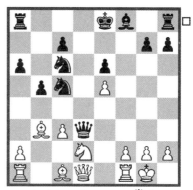

Position after: 13... ♕d3

1. e4 e5 2. ♘f3 ♘c6 3. ♗b5 a6 4. ♗a4 ♘f6 5. 0-0 ♘xe4

Almost every chess game starts with a theoretical duel. Who is the better prepared of the two players? Who will deliver the first blow? The Open Ruy Lopez, a favourite of Anand's in those days, had already featured in the sixth game of the match, causing Kasparov considerable trouble. In the eighth game he had avoided a further discussion of this line by choosing a different opening. Now his opening moves signal his readiness for a continuation of the fight.

6. d4 b5 7. ♗b3 d5 8. dxe5 ♗e6 9. ♘bd2 ♘c5 10. c3 d4 11. ♘g5!?

We have seen this spectacular move before, in the chapter on Smyslov, who now bravely played 11...♕xg5 in a game against Timman (page 121). Anand prefers the move that was played in the game where 11.♘g5 was first seen.

11... dxc3 12. ♘xe6 fxe6 13. bxc3 ♕d3

This is how Korchnoi defended himself when Karpov took him by surprise with 11.♘g5 in their 1978 match in Baguio City. Black gives up the pair of bishops,

but with his queen dominant on d3 aims to contain White's latent attacking chances. Karpov now saw nothing better than to offer an exchange of queens with 14.♘f3, which indeed gave him a slight advantage in the endgame after 14...♕xd1 15.♗xd1 thanks to White's bishop pair, although the game was eventually drawn.

In game 6 Anand had demonstrated that 14...0-0-0! is a more accurate move than 14...♕xd1. If White now initiates the exchange of queens with 15.♕xd3 ♖xd3, Black is left with a far more active position than is the case after 14...♕xd1 15.♗xd1, while avoiding the exchange is possible only with two rather passive moves: 15.♗d2 or 15.♕e1. Kasparov chose 15.♕e1, but after 15...♘xb3 16.axb3 ♔b7 had achieved no advantage at all.

Many would have given up the entire variation after a game like that, but the effect on Kasparov was the opposite. Together with his team of seconds he thoroughly researched every nook and cranny of the position after 13...♕d3, convinced that somewhere a sharper approach to this problem must be hidden.

14. ♗c2!

This pawn sacrifice had been recommended by none other than Mikhail Tal as far back as 1978, but without giving any variations in support. At first sight the idea looks rather speculative. Watch (and tremble at) how deeply Kasparov analyses a seemingly casual one-move suggestion like this.

14... ♛xc3

Now what? White has of course safeguarded his pair of bishops, but it doesn't look as if he has generated even the first hint of an attack. If 15.♖b1 0-0-0 White's pieces are tangled up far more seriously than they were two moves earlier.

15. ♘b3!!

A rook sacrifice that changes the picture completely. Black's king is robbed of an easy route to security, White's bishops dominate the board and the weakening of the h1-a8 diagonal (the result of b7-b5) is palpable. The only drawback is that it costs a rook. Is it worth that?

15... ♘xb3

There are many alternatives to this move (Kasparov mentions 15... ♘b4, 15... ♗e7 en 15... ♖d8), that both players had to take into account, Kasparov in his preparation and Anand (presumably) over the board, yet the text move is undoubtedly the critical one.

16. ♗xb3 ♘d4

To analyse this position in full is a time-consuming job (especially in the pre-computer era), which demands enormous if not total precision. The first move that comes to mind is of course 16... ♛xa1, when Kasparov gives 17. ♛h5+ followed by an array of dazzling variations both after 17... ♔d7 18. ♗xe6+ ♔xe6 19. ♛g4+ and after 17...g6 18. ♛f3 ♘d8 19. ♛f6 ♖g8 20. ♗xe6. These are simply too complicated and too deep to even begin to reproduce here. Kasparov's evaluation is that White has a winning attack in all of these lines. Perhaps Anand also reached this conclusion over the board, but it is quite possible that he simply chose 16... ♘d4 intuitively, for it certainly looks like an excellent move. After all, White's powerful bishop on b3 is under threat, the e6-pawn is protected, Black's queen remains dominant on c3 and all the while White's rook remains attacked. Hasn't White's initiative burnt itself out already?

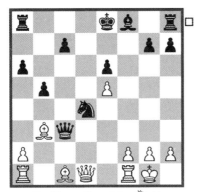

Position after: 16... ♘d4

17. ♕g4!!

Without a worry in the world White simply continues to reinforce his attack, a truly brilliant concept, especially when put into perspective by 'ordinary' moves like 17. ♗g5 and 17. ♗d2, which protect the rook on a1, but do not add sufficient fuel to the fire. Now Black no longer has a choice. Accepting the proffered rook is basically his only move. But then again, what's wrong with it?

17... ♕xa1 18. ♗xe6

Plumbing the depths of this incredibly complicated position over the board is impossible. Even in the peace and quiet (and unlimited time!) of home preparation this demands huge effort. Few players would have been prepared to allow their seconds to spend their time and energy on this position. Yet Kasparov must have 'felt' that it was worth it and the game has proved him right. His unique 'feeling' for the dynamics of

chess showed him the narrow path to the 'ultimate truth', the winning attack that justifies 14. ♗c2!, the move that started it all.

18... ♖d8

Anand continues to defend with sound, logical moves. 18... ♕c3 was a serious alternative, yet according to Kasparov 19. ♗d7+ ♔f7 20. ♗e3 would then keep the black king trapped in a mating net.

19. ♗h6!!

The last and decisive link in a chain of sledgehammer blows, every single one of them essential for the demolition of Black's position. Black is a rook up, his pieces are reasonably well-placed yet he has no defence. If 19... ♕xf1+ 20. ♔xf1 gxh6 21. ♕h5+ it is mate in two moves.

19... ♕c3 20. ♗xg7 ♕d3

This saves Black from getting mated with 21. ♕h5+, but it costs him his extra rook.

21. ♗xh8 ♕g6

An attempt to escape in an endgame a pawn down. He could have gained material again by playing 21... ♘e2+ 22. ♔h1 ♘g3+, but this would only have added new fuel to White's attack. After 23. hxg3 ♕xf1+ 24. ♔h2 and now for instance 24... ♕xf2 25. ♗f6 it is game over.

22. ♗f6 ♗e7 23. ♗xe7 ♕xg4 24. ♗xg4 ♔xe7

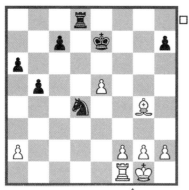

Position after: 24... ♔xe7

If it were Black's move now he could get in 25... c5 and the endgame would indeed have been very tricky, but of course it is White to move. **25. ♖c1!** allowed Kasparov to stop Black's c-pawn from storming forward. He still needed his excellent endgame technique in order to finish the job, but this he did.

For Anand it must have been a horrible blow. By any normal human standards his preparation of 11...dxc3 had been excellent, but the level of preparation that he unwittingly encountered in this game was simply out of this world. It cannot have been a coincidence that he lost three of the next four games, which effectively ended the match.

Vladimir Kramnik

Vladimir Borisovich Kramnik, who was born in 1975 in Tuapse on the Russian Black Sea coast will probably be remembered more than anything else as 'the man who beat Kasparov', a feat given extra symbolic weight by its taking place in the first year of the new millennium. In the midst of the tempestuous changes that have swept through the chess world over the last 25 years or so, no better line between the 'old' and the 'new' can be drawn than in the match Kramnik-Kasparov, London 2000. This is not to say that Kasparov represented 'old' chess in any way! On the contrary, if anyone can be said to have brought chess into the modern era it must surely be Kasparov. But he was the pioneer, the trail blazer, while Kramnik simply grew up in the modern world and became, by nature, its first champion, the first World Champion of the 21st century.

Kramnik was also the last of a long line of World Champions from the Soviet Union. When in 2007 he lost the title to Anand, an era of Soviet domination that began with Botvinnik in 1948 and lasted almost 60 years – interrupted only by Bobby Fischer – finally came to an end, sixteen years after the Soviet Union itself.

The changing of the chess world has been a gradual process. It wasn't that at one particular point in time one fundamental aspect of chess changed. Rather it was that at some point everything started changing and above all *kept* changing. Change has become a permanent feature of chess and the rate at which it is occurring is high. The main culprit, not just in the world of chess but in the entire world, is of course the computer, or more accurately the digitisation of our existence.

Restricting ourselves to the chess world, this era of change started in the latter half of the 1980s, with the abolition of adjournments and the related introduction of shorter time controls. Time in chess had always been regarded as something that was available for thinking, either unlimited or limited by a generous time frame. For a very long time the standard time control had been forty moves in two and a half hours, followed – after adjournment – by sessions of sixteen moves per hour. This was now changed to a time control where this generous amount of time was *not* continually renewed but finite (e.g. forty moves in two hours, followed by an extra thirty minutes to finish). The new time limits required players to be much more aware of their time situation. A game that would last 80 moves did not get a minute more than a game of 41 moves and there were no adjourn-

(photo Jos Sutmuller)

ments in which to catch your breath. It was a radical break with the past, where the basic principle had always been that in order to play a serious game players should be allowed plenty of thinking time until the very last move.

This radical change met with surprisingly little resistance. Apparently most players liked the idea of not having to adjourn anymore. Perhaps many even felt attracted to the added tension of time trouble duels, the fight against the clock, which with the new faster time controls became an essential part of the game. From now on, even in a lost position there would always be the chance of winning 'on time'. Time management became an essential part of a player's skills.

The next thing that changed was the clocks. The old analogue clocks, with their 'flag' that fell when a player's time had expired, were replaced by new, digital clocks that would indicate a cool and accurate '0.00' when the player's time was up. The digital clock in its turn paved the way for a whole new *method* of keeping time. It became possible to play with 'increment'. This means that time is added after each move so that a player will always have *some* time (depending on the amount of time added per move). This protects a player from losing on time in a

(photo Jos Sutmuller)

winning position, one of the most hateful aspects of playing with a fixed amount of time.

Parallel to this development, the *format* of chess tournaments also began to change in the 1990s. The round-robin formula (all participants playing each other once) had been the norm for over a century. In the 1970s 'open' tournaments became popular and for this format the Swiss system was used (a large group of players, who cannot all play against each other, are paired in each round with an opponent who is equal with them on points). Now, however, some organisers went back to the 19th century format of a knock-out tournament. The idea was not so much to allow more players into a tournament (the Swiss system already does that), but to increase the excitement by forcing players into a permanent do or die situation. A knock-out knows only winners and losers, so players are continually fighting for their lives. The problem with this format is of course that a game of chess, unlike for instance a tennis match, can end in a draw. What were knock-out organisers to do about this? In an era where changes were natural the answer came naturally. If a game (or more usually a short match consisting of two games) is drawn, a tiebreak is played at a faster time control, or – more precisely – at *ever* faster time controls until one of the players cracks. The final stage of this spiral of speed is the 'Armageddon' or sudden death game, where White gets an extra minute (e.g. 5 minutes against Black's 4) but a draw gives victory to Black.

So successful was the introduction of this system of tiebreaks with a faster time control, that it began to be used in events where a tiebreak was not strictly necessary: in open tournaments and even round-robin tournaments. Nowadays many chess players (or perhaps chess *fans*) regard a tiebreak as the highest form of chess *entertainment*. They look forward to the tiebreak of a match or tournament more than the main event. It is now quite common for even a World Championship match to end in a blitz orgy and nobody thinks twice about it.

Clearly then, anyone who wishes to become a strong and successful chess player these days needs to be a master at all formats and all time controls. Round-robins, opens and knock-out tournaments, with an endless variety of different time controls and increments – a top player has to be prepared for them all. Every organiser comes up with a tournament format and a time control of their own fancy and players just have to adapt to them, which is not always an easy matter. Even Magnus Carlsen, the current World Champion, once lost a game on time in a winning position, because he had forgotten about the particular time control that was being used. But let's not get ahead of ourselves...

Vladimir Kramnik was born at exactly the right time to both take full advantage of the unique Soviet coaching system for young chess players and then to profit from the disintegration of the Soviet Union. Borders opened and there was no one to stop him from playing as much as he liked. He was even able to settle in Western Europe, where it was now easier to develop a career as a professional chess player than in disorientated and impoverished Russia. He didn't even have to give up his Russian citizenship in order to make this move.

Kramnik's talent had of course been spotted at an early age, but he became world famous when, still only sixteen years of age, he won the open tournament that formed part of the *Dortmunder Schachtage* in 1992. The Crown Group of that event was particularly strong that year and was won by Kasparov, which meant that the whole tournament received huge media interest. So impressed was Kasparov by his young countryman that he made every effort to have him selected for the Russian team for the 1992 Olympiad in Manila, incredible for a player who was not even an International Master. Kramnik took his chance with both hands, scored 8½/9 and was awarded the Grandmaster(!) title at the FIDE Congress held alongside the Olympiad. Things continued to move fast for Kramnik. So fast in fact, that when, only two years later, he was eliminated in the quarter finals of both the PCA and FIDE Candidates tournaments, this was viewed as a rather disappointing performance, even though he was still only nineteen years old.

Kramnik probably just needed some more match experience. In this respect, his 'job' as Kasparov's second for the latter's World Championship match against Anand in 1995 would have taught him a lot. In fact Kramnik and Kasparov worked together for quite some time so to call Kasparov his early mentor would not be unduly exaggerated.

During the latter half of the 1990s Kramnik's talent blossomed and his tournament record was beginning to equal Kasparov's. Sometimes Kramnik even finished ahead of Kasparov and their mutual encounters were always tense and would go one way and then the other. As described in the previous chapter, the way in which their match for the World Championship in 2000 came about didn't deserve a brilliancy prize, but the fact that it was Kramnik who was chosen as the new 'challenger' was generally viewed with approval. The chess world was eagerly anticipating this match between the World Champion and his crown prince.

The Berlin wall

It turned out to be the end of an era. For the first time since his (first!) match against Karpov in 1984, Kasparov was unable to come to grips with his opponent's play. Kramnik was not overwhelmed by Kasparov's opening knowledge, probably because he partly helped build it. He seized every chance he was given, defended staunchly when in trouble and generally gave the impression of being extremely self-confident.

It must have been a sobering experience for Kasparov, who was used to his opponents to some extent at least, being afraid of him.

A large part of Kramnik's success in this match can be attributed to his choice of opening against Kasparov's then favourite opening move: **1. e4**. Kramnik chose the Berlin Wall, the main line of which begins: **1... e5 2. ♘f3 ♘c6 3. ♗b5 ♘f6** (the Berlin Defence) **4. 0-0 ♘xe4 5. d4** and now **5... ♘d6 6. ♗xc6 dxc6 7. dxe5 ♘f5 8. ♕xd8+ ♔xd8**

(see diagram next column)

Position after: 8... ♔xd8

This position occurred in four of the eight games where Kasparov played with the white pieces. By exchanging queens this early and by simplifying the pawn configuration, Black has made the position far less dynamic than Kasparov liked. It is indeed a wall that Black has built and White is challenged to try to tear it down. This Kasparov failed to achieve, which must have been a source of great irritation to him. Perhaps it even gave him a sense of powerlessness, which may well have affected his self-confidence in his games with the black pieces as well. Kramnik later noted that computers do not understand this type of position. Apparently, as early as 2000 (and possibly even earlier) Kramnik had come to

Kramnik against Deep Fritz (photo Cathy Rogers)

see the computer as Kasparov's most important assistant in opening preparation. The Berlin Wall remained very popular after the match, especially at the highest level. Nowadays White often avoids it by playing 4.d3 rather than 4.0-0.

In the end Kramnik won two (out of fifteen) games, while Kasparov was unable to win any games at all. Not since the match between Lasker and Capablanca had a World Champion lost his title without winning at least once. It is a bitter twist of fate that – of all people – these two great fighters, Lasker and Kasparov, had to suffer this ignominy. Yet it is also proof of how tremendously strong Capablanca was in 1921 and Kramnik in 2000.

Kramnik's first years as World Champion were very successful. He won several strong tournaments and a number of matches as well, often at faster time controls or otherwise deviating from the standard traditional elite tournament. For instance, he beat Anand in 2002 in a short match where both players were allowed to consult their computers. It shows how at home Kramnik felt in the new computer and rapid-play era. Following Kasparov's example he didn't shy away from meeting the strongest engines in public either. In 2002 he drew an eight game match against Deep Fritz, while in 2006 he lost 2-4 against the 'same' opponent (naturally Deep Fritz's hardware and software in 2006 were not to be compared with the 2002 version) in what is likely to have been the last ever match between a human World Champion and a supercomputer.

Nevertheless, his World Championship title was under a lot of pressure from the start. Not only did Kasparov maintain his position as number one on the international rating list until his retirement in 2005, FIDE was more active than ever in organising *their* version of the World Championship. Kramnik also had to compete for legitimacy against all the FIDE World Champions. ("Who is the real World Champion?")

In 2004 Kramnik defended his title against Hungarian grandmaster Péter Lékó (1979), who had qualified for the match in a short, but fairly representative Candidates Tournament. To the great surprise of all Kramnik was in huge trouble in this match. In fact he had to win the last game in order to level the score (which was enough to retain the title). Although this feat had only been performed before him by Lasker (against Schlechter) in 1910 and Kasparov (against Karpov) in 1987, it wasn't felt to be a sign of a true champion's predominance.

Péter Lékó (photo Jos Sutmuller)

The match was actually planned as part of an attempt at reunification of the chess world. The schism by now had come to be widely regarded (even by Kasparov) as an undesirable situation, which had to end. The plan was to have the winner of the Kramnik-Lékó match play the 'ultimate' reunification match against the winner of a match between Kasparov and the then current FIDE world champion Ruslan Ponomariov (1983) from Ukraine. For reasons which have never been fully disclosed (but can probably be summarized as 'power and money') the Kasparov-Ponomariov match never came about. Yet the urgency to resolve the situation was widely felt. Since 1993, FIDE had organised five World Championship tournaments in knock-out format, each giving a hundred or more players the chance of winning the title, but the formula was felt to have exhausted itself. Moreover these tournaments had done nothing to facilitate reunification, as both Kasparov and his successor Kramnik had always refused to take part. In 2005 FIDE had a change of heart and invited eight of the world's best players to a double round-robin World Championship tournament (without any prior qualification cycle) in San Luis, Argentina. (Neither Kramnik nor Kasparov participated). The tournament was won by Veselin Topalov (1975) from Bulgaria, who played superbly and finished 1½ points ahead of his closest rival Anand.

And then all of a sudden the seemingly impossible happened. After thirteen years of division, a reunification match was organised by FIDE between the two competing World Champions. This match, between Kramnik and Topalov, held in 2006 in Elista, the capital city of Kalmykia in Russia, has gone down in history for more reasons than one. Firstly because, of course, it *did* unite the two World Championships, which by now had universally come to be called the "Classical World Championship" and the "FIDE World Championship" respectively. Secondly, because it was the first time in history (apart from the FIDE championships during the years of separation) that the new time control and tiebreak system were used in a match for the World Championship. The match was the best of twelve games, with neither champion enjoying the privilege of retaining his title in case of a tie. Instead if the score was equal after twelve games, a tiebreak was to be played at faster and faster time limits: first four rapid games (25 minutes each plus a ten second increment per move) then, if needed, pairs of blitz games (5 minutes each plus increment). Finally, if the score was still level, a sudden death game of 6 against 5 minutes was to decide the match, with draw odds to the player taking Black.

Thirdly, and perhaps most prominently, this match has gone down in history as 'Toiletgate'. A disagreement between the two camps escalated completely out of proportion, making the atmosphere surrounding the match the most hostile since the notorious 1978 Karpov-Korchnoi match. Briefly, after four games, with Kramnik leading 3-1, Topalov's manager accused Kramnik of consulting a chess engine in his private toilet. (The players had separate toilets.) This was a very serious accusation indeed, since by now computer engines were strong enough to provide a player with vital information within seconds. Proof was not supplied, nor found, and of course Kramnik was beside himself with rage at the allegation, especially when FIDE decided to go along with the Topalov camp and require the players to share a neutral toilet. Kramnik refused to show up for game five if the

(photo Frans Peeters)

ruling was not reversed but FIDE stuck to its decision. So, for the second time in history, a game in a World Chess Championship match was lost by forfeit. (Game two of the match Fischer-Spassky in 1972 was the first.)

Naturally, chaos and talks behind the scenes went on for days, the upshot being that the match continued with game six, in an atmosphere of deep hatred and an increased risk of further explosions. The tension was palpable, both on and off the board. Topalov won games eight and nine, Kramnik struck back in game ten and after twelve games the match was tied 6-6. In the tiebreak the tension increased further. The first rapid game ended in a draw, Kramnik won the second, Topalov the third, and the climax came in game four which was won by Kramnik. He had retained his title, but what a dirty war it had been!

Cheating by using a computer engine has become a major problem in the chess world now that all you need is a an app on your smartphone. In the dozen years or so that have elapsed since 'Toiletgate' there have been countless incidents, especially in open tournaments where the sheer number of players forms a natural camouflage for cheating of any kind. Some players have been caught red-handed, there have been unfounded allegations, and rules have been changed. Mobile phones are no longer allowed in playing halls and huge events like Olympiads now use security gates. Yet the potential for computer cheating remains a problem.

For Kramnik, the victory over Topalov was in effect a comeback to the top of the chess world. His results in 2005 had been disappointing and he had dropped to number four on the world rankings; after Kasparov retired, Topalov was the number one. It transpired that Kramnik had been suffering from ankylosing spondylitis, an uncommon form of arthritis. This caused him considerable pain and even the painkillers he took had an adverse effect on his chess. Kramnik took a half year off chess to undergo some intensive treatment and this helped him both during and after the Topalov match. Unfortunately though, there is no cure for this affliction, so he is likely to be affected by it for the rest of his life.

Part of the complicated arrangements for the reunification match was that Kramnik, should he win, was to play for the title again in a double round-robin tournament in 2007, similar to the one Topalov had won in 2005. If Kramnik did not win this (and lose his title as a consequence) he would be allowed a revenge match against the winner one year later.
This proved to be the end of Kramnik's World Championship. Anand won the tournament (which was held in Mexico City) and thus became the next World Champion. He defended his title successfully in the match against Kramnik, held in Bonn in 2008, winning 6½-4½.

After the loss of his title Kramnik remained a highly successful player for a decade until his rather abrupt retirement in 2019. He won a number of elite tournaments, always had a very high ranking on the Elo list and came close to qualifying for another attempt at becoming World Champion several times. In 2013 he shared first place in the London Candidates tournament with Magnus Carlsen and

Anand versus Kramnik, Karpov making the first move (photo Cathy Rogers)

it was just bad luck for him that the tiebreak rules happened to be in favour of the player who had more wins, which was Carlsen. Like the time control, these rules vary from tournament to tournament and at times can be rather frustrating.

Kramnik officially ended his career as a professional chess player in January 2019 after the traditional Wijk aan Zee tournament. He explained that his motivation had dropped and that he had been planning to retire for some time, but wanted to play one last elite tournament.

Over the years Kramnik had impressed not just with results, but with his playing style as well. When he was young he worked very hard on his openings which made him particularly dangerous in sharp lines, more so because his powers of calculation were impressive. In these respects Kasparov's influence is clearly visible. At the same time Kramnik had a unique natural feeling for the positional nuances of the game, which allowed him to keep control of even the most complex positions and which made him invulnerable in his match against Kasparov. In this respect he was much closer to Petrosian or Karpov.

Above all Kramnik had the ability to create something out of nothing. The number of games where he seemed to have nothing at all – until he suddenly *did* have something! – is countless and his technique in converting tiny advantages has always been impeccable. This ability allowed him to sometimes play very modest openings, which then, often in the early middlegame, turned out to be not as harmless as they looked – for inexplicable reasons! Another resemblance to Petrosian, which became apparent in his final tournaments, was Kramnik's knack for purely positional sacrifices.

Let us first take a look at a supreme and very famous example of his 'early' style, based on opening preparation and enormous calculating power.

♙ Kasparov, Garry
♟ Kramnik, Vladimir
🌐 Dos Hermanas 1996

In 1996 Kasparov was still very much the man to beat. His occasional losses were almost always superbly well-played games, simply because that is what it took to beat him.

1. d4 d5 2. c4 c6 3. ♘c3 ♘f6 4. ♘f3 e6 5. e3 ♘bd7 6. ♗d3

Allowing the sharp Meran Variation. Nowadays the slightly more reticent 6. ♕c2 is a popular move.

6... dxc4 7. ♗xc4 b5 8. ♗d3 ♗b7 9. 0-0 a6 10. e4 c5 11. d5

This is where the position becomes complicated. There are many ways for Black to combat White's central breakthrough. What they all have in common is that Black has to play aggres-

sively in order to avoid being pushed back.

11... c4 12. ♗c2 ♕c7 13. ♘d4 ♘c5

Postponing the decision between an open (13...exd5) or a closed (13...e5) middlegame, Black is keeping as many options open as possible. There is also the question of where his king should go, which he also leaves unresolved for the moment. This is very ambitious opening play indeed. Kasparov now attempts to 'punish' Black by opening up the queenside, which he achieves – typically – at the cost of a pawn.

14. b4!? cxb3 e.p. 15. axb3 b4 16. ♘a4 ♘cxe4 17. ♗xe4

A novelty. White is hoping to improve upon the older move 17.dxe6, which after 17... ♖d8 18. exf7+ ♔xf7 leaves Black with beautifully developed pieces, compensating for the exposed position of his king.

17... ♘xe4 18. dxe6

Position after: 18. dxe6

18... ♗d6!

We are now entering the type of terri-
tory where both Kasparov and Kramnik
felt thoroughly at home; it requires not
just deep and precise calculation, but
also an intuitive feeling for 'what the
position wants'. Black's move may look
rather obvious at first sight, yet the
consequences are far-reaching. The
seemingly natural 18...0-0-0 would
have been met by 19. ♗e3 and Black is
in trouble.

19. exf7+ ♕xf7!

A crucial difference to the variation
17.dxe6, mentioned above, is that 19...
♔xf7 can now be met by 20. ♕h5+,
preventing Black's king from reaching a
safe haven.

20. f3

White's plan is simple – he intends to
chase the black knight away from e4,
check on e1 and start a king hunt. In
short, Kasparov wants to attack! But
Kramnik has no intention of obliging.
Instead, by sacrificing material, he
starts an attack of his own.

20... ♕h5 21. g3 0-0

I would like to give an exclamation
mark here, yet according to Kramnik
21... ♘xg3 22. hxg3 0-0 would have
been even stronger. He supports his
claim with frighteningly deep, razor-
sharp variations. Still, the move he
plays can hardly be called meek.

22. fxe4 ♕h3

Position after: 22... ♕h3

Black is a full piece down and if you
look at the position superficially you
could be forgiven for thinking that
White's pieces seem well-placed to
cope with the threats. But even Kasparov can't always find his way in a true
maze of variations. Besides, he didn't

like defending. Should Kramnik at this point have proposed to swap sides, Kasparov might readily have agreed.

23. ♘f3

This logical move (the knight defends the kingside and the bishop on d6 is attacked) is criticized by Kramnik. Instead, he recommends 23. ♖a2!, which is indeed even more logical. His main line runs 23... ♗xe4 24. ♖e1! ♗b7 25. ♕d3! when White is still a piece up, but has to endure the sight of that monstrously strong bishop on b7. He assesses the position to be roughly equal. It is an evaluation that might be disputed by a full-powered chess engine, but *mano a mano*, over the board?

23... ♗xg3! 24. ♘c5?

A question mark because White now loses by force, but how difficult it is to see this! Kramnik recommends 24. ♕e2, when Black's attack is awesome, yet perhaps not fatal for White. One variation he examines is 24... ♖xf3 25. ♖xf3 ♗xh2+ 26. ♔f2 ♕h4+ 27. ♔f1 when there does not seem to be a win for Black.

24... ♖xf3! 25. ♖xf3 ♕xh2+ 26. ♔f1

It looks as if White has found a strong defence, but now comes the crunch.

Position after: 26. ♔f1

26... ♗c6!

Who would have thought that a 'quiet move' would be the decider in a position where everything seems to revolve around speed? The threat of 27... ♗b5+ is lethal.

27. ♗g5

The alternative 27. ♖a5 is met by yet another quiet move: 27... ♗c7!, threatening both 28...♗xa5 and 28... ♖d8.

27... ♗b5+ 28. ♘d3 ♖e8!

Black is a rook down, yet White's king is surrounded by enemy pieces.

29. ♖a2 ♕h1+

Computer engines disapprove of this move and point out that 29... ♗xd3+! 30. ♖xd3 ♕h1+ 31. ♔e2 ♕g2+ 32. ♔e3 ♖xe4 would have been mate in four moves. But when a human being, in the heat of the battle, has spotted a certain win he doesn't always stop to look for a quicker one.

30. ♔e2 ♖xe4+ 31. ♔d2 ♕g2+ 32. ♔c1 ♕xa2 33. ♖xg3 ♕a1+ 34. ♔c2 ♕c3+ 35. ♔b1 ♖d4

Finally, an example of Kramnik's 'later', more intuitive style of play.

♙ Kramnik, Vladimir
♟ Blübaum, Matthias
🌐 Dortmund 2017

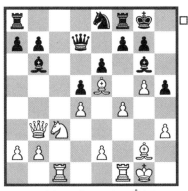

Position after: 18... ♗b6

Kramnik has played the early stages of the game modestly, yet ambitiously at the same time (if that is possible), a paradoxical way of playing that has become something of a trademark. His bishop on e5 is trapped, so something now *has* to happen. Many players would panic in a situation like this, but in the game of a truly great champion something usually *does* happen.

19. f5! ♗xf5 20. ♖xf5! exf5 21. ♘xd5

White resigned. He could have played on with 36. ♗f6, but the refutation is fairly simple: 36... ♗xd3+ 37.♔a2 ♗b1+! 38. ♕xb1 ♖d2+ with mate to follow.

There are no immediate threats facing the opponent – quite unlike the above game against Kasparov! White's pieces are excellently placed and 'that is all'. At first the young German Grandmaster defends himself well.

21... ♕e6 22. ♔h1 ♖d8 23. ♕f3 g6 24. e3 ♔h7

Black is hoping to (finally) be able to play ...♖d8-c8. He could also have chosen 24... ♖d7, followed by 25... ♗d8 and possibly ...f7-f6 sometime in the future.

25. ♘f4 ♕e7 26. ♕g3 ♗c7

Position after: 26... ♗c7

Exchanging White's powerful bishop on e5 would certainly improve Black's chances. So what is Kramnik thinking?

27. ♖xc7!

Sacrificing another exchange.

27... ♘xc7 28. ♗f6 ♕b4

Black may have been glad to finally play an aggressive move, but it quickly transpires that his queen is sorely missed for the defence of the kingside. 28... ♕d7 would have been more prudent.

29. ♘xh5! gxh5 30. g6+ ♔g8

If 30... fxg6 31. ♕xc7+ Black gets mated. Yet the text move seems to hold, thanks to Black's enormous material advantage.

31. ♕g5!

Another quiet move. The threat is simply to play 32. ♕h6.

31... h4?

A nice idea, but it is badly calculated. 31... ♘d5 was the only move, stopping 32. ♕h6 because of 32... ♘xf6. Instead, 32. ♗xd8! retains the advantage.

32. ♕h6 ♕e1+ 33. ♔h2 ♕g3+ 34. ♔g1 ♕e1+ 35. ♗f1!

Black resigned. If 35... ♕g3+ 36. ♔h1! ♕f3+ 37. ♗g2 ♕d1+ 38. ♔h2, when Black's queen has been sidetracked and there is no perpetual check. Mate is unavoidable.

Viswanathan Anand

Viswanathan Anand, or Anand Viswanathan, or simply Anand, or simpler yet Vishy – it is not so easy to translate Indian names to Western languages, so he is often called Vishy either as a term of endearment or as a matter of convenience – was born in 1969 in the city of Madras, now Chennai. At the time, India had no chess culture to speak of. Fifty years on it is a great chess nation with many tournaments and top players with Anand a superstar. *His* unique talent, *his* charisma and *his* extremely long list of titles have put India on the chess map. What's more, he has in effect woken up a sleeping giant: Asia. Spearheaded by China, many Asian countries have undergone a similar transformation to India and are now enjoying a more than healthy chess climate. As a result, at the turn of the 21st century, inspired by Anand and made possible by the multitude of new opportunities the internet has provided, chess has become a truly global sport at last. While Bobby Fischer may have interrupted the post-WW II hegemony of the Soviets for a few years, it was Anand who permanently ended the far older European-American domination in chess.

Anand's rise to the top was meteoric in more respects than one – not only was he very young when he made his way to the top of the game, he also played extremely fast. It was the first sign of his extraordinary talent, which allowed him to 'understand' a position intuitively and immediately. Time to think just wasn't necessary when he was young. In later years his speed of play has 'normalised'. He even finds himself in time trouble now and again, just like everybody else.
Anand first joined the battle for the World Championship in 1990 at the Manila Interzonal tournament, where he qualified for the Candidates Matches.

At these matches he made it to the quarterfinals, losing to Karpov in Brussels in 1991. Then, in 1993, the break-up between FIDE and Kasparov happened and suddenly there were *two* World Champions to beat. At first this seemed not a bad situation for Anand. In the years 1993-1995 he played a key role in both the FIDE and the PCA World Championship qualifying cycles, winning one and only just missing out on winning the other as well. As a result he played the match against Kasparov in New York 1995 that we discussed in a previous chapter, losing after an exciting struggle.

After that match the institution of the World Championship sank deeper and deeper into the morass of chaos. On one side there was the 'traditional' line of Kasparov (later Kramnik), legiti-

(photo Jos Sutmuller)

mised by the age-old principle that in order to become World Champion you need to beat the reigning champion, on the other side was FIDE with its reasoning of "that is for us to decide". After the 1995 match between Kasparov and Anand both sides were finding it increasingly difficult to legitimise their position; Kasparov because his organisation collapsed, and FIDE because their hurried attempts at modernising 'their' World Championship lost them credibility. In truth, little remained of the tough, narrow and demanding, yet ultimately fair and democratic path to the summit that had once been the crowning glory of the chess world.

For the best players in the world it was a difficult situation. Choices had to be made, loyalties had to be declared and every time a way out of the crisis seemed possible, disillusionment followed. The problems were further aggravated when in 1995 multimillionaire Kirsan Ilyumzhinov (then president of Kalmykia) was elected FIDE President. Though he spent a lot of money on chess, his fitful and far from transparent policies ultimately only worsened the existing chaos.

Anand with Trophy in Bonn 2008 (photo Cathy Rogers)

In hindsight, Anand can be said to have made the best of these difficult times. He won the first FIDE knock-out World Championship in Groningen 1997, although he didn't win the title because FIDE had decreed that the winner of Groningen should play a short final match against defending champion Anatoly Karpov, who hadn't had to play the knock-out tournament and was waiting, fresh as a daisy, for his worn-out opponent. Miraculously Anand managed to tie the regular match 3-3, but in the tiebreak his reserves were exhausted and he lost 0-2. For the next cycle FIDE abolished this 'champion's privilege', whereupon Karpov angrily retired (and took FIDE to court).

Neither did Anand participate in this FIDE World Championship, which took place in Las Vegas in 1999. This was probably because he was negotiating a new match against Kasparov at the time, although the match didn't come about and Kasparov played Kramnik instead. However the third FIDE knock-out World Championship, held in 2000 in New Delhi and Tehran, was a great success for Anand. He won and thus became World Champion, *FIDE* World Champion to be precise. He only held the title for a year. In the next FIDE knock-out World Championship, in Moscow 2001/2002, he lost in the semi-final stage to his brilliant yet erratic contemporary Vasily Ivanchuk from Ukraine.

Topalov versus Anand (photo Cathy Rogers)

Anand did not play in the fifth and final FIDE knock-out World Championship in 2004, perhaps because this tournament was held in Libya, the most controversial of the many 'Ilyumzhinov-locations' and – naturally – not a country everybody wanted (or was allowed) to visit. Ilyumzhinov saw no reason not to hold the tournament there, just as he saw no reason not to visit and play a friendly game of chess with "leader of the revolution" Muammar Gaddafi in the middle of a raging civil war seven years later, shortly before the latter died a violent death in 2011.
The next year saw FIDE abandon the knock-out format and organise an eight player double round-robin tournament for the World Championship in San Luis, Argentina. Anand participated, but was unable to keep pace with Topalov, who played the tournament of his life and won.

All in all, for Anand the 'era of the double World Championship' (1993-2006) resulted in one match against Kasparov (which he lost) and one FIDE title. Not a bad harvest! Nevertheless, he will have breathed a sigh of relief when the chess world was finally reunited and it became possible to simply play for the undisputed World Championship again. He seized his chance at the first opportunity: he was in top form at the World Championship tournament in Mexico City in 2007 and won the title, a point ahead of defending champion Vladimir Kramnik. It was the first time since Steinitz that a new World Champion was older than his predecessor (if we don't count the two revenge matches Botvinnik won against Smyslov and Tal).

A year later Anand beat Kramnik in a match as well (6½-4½), effectively silencing any possible questioning of the legitimacy of his title. The chess world had finally been reunited and Anand was its new champion.

It is easy in a book like this to lose sight of the fact that the World Championship isn't the only thing that counts in chess. Like his predecessors, Anand also won a great number of 'ordinary' elite tournaments. He also headed the world rankings for quite some time. He himself has insisted that we shouldn't attach more importance to the World Championship than to other tournament successes. Perhaps it is for this reason that Anand is the first World Champion who is more often called "Five-time winner of the World Championship" rather than "World Champion from 2000 to 2002 and from 2007 to 2013".

Anand with his wife Aruna (photo Cathy Rogers)

It is a shift from a static to a dynamic perspective, focussing on the number of times someone actually *wins* a title event rather than on the number of years he or she is sitting on the throne.

Of course Anand does very well in this respect. After he defeated Kramnik he defended his title successfully in two more matches, first against Topalov (in Sofia in 2010) and then against Boris Gelfand (in Moscow in 2012). Both matches were extremely close. Against Topalov, Anand won the final game to win the match 6½–5½. Against Gelfand (born 1968 in Minsk, later emigrating to Israel) the match was tied after twelve games and Anand had to win the rapid play-off to retain his title.

In the end, a representative of an entirely new generation (and a very special one at that) was needed to dethrone Anand. In 2013 he lost in what must have been (to him) a very disappointing match against Magnus Carlsen, 21 years his junior: 6½-3½.

Yet he immediately recovered from this setback, winning the Candidates Tournament in Khanty-Mansiysk only a year later. Even though he was the oldest competitor here, Anand remained well ahead not only of his old rivals Kramnik and Topalov, but also of the much younger Sergey Karjakin (1990). This victory earned him a second match against Carlsen, which was held later that year (2014) in Sochi, Russia. Anand lost

Anand with his Trophy in Moscow 2012
(photo Cathy Rogers)

again (6½-4½), but this was perhaps not a huge disappointment, since by now Carlsen was truly dominating the chess world.

In line with his publicly expressed views on the World Championship, Anand reacted stoically to the loss of the world title. He simply went on being one of the best players in the world. To this day he remains successful, even though he now has to compete against players twenty years or more his junior. He may well be on track to follow in the footsteps of Lasker, Smyslov and Korchnoi, who continued playing into their old age without losing (much of) their strength.

Anand's style is hard to describe, perhaps because he does not seem to 'steer' his games. He doesn't appear to have a preference for one type of position over another, is equally good at all aspects of the game and has an uncanny knack of conjuring brilliant moves out of thin air.

♙ Anand, Viswanathan
♟ Karpov, Anatoly
🌍 Las Palmas 1996

---

1. ♘f3 d5 2. d4 e6 3. c4 dxc4 4. e4 b5

A somewhat obscure sideline of the Queen's Gambit Accepted, which enjoyed a brief spell of popularity at the time. It is rare for Black to be able to protect his c4-pawn in this way, but in this particular case he gets away with it.

5. a4 c6 6. axb5 cxb5 7. b3 ♗b7

This attack on e4 is what allows Black to settle his queenside problems satisfactorily.

8. bxc4 ♗xe4 9. cxb5 ♘f6

Black has achieved a solid position. In order to be entirely safe he only needs to exchange his a-pawn for White's b-pawn.

10. ♗e2 ♗e7 11. 0-0 0-0 12. ♘c3 ♗b7

Everything is ready for a7-a6. White is unable to prevent this move, but Anand finds a way to keep the fight going anyway.

Position after: 12... ♗b7

13. ♘e5 a6 14. ♗f3!

Undermining the safety of Black's rook on a8. White is not worried about the possible loss of a pawn as after 14... ♗xf3 15. ♕xf3 ♕xd4 16. ♖e1 Black is in serious trouble.

14... ♘d5

A good defensive move, but a concession nevertheless. By closing the diagonal of his queen's bishop, Black accepts a diminishing of the elasticity of his position.

15. ♘xd5 exd5 16. ♖b1!

A highly unexpected move – to all outward appearances a1 is the perfect square for this rook. White is preparing to meet 16... axb5 (which looks like the most normal move in the world) with 17. ♖xb5, when all of a sudden Black has problems defending his pawn on d5 (17... ♗a6 18. ♖xd5).

16... ♕b6

A move which Karpov won't have made easily. It looks strange to put the queen on the same file as White's rook, yet it seems a good solution, as the pawn on b5 is now both blocked *and* pinned. If White now plays a 'routine' move like 17. ♕d3, Black will have time to reinforce d5 with 17... ♖d8 when everything is 'under control'.

17. ♗e2!

Three moves ago ♗e2-f3 was a strong move, now ♗f3-e2 is what the position needs. To *find* a manoeuvre like this demands a flexible mind; to actually *play* it requires unswerving self-confidence as well.

17... axb5

There are no useful alternatives. If 17... ♖d8 White plays 18. ♗d3 when capturing on b5 can no longer be avoided.

18. ♖xb5 ♕c7 19. ♗f4 ♗d6

It looks as if Black has found a successful defensive set-up. There is even a counter-threat looming: f7-f6.

20. ♗d3!

Instead of taking a step back White keeps moving forward. Suddenly, it is not just the d5-pawn that is under a cloud, but Black's entire kingside as

well. Seemingly out of nothing nasty moves like ♕d1-h5 or ♕d1-b1 have materialised.

20... ♗a6

Karpov is feeling the pressure. Hoping to exchange pieces, relieve the pressure and simplify the position, he offers a pawn.

Position after: 20... ♗a6

21. ♗xh7+!

Anand must have felt there is bigger game to be hunted than just a pawn. Still, to forego a perfectly reasonable option with an extra pawn and a draw in the bag, in favour of a piece sacrifice with unpredictable consequences, is not a decision many players would have made. It is a sign of self-confidence, great powers of calculation and bravery; in other words the hallmark of the most pure, sparkling talent.

21... ♔xh7 22. ♕h5+ ♔g8 23. ♖b3 ♗xe5?

In time trouble and probably irritated by the unexpected turn the game has taken, Karpov doesn't defend as well as he might have done. There are two better moves, 23... f6 and 23... ♗c8. The point of 23... f6 is that after 24. ♖h3 fxe5 25. dxe5 Black has the double attack 25... ♕c4! [not 25... ♖xf4 26. e6! and Black is mated]. The complications are unfathomable, yet according to Anand White maintains a winning attack with 26. ♖e1! ♕xf4 27. ♕h7+ ♔f7 28. exd6. The alternative 23... ♗c8 also demands an awful lot of violence and imagination to break down. Anand gives 24. ♖g3 ♕e7 25. ♗h6 ♗xe5 26. dxe5 g6 27. e6!! with the dual point 27... ♗xe6 28. ♕e5 or 27... ♕xe6 28. ♗xf8, winning for White in both cases.

24. ♖h3 f6 25. dxe5

White now has a fabulous attacking position at a relatively cheap price. Neither 25... ♗xf1 26. e6, nor 25... ♕c4 26. ♖e1 ♕xf4 27. ♕h7+ ♔f7 28. e6+! ♔e8 29. ♕g6+, holds.

25... ♕e7

Preventing 26.e6, but White has plenty of options.

26. ♕h7+ ♔f7 27. ♖g3 ♔e8 28. ♖xg7 ♕e6 29. exf6 ♘c6

Finally, the queen's knight is able to join the battle, but it is clear that Black is helpless against the onslaught, now that he has insufficient material compensation for the exposed position of his king. The concluding moves were **30. ♖a1 ♔d8 31. h4 ♗b7 32. ♖c1 ♗a6 33. ♖a1 ♗b7 34. ♖d1 ♗a6 35. ♕b1! ♖xf6 36. ♗g5.** In this position Karpov lost on time. He might as well have resigned.

It is Anand's unique gift for finding moves invisible to a lesser mortal that enables him to play games like this, again and again.

♙   Aronian, Levon
♟   Anand, Viswanathan
🌐   Wijk aan Zee 2013

1. d4 d5 2. c4 c6 3. ♘f3 ♘f6 4. ♘c3 e6 5. e3 ♘bd7 6. ♗d3 dxc4 7. ♗xc4 b5 8. ♗d3 ♗d6

Deviating from the classical plan of playing ...c6-c5 as fast as possible, which we saw in Kasparov-Kramnik (page 226). With a bishop on d6 Black has the alternative plan ...e6-e5, e.g. 9. e4 e5 10. dxe5 ♘xe5 11. ♘xe5 ♗xe5 when Black can be satisfied.

9. 0-0 0-0 10. ♕c2 ♗b7 11. a3

In this type of position the players are like boxers, dancing and circling around their opponent, apparently playing a waiting game but in reality fully alert and ready to strike at the first opportunity. White is looking for the right moment to play e3-e4, while keeping an eye on options like ♘c3-e4 or ♘f3-g5. Meanwhile he has to be alert to the possible counterthrusts ...c6-c5, ...e6-e5 and ...b5-b4. Black will also be carefully evaluating the pros and cons of these possibilities at every move, with a variety of preparatory queen or rook moves from which to choose.

Deep opening preparation and an open, flexible mind are essential for those wishing to play this variation. Precisely right for Anand!

11... ♖c8 12. ♘g5!?

White strikes first. Aronian probably counted on the tame reply 12...h6 or perhaps on the wildly aggressive 12... ♗xh2+. In the latter case he must have assessed his position after 13. ♔xh2 ♘g4+ 14. ♔g1 ♕xg5 15. f3 ♘gf6 16. b4 as promising in spite of the pawn deficit, thanks to White's strong pawn formation and pair of bishops. However, Anand has a huge surprise in store for him.

(see diagram next column)

12... c5!

The moment White's knight has 'left its post', Black seizes his chance to play this strategically important pawn push. In doing so he not only ignores the

Position after: 12. ♘g5!?

threat against h7, he also leaves his pawn on b5 *en prise*.

13. ♘xh7?!

Obviously, taking on h7 is critical, but *how* to take? With hindsight (and *only* with hindsight!) 13. ♗xh7+ would have been White's best chance, yet the ensuing complications are unfathomable, even in the peace and quiet of one's study. After 13... ♔h8 (not 13... ♘xh7 14. ♕xh7 mate) White faces the double threat of 14...g6 and 14... ♗xh2+. It is difficult to find a move which covers both threats. In a game So-Sevian, US Championship 2015, White played 14.f4 (to prevent 14... ♗xh2+), had his bishop trapped after 14... g6, sacrificed the bishop (15. ♗xg6) and after 15... fxg6 16. ♘xb5 ♕e7 17. ♕xg6 had captured every pawn Black had left unprotected. Yet despite having more than adequate material compensation (four pawns for a piece) the position was still highly unclear and So lost.

13... ♘g4!

Attacking h2 and making room for the queen as well. White has no time to take on f8, for in that case he gets mated via 14... ♗xh2+ 15. ♔h1 ♛h4, etc. Perhaps 14.h3 would have been best but according to Anand Black then plays 14... ♗h2+ 15. ♔h1 ♛h4 anyway, with sufficient compensation for the pawn. (The threat is then 16... ♛xh3!.)

14. f4

A logical move, blocking the diagonal h2-b8 and connecting the queen to the defence of the kingside. It quickly becomes clear however, that the price White has to pay for this is high, very high.

14... cxd4 15. exd4

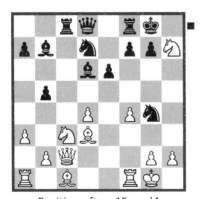

Position after: 15. exd4

15... ♗c5!!

An astonishing move. Once played, it is not so difficult to see that there is no real sacrifice involved, because after 16.dxc5 ♘xc5 the bishop on d3 is lost. But to even *think* of such a move! It is possible of course, that a computer engine lent a helping hand in finding it, but even that would be to Anand's credit. After all, even a computer needs to be steered in the right direction.

16. ♗e2

An unexpected defensive resource, but not quite of the same calibre as 15... ♗c5. It is understandable that Aronian is looking for an improvement on the natural 16.dxc5, when after 16... ♘xc5 17. ♘xf8 ♛d4+ 18. ♔h1 ♘xd3 19. h3 ♘df2+ 20. ♖xf2 ♘xf2+ 21. ♔h2 ♔xf8 material is equal, yet Black's positional advantage is undeniable.

In fact the text is a nice echo of 15...♗c5: ignoring two materialistic options (16.dxc5 and 16. ♘xf8) White sacrifices a pawn and invites moves like ...♛d8-h4 and ...♘g4xh2 (not to mention 16... ♗xd4+ 17. ♔h1 ♘f2+). But 16... ♗xd4+ 17. ♔h1 ♛h4 can be met by 18. ♗xg4, while 17... ♘xh2? gets punished by 18. ♘g5!, threatening mate on h7 while making it impossible for Black to play ...♛d8-h4. Naturally, Black can play 17... ♘f2+ instead, but after 18. ♖xf2 ♗xf2 19. ♘xf8 ♘xf8 at least White is still alive.

Even if after deep analysis 16.dxc5 should turn out to be the stronger move, Aronian still deserves credit for finding this ingenious alternative. Anand's reply though, comes from a different world.

Position after: 16. ♗e2

16... ♘de5!!

Even more than 15... ♗c5, this is a move any World Champion (and possibly even their computer engines) would be proud of. And yet, it is so simple and straightforward. "So you are attacking my knight? Right, I'll protect it."

Suddenly, White's back is well and truly against the wall. The option to play 17. ♘g5 (or 17. ♘xf8 or 17. fxe5) is ruled out, because of 17... ♕xd4+ 18. ♔h1 ♕g1+! 19. ♖xg1 ♘f2 mate. Nor is 17. dxc5 ♕d4+ 18. ♔h1 ♘f2+ 19. ♖xf2 ♕xf2 playable with the killer bishop on b7. In fact, complicated as the position may look, White has only one move.

17. ♗xg4 ♗xd4+ 18. ♔h1 ♘xg4 19. ♘xf8

Now that the queen covers the vital squares f2 and g2, White can afford this. But the *real* point of Anand's combination is yet to be revealed.

Position after: 19. ♘xf8

19... f5!!

In a game like this (*are* there 'games like this'?) a commentator cannot possibly be sparing with exclamation marks. In the heat of the battle and a rook down, Black calmly plays a defensive move (avoiding the trap 19... ♕h4? 20. ♕h7+!) without his attack losing momentum. The threat of 20...♕h4 is disastrous. Again, White has only one possible reply.

20. ♘g6 ♕f6

Another quiet move. With his two powerful bishops trained on White's king, Black has his opponent in an iron grip. If 21. ♘e5, the reply 21... ♘xh2! is decisive.

21. h3 ♕xg6 22. ♕e2 ♕h5 23. ♕d3?

In truth, this is White's only real mistake in the entire game, but who wouldn't lose courage after a battering like this. The only defence against the threat of 23... ♕xh3+ is 23. ♖f3, even though 23... ♗xf3 24. ♕xf3 ♘f2+ 25. ♔h2 ♕xf3 26. gxf3 ♘d3! would then transpose into an ending which looks rather hopeless for White.

23... ♗e3!

White resigned. The threat of 24... ♕xh3+ is lethal.

To round off, let's take a look at the 'early Anand', where speed and depth of play merge beautifully.

♙ Kuijf, Rini
♟ Anand, Viswanathan
🌐 Wijk aan Zee 1990

1. e4 e5 2. ♘f3 ♘c6 3. c3

The Ponziani Opening is a rare bird in modern tournament practice. No doubt Rini Kuijf, who was the reigning Dutch champion at the time, chose it in order to surprise his opponent. And no doubt he did! But the first blow is not always half the battle.

3... ♘f6 4. d4 ♘xe4 5. d5 ♘e7 6. ♘xe5

White has a space advantage, Black has a slight lead in development.

6... ♘g6 7. ♗d3

A useful developing move, yet it also contains a trap: 7... ♘xf2?, thinking to win a pawn, runs into 8. ♗xg6! ♘xd1 9. ♗xf7+ ♔e7 10. ♗g5+ and it is White who wins material.

7... ♘xe5 8. ♗xe4 ♗c5 9. ♕h5

In combination with White's next move, this attempt to keep the initiative is too ambitious. But in 1990 9. ♕h5 was still established theory! The computer era had not yet arrived and when preparing for our games 'we' were still relying on books and magazines. It was far from unusual for a player not to be sufficiently critical when reading these and inadvertently follow some bad advice. This is what happened here.

9... d6 10. ♗g5?!

White's play looks logical, even solid. Indeed, if Black were to follow the 'theoretical recommendation' 10... ♕d7, White would have every reason to be satisfied with the opening.

(see diagram next page)

10... ♗g4!

This hits the nail on the head! One

Position after: 10. ♗g5?!

seemingly effortless move, played almost without thinking by Anand, turns out to be sufficient to totally refute the theoretical evaluation of the line. If White exchanges queens Black's lead in development makes itself felt, e.g. 11. ♗xd8 ♗xh5 12. ♗h4 0-0 or 12. ♗xc7?! ♖c8 13. ♗a5 b6. There are no tactical escape routes; if 11. ♕xh7 Black might even play 11... ♕xg5! 12. ♕xh8+ ♔e7, winning.

11. ♕h4?

Understandably, White isn't ready to make the mental switch to defensive play, but this pseudo-agressive move only makes matters worse.

11... f6!

Little now remains of White's 'initiative'.

12. ♗c1

12. ♗e3 ♗xe3 13. fxe3 would have been relatively best. The text loses a piece.

12... ♕e7 13. 0-0 g5! 14. ♕g3 f5

Attacking the bishop on e4 and threatening 15...f4 as well. Resignation would have been perfectly reasonable at this point. Instead White played **15. ♗xf5 ♗xf5 16. ♗xg5**, hoping to get some compensation for the piece, but after **16... ♕f7 17. ♘d2 ♖g8** Black had consolidated. The remaining moves were **18. ♖ae1 h6 19. ♖xe5+ dxe5 20. ♕xe5+ ♔d7 21. ♗e3 ♖ae8 22. ♕f4 ♕xd5 23. ♘f3 ♗d6 24. ♕a4+ b5** and White finally resigned.

This game, which took Anand less than twenty minutes and lasted under an hour in total, was played in the first round. For the rest of the tournament it was a running gag among the other participants, when the games had only just started to ask each other jokingly "Has Anand finished yet?"

Magnus Carlsen

With Sven Magnus Øen Carlsen, born in the Norwegian city of Tønsberg in 1990, the chess world once and for all closes the book on the 20th century, entering a new age and a new millennium. Everything about Magnus is new and very different from the World Champions before him: his personal appearance, his demeanour at the board, his views on the wide variety of time controls and tournament formats. More than anything else though, it is the way he interacts with the non-chess world that sets Carlsen apart from his predecessors. He has made chess cool again. He is a star. He is the standard-bearer of a new generation.

His match against Anand in 2013, which brought him the title of World Champion, was a battle of the generations. An age gap of 21 years is unheard of in modern World Chess Championship history. Only the matches Steinitz-Lasker and Botvinnik-Tal had known a greater gap than theirs. Because of his youth and because in 2013 he had already held the number one position on the world rankings for a couple of years, Carlsen was the clear favourite to win the match. Many were actually hoping he would win. Perhaps the chess world simply *needed* a new, young champion, no matter how good the old one had been.

It was almost ten years before he became World Champion that Carlsen first captured the international limelight, when as a thirteen-year-old, he won the C group at the world famous annual Wijk aan Zee tournament in 2004. Anyone who was present there will find it hard to forget the impression Magnus made with games such as the following.

The young Magnus against Ernst in Wijk aan Zee 2004 (photo Cathy Rogers)

♙ Carlsen, Magnus
♟ Ernst, Sipke
🌐 Wijk aan Zee 2004

Position after: 17... c5

Black's last move (17...c5?) allows a combination which is fairly common in

this type of position, yet rarely with the devastating effect it has here.

18. ♘g6!

Had Black looked deeply into the consequences of this move, he would have refused the sacrifice and played 18... ♖fe8, even though this would have cost him a pawn after 19. ♘xe7+ ♖xe7 20. dxc5. Is it possible that he underestimated his opponent: wasn't he after all just a cute little boy of thirteen?

Dutchman Sipke Ernst was himself in great shape in this tournament. Like Carlsen, he would go on to fulfil the requirements for a Grandmaster 'norm' and, with a score of 10/13, won second prize, just half a point behind the Norwegian prodigy.

18... fxg6? 19. ♕xe6+ ♔h8 20. hxg6!

This is the point, rather than 20. ♕xe7? ♘d5 which is losing. Black's king is trapped and a crushing sacrifice on h6 is already threatened.

20... ♘g8

On the other hand, isn't this move defending everything? Unfortunately for Black the biggest surprise is yet to come.

21. ♗xh6! gxh6 22. ♖xh6+! ♘xh6 23. ♕xe7

Threatening mate on h7. Black has only one defence.

23... ♘f7

Incredible though it may seem, all this had been played before. In the game Almagro Llanes-Gustafsson, Madrid

2003, White couldn't find a win here and settled for a draw by repetition after 24. ♕f6+ ♔g8 25. ♖h1 ♘h6! 26. ♕e7 ♘f7 27. ♕f6 ♘h6.

24. gxf7!

Position after: 24. gxf7!

This wins on the spot. Although Black is a full rook up, he is powerless against the straightforward threat of mate. Ernst tried **24... ♔g7**, but was mated mercilessly: **25. ♖d3 ♖d6 26. ♖g3+ ♖g6 27. ♕e5+ ♔xf7 28. ♕f5+ ♖f6 29. ♕d7** mate. What a way for a thirteen-year-old to make his entree into the big world!

After this splendid first international performance Carlsen's progress was very rapid indeed. 'Only' an International Master when he travelled to Wijk aan Zee, three months and two tournaments later he was already a Grandmaster.

Carlsen then set his sights even higher. In a very strong blitz tournament in Reykjavik he managed to beat Karpov. In the ensuing (knock-out) rapid tournament Kasparov (who headed the world rating list at the time) only managed to knock out the teenager with great difficulty. Shortly afterwards, Carlsen was invited to take part in the FIDE knock-out World Championship in Libya. He lost in the tie-

With the great Garry Kasparov in 2004 (photo Cathy Rogers)

break of the first round, but against the formidable Levon Aronian, an impressive first step on the long and narrow road to the summit.

A year later, in 2005, he was given a place in the World Cup in Khanty-Mansiysk, again a knock-out tournament and part of the next qualification cycle for the FIDE World Championship. There were ten tickets at stake for a place in the next Candidates Tournament. Carlsen, who turned fifteen during the tournament, showed himself to be completely at home in this hyper-competitive environment, finishing exactly in tenth place. He thus qualified for the Candidates, the youngest ever player to do so.

During the following years Carlsen's results became steadily more impressive and it was clear that it would be just a matter of time before he would outshine his rivals. However, the obstacles an aspiring world champion has to conquer become higher with every step and very few make it to the top without any hiccups. In Carlsen's case (and not just in his case), FIDE itself turned out to be one of the

The World Championship Match in 2013 against Anand (photo Cathy Rogers)

main obstacles, their ideas about the format of the World Championship changing continuously. Even when the reunification match between Kramnik and Topalov in 2006 finally ended the era of the two conflicting World Championships, the drama continued.

The Candidates Tournament for which Carlsen had qualified didn't take place until 2007, again in a knock-out format. Carlsen, who was sixteen by now, lost in the opening round to the favourite, Levon Aronian of Armenia, after a fierce battle which was decided in the tiebreak.

The next cycle was again a new format, a series of Grand Prix tournaments with a fixed set of participants, with the winner challenging for the world title. Carlsen made an excellent start before FIDE suddenly decided that an extra Candidates Tournament on top of the existing series would be held. Disregarding massive protests by the players, FIDE President Ilyumzhinov stuck to his guns, with the result that Carlsen withdrew from further participation in the cycle, declaring the changes unfair. FIDE of course had shot itself in the foot, because by now Carlsen had become the biggest media magnet in the chess world and to have a World Championship without him was just stupid. For this reason it was not a big surprise when, two years later, Carlsen was actually *invited* to take part in the offend-

The World Championship Match in 2018 against Caruana (photo Cathy Rogers)

ing Candidates Tournament. He refused however, arguing that the whole qualification cycle was unfair and that it was far too long anyway. More than anything else he must have been fed up with the way FIDE were treating him.

Next came a case of history repeating itself. What happened to Bobby Fischer in the late 1960s now happened to Carlsen. Although he had chosen not to be a part of the FIDE World Championship cycle, his results in 'ordinary' tournaments were so outstanding and people were clamouring for him to have a go at the World Championship so loudly, that neither Carlsen himself nor FIDE could ignore it, even if they wanted to. And, just as Fischer and Spassky had been involved in a kind of ongoing duel for prestige for years before they officially played for the title in 1972, Anand and Carlsen were constantly playing prestige duels against each other in every tournament in which they met.

In 2013 matters came to a head. FIDE had started yet another World Championship cycle and gave Carlsen (and Aronian and Kramnik) a place in the Candidates Tournament because of their high ratings. This time Carlsen accepted. The Candidates Tournament, held in London, was fiercely contested and culminated in a hair-raising last round. Both leaders, Carlsen and Kramnik, lost (to Svidler and Ivanchuk respectively), but remained in shared first place. Carlsen was then declared the winner, because he had won more games with the black pieces. Not exactly fair or even reasonable and not at all a glamorous way for Carlsen to win, but overall the chess world was happy that he had finally been given the chance everyone thought he deserved.

The match itself, held in Chennai half a year after the Candidates, went like a dream for Magnus. Three wins and seven draws were sufficient for him to win 6½-3½. At 23 Carlsen was the new World Champion. Only Kasparov had been (slightly) younger when he won the title – and Morphy of course, but for some reason *he* never gets included in this list.

The crucial game of the match was the 9th. Anand, who was trailing by two points, made a fantastic effort to win, took enormous risks and *seemed* to be on the verge of victory when this happened...

♙ Anand, Viswanathan
♟ Carlsen, Magnus
🌐 9th game Chennai 2013

Position after: 26. ♕h6

White has his opponent almost in a stranglehold. Almost, for Black can still move one little toe.

26... b2

On the other hand, it is an exceptionally dangerous little toe since the pawn cannot be stopped (27. ♖b1 ♕a5 28. ♖xb2 ♕a1+). However Anand has calculated that he can (and must) persevere with his attack.

27. ♖f4!

A rarity. Black is allowed to promote his pawn with check.

27... b1=♕+

Black is now a full queen up, but what's the use? The threat of ♖f4-h4 seems lethal.

28. ♘f1??

A blunder, based on some truly brilliant calculation. (Does that make sense?)

Anand had seen that after 28. ♗f1 Black holds by returning the extra queen: 28... ♕d1! 29. ♖h4 ♕h5 30. ♘xh5 gxh5 31. ♖xh5 ♗f5. An astonishing way of covering h7! Later analysis has confirmed that although Black is still in great danger he has sufficient resources to withstand the attack. If 32. g6 ♗xg6 33. ♖g5, for instance, Black has 33... ♘xf6! 34. exf6 ♕xf6 and a draw is the most likely outcome. The point of 28. ♘f1 is that now 28... ♕d1 29. ♖h4 ♕h5 loses to 30. ♖xh5 gxh5 31. ♘e3! destroying Black's fortress. There is the terrible threat of ♘e3xd5-e7+, while 31... ♗e6 runs into

32. ♗xd5! (threatening 33. ♗e4) 32...♗xd5 33. ♘f5! followed by 34. ♘e7+. A fantastic variation, which Anand must have calculated many moves in advance. Unfortunately what he had missed (or forgotten about) was the simple...

28... ♕e1!

In order to meet 29. ♖h4 with the sobering 29... ♕xh4. End of attack, end of story, end of game. White resigned. One of the great anticlimaxes in the history of the World Championship.

During his first year as World Champion Carlsen reigned supreme. He won or finished near the top in every tournament he played, won the world title in both blitz (3 minutes plus a 2 second increment per move) and rapid chess (15 minutes plus 10 seconds per move) and to crown it all he again beat Anand in a match for the World Championship, this time with a score of 6½-4½.

But competition is tough nowadays. Never before in the history of chess has a World Champion had so many rivals and there are so many elite tournaments, where these players constantly have to prove themselves!

In effect the world's best players are locked in an almost continuous battle, not in an official World Championship, but in all kinds of tournaments. It has become inevitable that not even the World Champion can play his very best all the time, nor win everything.

For his rivals are very strong players indeed. There is the 'old guard', refusing to go away, there are Carlsen's contemporaries, desperate to finally surpass him, and there are the even younger players, ready to remove the generation before them.

Anand (1969) and – to a lesser degree – Aronian (1982), have already featured. Hikaru Nakamura (1987), Maxime Vachier-Lagrave (1990), Sergey Karjakin (1990), Fabiano Caruana (1992), Wesley So (1993) and Anish Giri (1994) are just some of the young stars who are constantly treading on Carlsen's toes and occasionally manage to defeat him or finish ahead of him in a tournament.

Admittedly, opportunities to dethrone Magnus are thin on the ground. After Anand, the next player to qualify for a World Championship match was Sergey Karjakin from Russia (formerly representing Ukraine), an almost exact contemporary of Carlsen. Their match took place in New York in 2016 and resulted in a 6-6 tie. In the ensuing rapid chess tiebreak, Karjakin, after drawing the first two games, finally cracked under the pressure and lost the last two. Carlsen finished the match with one of the most beautiful moves ever played.

♟ Carlsen, Magnus
♟ Karjakin, Sergey
🌐 New York 2016

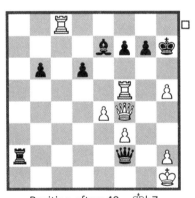

Position after: 49... ♔h7

White to play and mate in two moves.

50. ♕h6+!!

What a picture! Black resigned. Whichever way he takes the queen, it is mate on the next move (50... ♔xh6 51. ♖h8 or 50... gxh6 51. ♖xf7).

Two years later it was Fabiano Caruana's turn. Interest in this match was huge, not only because Caruana represents the USA and was thus the first American to play for the World Championship since Bobby Fischer in 1972, but also because of his fantastic results before the match. Apart from winning the 2018 Candidates Tournament in Berlin in great style, he also finished first in three other elite tournaments during the year, two ahead of Carlsen and one in which first place was shared between Caruana, Carlsen and Aronian. To top it all, Caruana came within an inch of Carlsen's number one spot on the world rankings, a position Carlsen covets and which he has held uninterruptedly since 2011. At the start of the match, held in London in November 2018, the difference between their respective ratings was a mere 3 points.

This near-equality between the two players was reflected in the result: all twelve regular games were drawn, which set a new record for World Championship matches. Carlsen then demonstrated his superiority in the tiebreaks, winning the series of rapid games 3-0, thus maintaining his title *and* his number one spot on the rating list.

And so the Carlsen era continues. The fact that he needed a rapid play tiebreak in both the matches against Karjakin in 2016 and Caruana in 2018 reflects the importance speed chess has gained in this era. In the twelfth and final classical game of his match against Caruana, Carlsen offered a draw in a better position because to him a tie-breaker was almost as good as a win, such is his self-confidence in

With the Trophy again in 2018!
(photo Cathy Rogers)

rapid playoffs. His intuitive genius, the way in which he *knows* what the best move is without having to calculate, sets him apart from his contemporaries and it is precisely this quality that is of vital importance in speed chess.

It will probably take a representative of a completely new generation, a new genius, to beat him. Until then chapter Carlsen can't be closed. Fortunately, as long as he continues to play as brilliantly as he does, no one is in any hurry for this to happen. We, the chess world, can just enjoy his reign as long as it lasts and wait to see how the story continues.

As the above fragments show, Carlsen is both a brilliant attacker and an extremely tough defender, but these are qualities that really are normal – for a World

Champion. Likewise, his mastery of the endgame is of the highest calibre, yet even this cannot be called exceptional – for a World Champion. Perhaps what sets him apart more than anything else is his treatment of the openings, which could be called revolutionary if it weren't for the fact that he is always looking for the complete opposite of a revolution. His aim is not to play sharp lines (which are in effect a way of creating clarity as quickly as possible), but to *postpone* clarity for as long as possible. Carlsen wants to fight, but – like Lasker before him – it is in the middlegame where he wants the battle to take place, rather than in the opening. Via 'harmless, innocuous' openings his opponents are led into a middlegame for which they are unprepared, where strategy is of the utmost importance, and where the tension is still very much alive, not killed by deep opening preparation. In short, Carlsen is never in a hurry. Since most of the top players of today *are*, it is very difficult for them to play against him.

♙ Carlsen, Magnus
♟ Anand, Viswanathan
♟ Sao Paulo/Bilbao 2012

This game dates from the "ongoing prestige duel" before their first World Championship match. Anand was the reigning World Champion, Carlsen the number one on the world rating list.

1. e4 c5 2. ♘f3 d6 3. ♗b5+

Like most of the top players of today, Carlsen varies his strategy against the Sicilian Defence. Sometimes he goes for the main lines (starting with 3.d4), sometimes he goes for a side line.

3... ♗d7 4. ♗xd7+ ♕xd7 5. c4 ♘f6 6. ♘c3 g6 7. d4 cxd4 8. ♘xd4

This variation is all about pawn structure. White has a space advantage but,

as one pair of bishops has already been traded and Black has been given the (arguably useful) developing move ...♕d8-d7 for free, Black has little difficulty in finding good squares for his pieces. What matters to Carlsen is that there is enough 'play' left.

8... ♗g7 9. f3 ♕c7

This was a new move, which shows that Anand came to the game well prepared. He intends to use his queen for active play along the a5-d8 diagonal. 9...♘c6 10. ♗e3 0-0 11.0-0 a6 12.a4 e6 would have been standard.

10. b3

Carlsen reacts warily. The pawn sacrifice 10. ♗e3 ♕xc4 11. ♖c1 would have been sharper, but to play this without preparation against Anand, who obviously knows what he is doing...

10... ♛a5 11. ♗b2 ♞c6 12. 0-0 0-0 13. ♞ce2 ♖fd8 14. ♗c3 ♛b6 15. ♔h1

White's first and foremost concern is to consolidate his pawn structure, while Black is on the lookout for ways to effectively use his well placed pieces. The obvious way to do this would be 15...e6, preparing the central advance ...d6-d5. Anand comes up with a truly spectacular alternative; he simply skips the preparatory move.

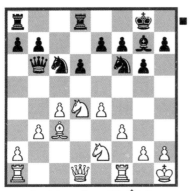

Position after: 15. ♔h1

15... d5!

This move is based on a sacrifice that isn't a sacrifice: 16. exd5 ♞xd5! 17.cxd5 ♖xd5 and White's knight on d4 is pinned and can't be saved.

16. ♞xc6 bxc6 17. ♛e1

The threat of 18. ♗a5 gives White the time needed to neutralise Black's initiative. But does he still have attacking chances? Carlsen has spotted one: the advance e4-e5-e6. That's enough for him.

17... ♖dc8?!

17... a5 looks more natural. Did Anand count on the c-file being opened?

18. e5 ♞e8 19. e6!

It is only four moves ago that Black seemed to be firmly in control, but this pawn sacrifice makes it abundantly clear that the real struggle is only starting. To begin with, Black faces a difficult long-term decision: 19...fxe6, 19...f6 and 19...f5 all look sound, but they all lead to totally different types of position. Which one to choose? Anand decides to eliminate White's far advanced pawn.

19... fxe6 20. ♞f4

This is how it often goes in Carlsen's games. On move 13 the knight seemed to be condemned to a passive role, now all of a sudden it is leading the charge.

20... ♗xc3 21. ♛xc3 d4 22. ♛d2 c5 23. ♖ae1 ♞g7

It looks as if Black has consolidated his position. So long as he can defend his pawn on e6 he seems safe.

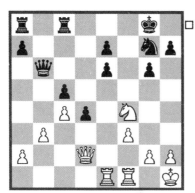

Position after: 23... ♘g7

24. g4!

A move that simply radiates self-confidence. It is obvious that White has a possible pawn storm h2-h4-h5 in mind and it is also clear that he is preventing ♘g7-f5, but there is even more to it than that.

24... ♖c6 25. ♘h3!

A big surprise. The position seems to be screaming for the much more conventional 25. ♘d3 until you realise that 25. ♘h3 introduces the simple threat of 26. ♕h6 followed by 27. ♘g5 and mate is unavoidable. The knight on g7, so well-placed for defending e6, is powerless against this straightforward mating attack, because it no longer has access to f5.

25... ♘e8 26. ♕h6 ♘f6 27. ♘g5 d3?!

Black plays his only trump card. This is understandable, but he soon gets over-trumped by yet another unconvention-

al yet very efficient attacking manoeuvre.

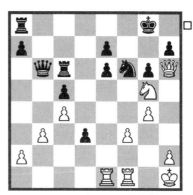

Position after: 27... d3?!

28. ♖e5!

The idea behind this move is not to routinely double rooks on the e-file in order to increase the pressure on e6 (that is precisely what Black's last move *has* made unattractive), but to enable the rook to join in the attack against Black's king. The threat is 29. ♘xh7! ♘xh7 30. ♕xg6+ ♚h8 31. ♖h5 and mate is inevitable.

28... ♚h8

Although this defends against the mating threat (for now 29. ♘xh7 ♘xh7 30. ♕xg6 is not check, which allows Black time for 30... ♖g8), it is a move that shows up the hopelessness of Black's position very clearly.

29. ♖d1!

The d-pawn is indefensible, as 29... ♖d6 loses to 30. ♘f7+ while 29... ♖d8 would not even prevent 30. ♖xd3 (30... ♖xd3 31. ♕f8+ ♘g8 32. ♘f7 mate). Worse for Black is that he finds himself unable to strengthen the defences around his king: 29... ♖g8? 30. ♘f7 is mate.

29... ♕a6

It is too late for a counterattack with 29... a5 30. ♖xd3 a4, as White wins easily after 31. ♖d7! axb3 32. ♖xe7 and mate to follow.

30. a4

Black resigned, perhaps surprisingly so, since his previous move seemed to indicate that he was preparing for the defensive manoeuvre ...♕a6-c8-f8. However, the endgame after 30... ♕c8 31. ♖xd3 ♕f8 32. ♕xf8+ ♖xf8 33. ♘xe6 ♖fc8 34. g5 is so utterly hopeless that resignation is indeed understandable and perhaps even preferable. Instead of 31.... ♕f8, Black could have considered. 31... ♕g8, yet even then after 32. ♖de3 his prospects are bleak indeed.

This was Carlsen's first victory over Anand in a regular game (not blitz or rapid chess). It is a prime example of the way in which he puts pressure on even his greatest rivals not in the opening but in the middlegame. Somehow he manages to disorientate them – even intimidate them. With his sometimes unconventional but always aggressive ideas he offers his opponents a lot of scope for making errors. It is not a coincidence therefore that, very often, they do.

Epilogue

In more ways than one, the future of chess is uncertain. Dutch professor of Computer Science, Jaap van den Herik, amongst others, has said he expects the game of chess to be completely 'solved' by the year 2035. So are we sitting on a time bomb? Will chess lose its fascination when every possible position on the board has a fixed and irrefutable engine evaluation? Or will this technological development simply be integrated in what has so far proved to be an indestructible living organism, capable of adapting to any form of climate change? After all, chess has already changed beyond recognition since the computer joined us and that hasn't killed the game.

And what about the World Championship itself? Is that still safe in the hands of an organisation that has been treating it for many years primarily as a way of making money? Well, perhaps it is a big step forward that we no longer have a FIDE President who in 2016 did not dare to attend his 'own' World Championship match in New York for fear of being arrested for being in violation of the US sanctions against those trading with the Syrian government (sanctions which also caused FIDE to have all its bank accounts closed). But the deep-rooted problem of 'buying votes in order to stay in power', of which Ilyumzhinov was such a past master, is unlikely to be easily solved.

Perhaps FIDE will be able to reinvent itself morally. Perhaps the players can bypass the old, weary organisation as did Kasparov in 1993, heralding a new beginning. Or perhaps we shouldn't have any illusions about the chess world being better than the world itself, or try to look too deeply into the future.

With a World Champion on a par with a movie star, more elite tournaments than ever before and chess lovers from all over the world playing and discussing chess online, the present looks very bright indeed.

We have come a long way in this book. Between the days of Philidor and Carlsen the world has changed beyond recognition. Neither of these two great players would be able to make the way they live understandable to the other. Except on the chessboard! They would be able to show each other their games and appreciate them. Chess is a universal language. Let's just keep speaking it and see what happens.

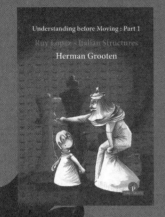
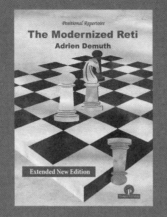

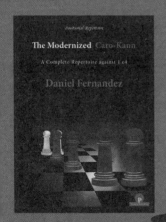

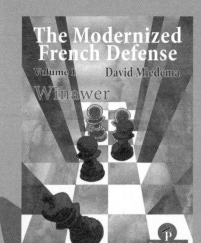

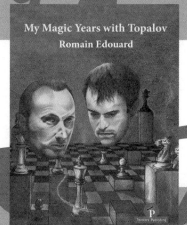

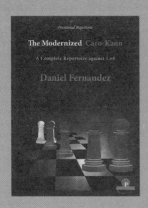

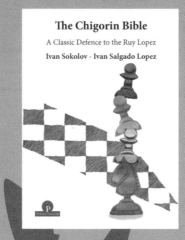

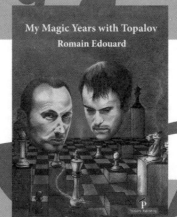

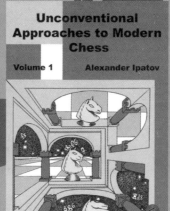